LIBERAL EDUCATION AND THE CORPORATION

The Hiring and Advancement of College Graduates

LIBERAL EDUCATION AND THE CORPORATION

The Hiring and Advancement of College Graduates

Michael Useem

Aldine de Gruyter
New York

About the Author

Michael Useem is Professor of Sociology and Director, Center for Applied Social Science, Boston University. Dr. Useem has written extensively on business and is a major contributor to professional journals. He has authored research-based articles for major newspapers including the *New York Times, Boston Globe, Washington Post, Miami Herald,* and *Chicago Tribune.* He has acted as consultant and active member of numerous panels for international and domestic programs, and serves on the editorial boards of several professional journals. Dr. Useem is the author of *The Inner Circle: Large Corporations and the Rise of Business Political Activity in the U.S. and U.K.* (co-winner of the 1985 C. Wright Mills award), and he is the co-author of *Educating Managers: Executiveness Effectiveness Through Liberal Learning.*

Copyright © 1989 by Aldine de Gruyter

ALDINE DE GRUYTER
A Division of Walter de Gruyter, Inc.
200 Saw Mill River Road
Hawthorne, New York 10532

Library of Congress Cataloging-in-Publication Data
Useem, Michael.
    Liberal education and the corporation : the hiring and advancement
of college graduates / Michael Useem.
        p.   cm. — (Social institutions and social change)
    Bibliography: p.
    Includes index.
    ISBN 0-202-30356-X. — ISBN 0-202-30357-8 (pbk.)
    1. College graduates—Employment—United States. 2. Corporate
culture—United States. I. Title. II. Series.
HD6278.U5U84   1989
331.11'423—dc19   88-33649
                                                                              CIP

Printed in the United States of America
10   9   8   7   6   5   4   3   2   1

Contents

Foreword: Liberal Education and Corporate America

America is at a critical juncture in developing an economic compass for the generations ahead. One response to the current debate on the qualitative aspects of higher education was the formation in 1985 of the Corporate Council on the Liberal Arts. The Council has pursued a program to advance the understanding of the subtle but positive relationship between a liberal-arts education and effective management in the corporate world. Originally located at the American Academy of Arts and Sciences, the Council has been affiliated with the Center for Advanced Study in Education of the Graduate Center of the City University of New York since 1987. The Council represents an innovative partnership designed to develop an empirical base that will demonstrate linkages between a liberal education and business.

It is an understanding of this complex universe that the Council seeks to reaffirm. As University of Chicago President, Hanna Holborn Gray, has put it: "Thinking about education is a way of reflecting on the future, and the future that one would like to see; it is a way of thinking about the present; and finally, it is a way of thinking about the past, and seeing what it is within the past that needs either to be repudiated or renewed. Education then becomes the instrument, or the vehicle, for this way of thinking about a larger world and about the essence of what human possibility, human personality, and human competence might ideally become within a social order." When the Corporate Council, in association with the President's Committee on the Arts and the Humanities, undertook a comprehensive examination of hiring and progression patterns of liberal-arts graduates among the nation's major corporate employers, our goal was to provide a profile of corporate perceptions of liberal-arts graduates. We wanted to know whether a liberal-arts education is a strategic attribute in today's workplace. The results are presented and discussed in this book.

   Michael Useem, Director of the Center for Applied Social Science at Boston University, has organized data that confirm what many policymakers, corporate executives, and members of the academy intuitively regard as unassailable—that a liberal education can be an invaluable asset in corporate management.

   Professor Useem's research and conclusions offer a detailed evaluation of these contrasts. In the context of assessing public pronouncements of corporate executives who stress the primacy of the liberal arts, he offers a framework for understanding why such pronouncements are not always embraced by line managers who stress the practical skills needed to do the job. To reconcile this paradoxical situation, Professor Useem posits a set of proactive variables. They are close to what Ernest L. Boyer calls for in his report for the Carnegie Foundation for the Advancement of Teaching. "College education," according to Boyer, "should combine the liberal arts and the useful arts throughout the undergraduate curriculum." Our report, therefore, becomes the start of what we expect will become a substantive debate on the relationship of the liberal arts to corporate management.

   The universal call for educational reform must not be dismissed as a short-term phenomenon. Educators and corporate executives must join together in shaping the industrial policies that will guide this nation into the next decade and beyond. The blueprint for achieving this objective will not materialize without the commitment of our nation's resources and considerable talent. Nor will reforms be structured necessarily from the policies and practices offered by offshore models.

   While "competitiveness" has become the call from Washington, education reform advocates have advanced the clear message that intellectual mediocrity is unacceptable for America's future. The basic mission for higher education has been undermined by artificial disciplinary boundaries and a lost sense of the mission within the liberal arts. Louis Harris, the public opinion analyst, comments in *Inside America* that "this may well be a major and historic moment for education, for the economy and for America's role in the world in the next half century."

   My own experience confirms this observation. Whatever the job category or classification, the intellectual skills that a liberal education provides, including the ability to cope with the complex atmosphere of a communications company as well as the training to evaluate historical fact and the ability to know the limits of one's knowledge, were of critical importance.

To achieve a workable matrix which policymakers, industrial and labor leadership, and academics nationwide can embrace, as well as implement, will require a renewal of spirit and the commitment of resources to frame the agenda of American higher education. There are no easy answers. Harvard President Derek Bok has called for such a reaffirmation of a partnership with the federal government and the private sector that colleges and universities must build to keep pace with the changing character of the American workplace and the nation's global competitiveness.

Underlying the work of the Corporate Council, including this report, is an assumption that a liberal education should be available to all individuals regardless of wealth or status. Exposure to a quality liberal education is an imperative if we are to cultivate a future generation which will assume leadership roles in a pluralistic nation.

John Gardner believes that a liberal education is the best way to develop this talent pool. He writes, "At the college level, the best preparation for leadership is a liberal arts education. It is essential to broaden and deepen the understanding of those individuals who will have in their hands the future of our communities and our society. That means covering the whole range of the liberal arts, from science to literature, from mathematics to history. By absorbing, through religion, literature, psychology, sociology, drama and the like, the hopes, fears, aspirations and dilemmas of their people and of the species, by coming to understand what our ancestors valued and fought for, by coming to know through history and biography the extraordinary outlines of the human story, they may hope to discharge their leadership duties with wisdom."

Corporate leadership should not overlook its own role in the current debate. A renewed commitment to the quality and depth which an enlightened student population will assume in leadership in the private sector is essential.

It is with this spirit and sense of renewed commitment that *Liberal Education and The Corporation* should be read. The guidance this document can provide for shaping and altering company hiring and promotion practices for years to come makes its utility as a resource tool and reference guide most worthwhile.

Frank Stanton
Chairman, Corporate Council on the Liberal Arts

Introduction: A Study of Liberal-Arts Graduates in the Corporate Workplace

The director of admissions for a large private university was explaining to the 20 chairs of the liberal-arts departments why the 1987 freshman class was to be the largest in recent memory. To the department heads who listened, the news was not an unalloyed blessing. They would soon be contending with oversubscribed courses and undersized classrooms. But otherwise the message was very welcome. The burgeoning flow of students seemed to imply a long-awaited restoration of confidence in the mission of the liberal arts.

Was the 10% growth over the previous year's entering class in the liberal arts shared by other universities? The admissions director replied that it was: conversations with his counterparts at other institutions had confirmed that first-year-student interest in the liberal arts was vigorous at many schools. But what explained the growth? The university had long been worried about the demographic decline of college-age youth in the late 1980s. The admissions director offered two explanations to the department chairs. First, he suggested, the "economy was strong." And second, the "chief executives of corporations have been getting out the word that they want liberal-arts graduates."

The 1987 renewal of campus optimism on the future of liberal arts was in stark contrast to widespread gloom just 5 years earlier. Enrollments in the arts and sciences had been plummeting for a decade as undergraduates flocked to business and other preprofessional majors that seemed to guarantee future employment in a slack economy.

Alarmed at the precipitous student slide toward purely business studies, a number of business leaders had openly warned in the mid-1980s against the loss of curricular breadth. If the admissions officer's impressions were correct, their warnings had had the intended impact. In all likelihood general prosperity, too, had been a factor. With less anxiety about securing a job upon graduation, students could confidently pursue the liberal arts without seemingly consigning themselves to a future of underemployment.

If the corporate warnings and economic growth have helped restore the mission of the liberal arts in America, the renewal may be
short-lived and shortsighted if we fail to understand the reasons for
the enduring value of liberal learning for careers and performance in
the private sector. We know that most college graduates will find employment there: approximately three quarters take their first job with
a company. What we know relatively little about, however, is the experience of the graduates once they enter corporate employment. We
have little systematic information on the hiring of liberal-arts graduates and the graduates of other programs, and only scant data on
their experiences once employed. Even less well described are corporate policies and practices in the hiring and promotion of liberal-arts
and other college graduates.

For current and future college students and their parents to make
informed choices, however, such information is essential. It can be
critical as well for educators concerned with curricular change; for
corporate employers concerned with further development of their
hiring and promotion policies; and for policymakers concerned with
the future of American higher education and corporate performance.
With parental guidance, college students are making critical choices
in the selection of majors and courses of study; university administrators and faculty committees are deciding on new programs and
curricular change bearing directly on preparation for careers in the
private sector; and companies are recruiting large numbers of graduates to start those careers.

The results of the research study reported in this book are intended to help inform these choices. The project has gathered information from a large cross section of major American corporations;
a representative cross section of middle and senior managers of
the nation's larger firms; and more detailed information on the hiring
and promotion practices of five diverse corporations. A number
of colleges have conducted studies of their alumni, many of whom
have entered the private sector; several companies have completed
studies of the importance of educational background in the careers
of their managers; and various inquiries have looked to identify
the qualities sought in corporate managers that might be cultivated
by a good college education. No prior study, however, is available
that systematically acquired information on the policies and practices
of a large and representative sample of the nation's major private
employers.

We know that large numbers of liberal-arts graduates have entered and will continue to enter the corporate workplace. Information is now needed regarding which companies are most likely

to want liberal-arts graduates; what companies look for in hiring liberal-arts and other college graduates; which functional areas within the company are most frequently staffed with liberal-arts graduates; how liberal-arts graduates fare compared with other college graduates; and what educational reforms corporations and their managers would urge upon higher education. The present study is intended to help generate that information. The information is needed to properly assess the critical choices facing those entering, managing, or recruiting from higher education, but it is also intended to contribute to an informed approach to the reform of higher education. This is a period of intense educational debate, an era in which educational change is on the national political agenda. The policy decisions of the period will shape the college curriculum and the educational experience of the next generation of managers who will influence corporate decisions and industrial policies for decades to come. More extensive information is needed on the educational requirement of the nation's white-collar work force if those decisions are to be effectively undertaken.

I. Project Design

The research draws upon three primary sources of information. The *first* source consists of a survey of 535 major American corporations, focusing on their policies and practices in hiring and promoting liberal-arts and other college graduates. The *second* source is a parallel survey of 505 middle and senior managers of large companies, concentrating on their experiences in their own career and in working with other managers of varying educational backgrounds. The *third* primary source of information is a more detailed examination of the experience of five major corporations in the hiring and promotion of college graduates.

Supplementing the primary sources of information are numerous other forms of information: informal interviews with a number of individuals familiar with the concerns of the study, ranging from campus placement officers and college administrators to company managers and government officials; statistics on education and employment compiled by government agencies; technical research on college graduates in the employment market; studies of liberal education by the Association of American Colleges and other organizations; and recent efforts by colleges and universities to adapt their liberal-arts curricula to intensified student interest in private-sector careers.

A *liberal-arts graduate* is defined here as an individual holding a 4-year undergraduate degree in the humanities, social sciences, or natural sciences (including physics, chemistry, biology, and mathematics). Liberal-arts degrees are typically granted by 4-year colleges and by college units within universities, units that usually carry the title of "arts and sciences," though "liberal arts" and other variants are also common. The University of Washington's core unit is the College of Arts and Sciences, while the University of Michigan offers its degree through the College of Literature, Science, and the Arts. Following a convention within higher education, liberal arts is used interchangeably with arts and sciences.

Liberal learning and liberal education are certainly not limited to students enrolled in liberal-arts degree programs. Most business and engineering undergraduate students take courses in the liberal-arts curriculum; some business and engineering courses incorporate the principles of the liberal arts in their substantive content and didactic style; and company managers often enter executive-development programs that stress the humanities and other areas of the liberal arts. The concept of liberal learning is used here to include both study toward a liberal-arts degree and study in other courses and programs that involve critical inquiry, individual judgment, and the development of broad-gauged skills. It should also be noted that the liberal-arts curriculum certainly has no monopoly on liberal learning. Many liberal-arts courses fail to provide a liberal learning experience, and many courses in business, engineering, and other professional programs approach their subjects in a fashion that represents the best of liberal education.[1]

The analysis that follows will frequently compare liberal-arts graduates with other bachelor-degree holders, especially in business and engineering. When liberal-arts graduates are found to perform comparatively well, it might be their liberal learning rather than graduation from a liberal-arts program that has made the difference. Also, it should be noted that managerial performance and career advancement are shaped by many factors in addition to education, including motivation, intelligence, family background, and networks of contacts. In the present research and other studies upon which we draw, information on many of these factors is unavailable. Causal inferences must thus be undertaken cautiously, since a reported correlation between educational background and career experience in the private sector may be partly an indirect product of these other factors. Finally, it should be kept in mind that the present and other studies are inherently time-bound—both educational policies and managerial practices are in flux, and results from all of the research should be interpreted in terms of contemporaneous realities.

II. Survey of Company Policies and Practices

To obtain systematic information on corporate practices in the hiring and promotion of liberal-arts and other graduates, 535 large and middle-sized companies were surveyed. The survey was executed by the Opinion Research Corporation of Princeton, New Jersey. The research focused on the nation's 1000 largest firms and 200 middle-sized companies.

The top 1000 consisted of the *Fortune* magazine annual compilation of the 500 largest manufacturing companies and the largest companies in eight service sectors. The product sectors, the number of companies included in the sectors, and the two largest corporations in each sector are as follows:

Product sector	Number of companies	Largest companies
Manufacturing companies	500	General Motors; Exxon
Commercial banks	100	Citicorp; Bank of America
Diversified financial firms	50	Federal National Mortgage Association; American Express
Savings institutions	50	Financial Corporation of America
Insurance firms	50	Prudential; Metropolitan Life
Retail companies	50	Sears Roebuck; K Mart
Transportation corporations	50	UAL (United Airlines); United Parcel Service
Utilities	50	GTE; Bell South
Diversified services	100	Browning-Ferris Industries

While these firms account for the vast majority of the sales and assets of all U.S. firms, much of the nation's employment growth is among smaller companies. For this reason, 200 middle-sized firms were sampled as well. They were selected at random from those companies with annual sales of $100 to $200 million, as listed in Dun and Bradstreet's *Top 50,000 Companies*. By way of contrast, America's top 500 manufacturing firms have annual sales from $420 million (Rochester and Pittsburgh Coal) to $103 billion (General Motors).

Of the 535 responding companies, 240 are among the top 500 manufacturing firms, 227 among the top 500 service-sector firms, and 68 among the middle-sized firms. The cooperation rate among the top 500 manufacturing firms was slightly above the overall response rate (48 vs. 45%); among the service sector on the average (45%); and among the middle-sized firms below average (34%). More generally, larger firms were slightly more likely to respond than smaller companies: 50% of the top 200 manufacturing firms cooperated, while 47% of the next 300 responded. Yet overall the 535 firms constitute a representative cross section of the nation's major corporations.

Companies were approached through an initial letter to the chief executive officer from the chairmen of the Corporate Council on the Liberal Arts and the President's Committee on the Arts and the Humanities. The executive officer was asked to forward an 8-page survey form to an appropriate manager for response, generally the vice-president or director of human resources or personnel. Of the 535 companies cooperating, information on 412 was acquired from a completed survey form (the survey form appears in Appendix I). Information on the policies and practices of the remaining 123, using a slightly shortened set of questions, was obtained from a telephone interview with the designated manager.

As a representative national survey of major companies, this study provides an opportunity to present an overall portrait of corporate practices in the hiring and promotion of college graduates. Yet it is also recognized that companies vary vastly in their needs and policies in hiring educated employees. Large firms place more emphasis on college credentials than do smaller firms, and some companies have a long history of hiring liberal-arts graduates while others hire few college graduates outside of engineering. Specification of typical corporate practices can thus mask considerable variation among companies. Much of the variation itself, however, is subject to analysis, and part of our task here is to identify the major reasons why companies differ so sharply in their practices.

III. Survey of Managerial Experience

To acquire systematic information on the experience and assessments of managers, 505 upper-middle and senior managers with major American firms were surveyed. This manager survey was also executed by Opinion Research Corporation as part of its quarterly Executive Caravan Survey in July 1987. The sampling frame was the nation's 1000 largest manufacturing corporations and the 500 largest service-sector firms, a set of companies significantly overlapping though not identical to those approached in the corporate survey. While both studies surveyed the top 500 manufacturing and top 500 service-sector companies, the manager survey included 500 middle-sized manufacturing corporations. Nonetheless, both studies draw on relatively similar cross sections of the nation's middle-range and large corporations.

The first step in the procedure for selecting managers to participate in the survey was to take a random sample of 505 of the eligible 1500 companies. The companies were approached by telephone, and one manager was selected from each of the 505 companies for telephone interview (the interview schedule appears in Appendix II). The managers were selected by the Opinion Research Corporation in a way to ensure a balance in the functions that they performed and in the managerial level at which they worked. One third of the interviewed managers are in service-sector companies, and two thirds work in manufacturing companies. The 505 managers were distributed among management levels and functions as follows:

Management levels	
Officers	44%
Nonofficers reporting to officers	39
Managers reporting to nonofficers	17

Management functions	
Marketing and sales	24%
Finance and accounting	20
Human resources and personnel	15
General management and administration	10
Information and data processing	10
R&D, technical, and engineering	7
Plant and production management	6
Other	8

Four out of five managers are relatively senior in position, either serving as a corporate officer or reporting to an officer. The managers are spread among a range of functions, with marketing and finance well represented; comparatively few managers are directly involved in overseeing production, though this reflects the senior ranks from which they are drawn and the fact that a third of the companies are not engaged in manufacturing.

IV. Select Company Policies and Managerial Experiences

To acquire deeper information on the policies, practices, and general hiring and promotion climates of companies, the experiences of a select set of companies is examined in more detail. Five corporations that represent diverse product sectors and practices in the hiring and promotion of college graduates were selected. Company product areas ranged from diversified financial services to household consumer products and military hardware; the practices varied from aggressive recruitment of liberal-arts graduates to almost no hiring of them whatsoever. Information was acquired from the corporations through direct visits by a research team to company headquarters and ancillary offices. Among those usually interviewed were human-resource and personnel managers, college recruiters, organizational planners and developers, directors of personnel information systems, general managers with a special interest in the issue, and other managers. Information was acquired on the premise that the identity of all individuals and companies would remain confidential, a practice followed in the company and managerial surveys as well. The five firms are:

- *A consumer-products company* that has successfully placed liberal-arts graduates in the management of marketing.
- *A high-technology firm* that has stressed the value of a college education and communication abilities.
- *An industrial-products corporation* that is engineering oriented and has little interest in hiring either liberal-arts or business graduates.
- *A maker of health products* that has opportunities for liberal-arts graduates who also have significant postgraduate work experience.
- *A diversified financial-services company* that hires a limited number of liberal-arts graduates, but substantial numbers of MBA holders with liberal-arts background.

The experiences of the five companies in the hiring and promotion of liberal-arts and other college graduates are described in appendixes at the end of Chapters 2, 3, and 4. It should be noted that the policies and practices of these companies are evolving and the accounts provide a picture of the company experiences in late 1987 and early 1988.

V. Plan of the Book

While the book focuses on liberal-arts graduates, much of the analysis is concerned with the differences and comparative advantages of liberal-arts, business, and engineering education and with the special value of the premier postgraduate degree for careers in management, the MBA. Information has been collected, for example, on the undergraduate studies of the 505 managers now in middle and senior positions in the Fortune 1500 firms. Those with varying undergraduate backgrounds are compared in regard to such issues as the kinds of companies in which they are most often working, the managers' primary areas of responsibility, and the perceived value of their college education for the tasks they are now performing.

The plan of the book is as follows. Chapter 1 assesses recent trends in college-student interest in the liberal arts, business, and engineering and reviews major factors that account for the decline of student interest in liberal-arts majors and the rise of student interest in business programs in the 1970s and early 1980s. The chapter then turns to a host of proposals for educational reform in the mid-1980s that were intended to restore the place of liberal arts in the undergraduate curriculum, reforms that would often have the effect, intended or otherwise, of strengthening exposure to liberal arts among those who would later enter the private sector. The chapter concludes with an assessment of what is known about the importance of higher education for work and careers in the private sector.

This is followed by a chapter (Chapter 2) that examines company practices in the hiring and promotion of college graduates. The focus is on determining where corporate interest in liberal-arts graduates is strongest or weakest. Survey information is used to identify the kinds of companies that most often recruit liberal-arts graduates and the kinds of functions within the company to which liberal-arts graduates are most often assigned.

The next chapter (Chapter 3) considers what companies look for in the liberal-arts graduates that they hire and what they would urge college students and educational administrators to do to prepare the next generation of company managers. How important, for instance, are an applicant's specific courses in business subjects, internship experiences, and general field of study when company recruiters come to campus for job interviews? What general balance do companies expect between study in the liberal arts and more "practical" curricula?

The experience of managers in moving up the corporate ladder and into various areas of responsibility, from marketing to plant management, is considered in Chapter 4. The question is examined from the perspective of both the company and the individual manager, focusing on the impact of educational background on managerial development and promotion. The contribution of a liberal education to a manager's leadership skills, innovativeness, and community outreach on behalf of the company is one of the special issues considered.

In Chapter 5 the focus is on the power of distinctive "educational cultures" within companies, cultures that encourage the hiring of those with educational backgrounds similar to managers already at the helm. It also examines the organizational basis for a notable variation in that culture: senior managers are often more favorably disposed toward the hiring of liberal-arts graduates than are the managers who are directly involved in the hiring and supervision of new college graduates. This is the variation that gives rise to the seeming policy inconsistency in which top executives sometimes extoll the virtues of the liberal arts while their own college recruiters are primarily looking for graduates with practical skills.

The next chapter (Chapter 6) identifies the study's implications and offers recommendations for groups with special stakes in the linkage of college education to corporate careers: liberal-arts colleges, business programs, company employers of college graduates, and of course college students themselves. If a single summary line could be extrapolated for college students who are interested in entering the private sector, it would be to stress both liberal learning and the acquisition of practical skills, combining the best of what higher education can offer in the liberal arts and the "useful arts." For colleges and universities, the main message is to expand opportunities for liberal-arts students to acquire business courses and internships and to strengthen the exposure of business students to liberal-arts coursework. For corporate employers, the central conclusion is to make their interest in liberal education more evident to those in college or approaching college age, and—equally important—to make their interest in liberal education clear as well to those within the company who are involved in recruiting and supervising college graduates.

The last chapter (Chapter 7) suggests that liberal learning is important not only for individual careers, but also for company performance. Liberally educated managers can make a significant difference in the kinds of policies that companies evolve both inside the company and in the company's relations with the outside world. Liberal learning can also be important for managers themselves in coping with the vagaries of career experiences, reduced prospects of promotion, and even periods of unemployment in an era of company downsizing.

Practical issues of educational choice and career development are of central concern in this book, yet it also has a more general research purpose—to further illuminate the role, impact, and decision making of corporations. Business firms are a critical, if not *the* critical, institution in American life. Company decisions on plant locations, product development, and corporate takeovers influence the lives of millions. Moreover, while corporations have long been America's premier economic actors, since the early 1970s they have become major political actors as well. Many now manage their environment with the same strategic attitude with which they have long managed their products and investments, drawing on tactics ranging from grass-roots mobilization to political-action-committee giving and cause-related marketing.

Corporations have come to be major cultural actors in American life as well. Accounts of managerial success, topped by such works as *In Search of Excellence* and Lee Iacocca's autobiography, have acquired widespread public attention, as have stories of corporate struggles and battles instigated by corporate raiders and Wall Street brokers. Sensing the shift in public mood toward business in the mid-1980s, community leaders and elected officials have welcomed public-private partnerships and other visible signs of cooperation with local business. College students in large numbers gravitated toward high-income opportunities in the private sector, shedding the antibusiness ethos of the 1970s in favor of getting ahead in the 1980s. So different had become that campus mood that the President of New York University, John Brademas, was led to complain in 1986 that the spreading popularity of prebusiness studies had transformed his campus into a "hotbed of student rest."[2]

If corporations are more central to American economic, political, and cultural life than ever before, our understanding of their role too often remains poorly developed or shrouded in myth. By focusing on the recruitment and promotion of college graduates by the nation's major private employers, the present study is intended to contribute to a better understanding of critical aspects of company decision making and management development. Through detailed examination of the company practices and managerial experiences in this area, we hope to show how corporations operate more generally in shaping the quality and experience of American life.

Notes

1. See Johnston (1986).
2. John Brademas, remarks at the Symposium on "Corporations at Risk: Liberal Learning and Private Enterprise," sponsored by the Corporate Council on the Liberal Arts in association with the American Academy of Arts and Sciences, Cambridge, Ma., September 3, 1986.

Acknowledgments

The research project on which this study is based has been supported by the Corporate Council on the Liberal Arts, in affiliation with the President's Committee on the Arts and the Humanities. These two organizations, their leadership, and a number of other individuals rendered assistance essential to the completion of the project.

The Corporate Council was established in 1985, through the support of CBS Inc., with the primary goal of furthering public understanding of the relationship between education and effective management and leadership in the corporate world. The Corporate Council's Chairman, Frank Stanton (President Emeritus of CBS Inc.), and its Executive Director, Andrew I. Wolf, provided invaluable encouragement and skilled guidance throughout the endeavor. Nancy Risser, Research Consultant to the Corporate Council, assisted many aspects of the project, and her fine research services have been critical to the shaping and completion of the study. A number of the current and former representatives of the fourteen corporate members of the Corporate Council's Executive Board have given generously of their time in developing the project, and many of the issues addressed in this report reflect their thoughtful suggestions. The members of the Executive Board were: American Express Company; AT&T; Cabot Corporation; Carter Hawley Hale Stores, Inc.; CBS Inc.; Exxon Corporation; General Foods Corporation; General Motors Corporation; Honeywell Inc.; Johnson & Johnson; The New York Times Company Foundation; Prudential Insurance Company of America; Time Inc.; and Union Pacific Corporation. The American Express Company provided additional support for the completion of the study.

The Corporate Council is affiliated with the Center for Advanced Study in Education of the Graduate School and University Center of the City University of New York. Helpful commentary and guidance are gratefully acknowledged from the Graduate School and University Center President Harold M. Proshansky; Bert Flugman, Director of the Center for Advanced Study in Education; Solomon Goldstein, Dean of the Graduate School for Research and University

Programs; and Professors David Lavin, Kathleen McCarthy, Floyd Moreland, and Saliah Neftci. Valuable suggestions have also been received from two other individuals who, along with the above members of the CUNY Graduate Center, have served on the Corporate Council's Academic Review Panel: Eve Katz, Director of Public Affairs Projects of the American Council of Life Insurance and Health Insurance Association of America, and John Chandler, President of the Association of American Colleges.

The President's Committee on the Arts and the Humanities served as a collaborating sponsor of the project. The President's Committee was created in 1982 for the purpose of analyzing and recommending ways to promote private sector support for the arts and the humanities. Very helpful guidance and support have been furnished by the President Committee's Chairman, Andrew H. Heiskel (former Chairman of Time Inc.); the Executive Director, Diane J. Paton; and the Assistant to the Director for Humanities, Tracy J. Joselson.

The project included two national surveys, one a cross-section of large U.S. corporations and the other of managers in major companies, and both were executed on behalf of the project by the Opinion Research Corporation of Princeton, New Jersey. The untiring assistance of the corporation's manager responsible for the surveys, Kenneth G. Patrick, Jr., Research Executive, is greatly appreciated.

A number of managers and executives within the corporations on which we conducted short case studies were most helpful in giving of their own time and in opening the doors to other offices within the company. While they cannot be identified here because of the constraints of confidentiality, a strong expression of appreciation for their indispensable assistance is extended.

Valuable discussions in the course of this project have been held with Joseph S. Johnston, Jr., of the Association of American Colleges; Anne Klepper, of the Conference Board; Robert Zemsky, of the Institute for Research on Higher Education of the University of Pennsylvania; and Meredith Gould, formerly Project Manager of the Business/Humanities Project of the Department of Higher Education, State of New Jersey. Useful suggestions have also been provided at a number of conferences and seminars at which preliminary results of the study were presented, and special thanks for these opportunities are extended to Peter Gouervitch of the Graduate School for Pacific and International Studies of the University of California, San Diego; David Atkinson of Pacific Lutheran University; Audrey Friedman of the Conference Board; John D. Kasarda and Howard Aldrich of the University of North Carolina, Chapel Hill; and Harriet B. Joseph and Stephen P. Steinberg of the University of Pennsylvania.

Helpful guidance and assistance have also been provided by my colleagues and university associates, including Geoffrey Bannister, of Butler University and formerly of Boston University; Dennis D. Berkey and Milton Kornfeld of the College of Liberal Arts, Boston University; Leonard Saxe, Peter Doeringer, Harold Salzman, and Meryl Louis of the Center for Applied Social Science, Boston University; Lori King of the Career Planning and Placement Center, Boston University; Paul Osterman of the Massachusetts Institute of Technology; and John Useem and Ruth Useem of Michigan State University. The unstinting support and frequent guidance of my wife, Elizabeth L. Useem, are deeply appreciated, as are the understanding and forbearance of my three children, Jerry, Andrea, and Susan. The latter, a preschooler, provided special incentive with her frequent plaintive query, "how soon will you be done with the college book?"

1

Higher Education and Corporate Careers

American business has looked to higher education for over half a century for the training of its managers. Until the 1920s, few future managers would have sought a college education for entry into management. Although college degrees have long been the expected foundation for the medical and legal professions, it was not until this era that business turned to higher education for the socialization and preparation of its future leadership. The emergence of the large, multidivisional corporation, the rise of what business historian Alfred Chandler has termed the "visible hand," placed a premium on sophisticated decision making, increasingly recognized as a developed rather than intuitive skill. As the first generation of entrepreneurial founders was gradually losing its grip on the executive suite to a new generation of professionally trained managers, college came to be viewed as a major avenue of preparation. Once it was so defined, a rising flow of interest would be assured. David O. Levine, an historian of the era, writes: "There could be no greater incentive for the pursuit of higher learning than individual ambition."[1]

By the 1970s and early 1980s, the exercise of that ambition had moved hundreds of thousands of students to concentrate their undergraduate studies in business. Liberal arts, long viewed as an appropriate general preparation for the responsibilities of business leadership, declined in appeal as courses in accounting, finance, and management drew more and more students. The number of liberal-arts majors went into decline, whereas the number of undergraduate business majors was growing steadily. The business degree came to be perceived as the avenue for the managerially ambitious, the liberal-arts degree for the career ambivalent. Yet new forces within both the business world and higher education now challenge this perception.

I. Corporate Challenge

American companies are facing unprecedented challenge from European, Japanese, and other Far Eastern companies, and many

1

are facing unusual competitive pressures at home as well. The threat of corporate raiders, hostile acquisitions, and profit squeezes have added "downsizing" to the lexicon of corporate strategists and spread fears of employment termination through the ranks of many companies. By one estimate, half a million middle managers with 300 companies lost their positions between 1984 and 1986 as a result of mergers and divestitures. Surveys of managers reveal, as a result, widespread career anxieties and fragile employee loyalties. Almost half of the managers of the nation's 1000 largest corporations surveyed in a 1987 poll expected their employer to "cut back its salaried work force in the next few years." Corporate response to the competitive challenges from abroad and at home, and to the task of retaining a committed work force during a period of uncertainty, will require innovation and change in the kinds of products marketed, the organization and culture of the company, and the ways of doing business.[2]

The educational preparation of the next generation of managers is critical as well. Rosabeth Kanter in her study of innovation and change in U.S. industry concludes that "The potential for an American Renaissance" is enhanced by managers who "are broader-gauged, more able to move across specialist boundaries, comfortable working in teams that may include many disciplines, knowledgeable about how to manage ambiguous assignments and webs of interdependencies." A liberal education is, in her view, the foundation: "The style of thought and problem-solving capacity associated with such Renaissance people are encouraged by a strong, affordable educational system that combats narrow vocationalism and permits people the luxury of studying a variety of fields before becoming too specialized." The next generation of managers must have the broadest possible vision, and a liberal education remains one of the effective avenues for engendering a breadth of understanding among the hundreds of thousands of college graduates who enter the private sector every year.[3]

Corporations are also more active than ever in the social and political arenas of American life. Nearly all major corporations operate programs for giving to community and nonprofit organizations, contributing to political candidates, and lobbying for legislation in Washington and state capitals. The practice of assigning managers to take an active part in community affairs, a kind of "grass-roots" political action, is increasingly widespread. Effective management of external affairs is becoming an important complement to the traditional internal management functions, particularly among the company's middle and senior ranks. Here, too, managers who are broadly educated can be more effective. A capacity to understand and move in circles far beyond those of the company is essential, and a liberal education may be one of the avenues for better comprehending the divergent cultures and values certain to be encountered. This is implicit, for example, in the conclusions of a 1985 study of business-school programs by the Business–Higher Education Forum, a select association of more than 90 chief executives of corporations and universities. Its report recommends that coursework "should be designed to enable students to recognize that problem-solving and managerial decision-making require an understanding of the total political and social environment within which the modern business firm operates."[4]

II. Liberal-Arts Challenge

If American corporations were battered by international competition and domestic takeovers, liberal-arts programs were battered by the rise of undergraduate interest in more practically oriented programs, above all—business. Few eras in American higher education have witnessed as profound a change in student preferences as occurred during the 1970s and early 1980s.

Between 1970 and 1985, the proportion of first-year college students professing an interest in the liberal arts declined from 40 to 21% (Table 1.1 and Figure 1.1). Within the liberal arts, freshmen preferences for the arts and humanities declined most sharply. Between 1970 and 1985, the percentage of first-year students intending to major in the arts and humanities dropped from 21 to 8%. The natural-science interest declined less precipitously, from 10 to 6%; social-science interest, however, remained relatively constant at 8 to 9%.

The decline of freshmen interest in the liberal arts was primarily a phenomenon of the 1970s. After dropping by 16 points between 1970 and 1978—from 40% of entering freshmen to 24%—the proportions of entering classes with intentions of majoring in the liberal arts stabilized at just over a fifth. By the mid-1980s, there were even signs that the liberal-arts proportions were again on the rise. The fraction of the freshmen reporting an interest in the liberal arts in the fall of 1986 stood at 24%, up from 21% the preceding year, prompting the *New York Times* to headline a front-page story in late 1986, "Liberal Arts, Long in Decline, Are Reviving Around Nation." In the fall of 1987, the proportion edged up further, reaching 25%, the highest proportion since 1978.[5]

The intertwined fates of undergraduate programs in liberal arts

Table 1.1 Percentage of Entering College Freshmen Intending
to Major in the Liberal Arts, Business,
or Engineering[a]

Year	Liberal arts	Business	Engineering
1970	40	16	9
1975	29	19	9
1977	25	22	9
1978	24	24	10
1979	24	24	11
1980	22	24	12
1981	22	24	12
1982	21	24	13
1983	21	24	12
1984	22	26	11
1985	21	27	11
1986	24	27	11
1987	25	27	9

[a]Liberal-arts fields of study include the arts and humanities and the
biological, physical, and social sciences.
Source: Astin, Green, and Korn (1987); Astin *et al.* (1987a,b);
Boyer (1987).

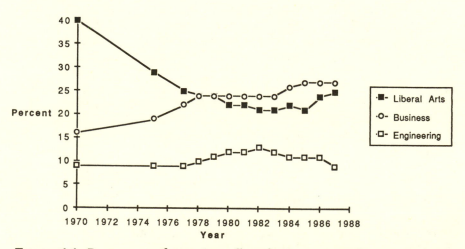

FIGURE 1.1. Percentage of entering college freshmen intending to major in
the liberal arts, business, or engineering, 1970–1987.

and business in the 1970s can be seen in the trends of first-year students intending to major in business. As the liberal arts went sharply down, business fields went sharply up, rising by half—from 16 to 24%—over the decade of the 1970s. More recently, however, the proportion of freshmen with plans to major in business displayed a far more moderate growth rate, rising from 24% in 1980 to a plateau of 27% in 1985–1987. Interest in engineering grew along with business in the 1970s, but it peaked in 1982 with 13% of first-year students intending to major in the area, and since then it slowly declined. By 1987, the proportion of freshmen with engineering plans had dropped back to 9%, the same as in 1978.

These patterns are also evident, albeit in a lagging way, in trends in the volume of baccalaureate degrees in the liberal arts and business. From 1971 to 1986, the number of bachelor's degrees earned in all fields grew slightly, rising to about 1 million in 1986. But the proportion of these degrees earned in liberal-arts fields dropped from 45% in 1971 to 28% in 1985, while the percentage in business grew from 14 to 24 and the percentage in engineering from 6 to 10 (Table 1.2 and Figure 1.2). During this 15-year period, the ratio of the number of liberal-arts degrees to business and engineering degrees

Table 1.2 Percentage and Total Number of Degrees Awarded in the Liberal Arts, Business, and Engineering[a]

Year	Liberal arts (%)	Business (%)	Engineering (%)	Total number, all fields (1000s)
1971	45	14	6	840
1975	40	14	5	923
1977	36	16	5	920
1978	35	17	6	921
1979	33	19	7	921
1980	32	20	7	929
1981	31	21	8	935
1982	30	23	8	953
1983	29	23	9	970
1984	28	24	10	974
1985	28	24	10	979
1986	29	24	10	989

[a]Liberal arts includes degrees classified in the life, physical, and social sciences, foreign languages, letters, and philosophy, and mathematics.
Source: U.S. Department of Education (1987a,b).

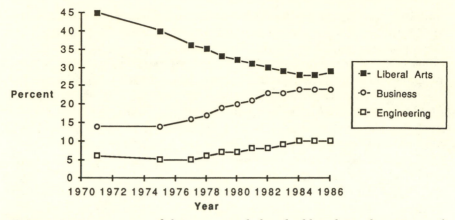

FIGURE 1.2. Percentage of degrees awarded in the liberal arts, business, and engineering, 1971–1986.

reversed from 2.3 to 0.8. "Higher education has a stake as never before in the study of business," observed the Carnegie Foundation for the Advancement of Teaching in 1987. It called the change "certainly one of the most important trends in higher education during the last decade."[6]

However, the proportion of baccalaureate degrees awarded in the arts and sciences increased from 28% in 1985 to 29% in 1986, the first sign of growth in 15 years. Since shifting freshmen preferences would not be mirrored in graduation majors until at least 4 years later, the even stronger recent upturn in freshmen interest in the liberal arts may push this proportion still higher in the years ahead. At the same time, business held its own, with an historic high of 24% of the graduating seniors majoring in this area in 1984, 1985, and 1986. Thus what have been opposing trends between the liberal-arts and business enrollments may be becoming parallel trends, with both the liberal-arts and the business level holding steady if not increasing.

The decline in the fortunes of the liberal arts during the 1970s was in all likelihood symptomatic of several concurrent trends: (1) a slack job market that made all new employment, including that of new college graduates, more difficult; (2) a more career-oriented and income-conscious cultural climate on campus; and (3) a decline in student academic abilities.

A. Employment Market for College Graduates

The employment market for college graduates generally worsened in the early 1970s, partly because the rise in the number of college

graduates during that period was not accompanied by a corresponding rise in the skill levels of the employment market. Comparing conditions in 1976 with those in 1960, for instance, one analyst found that
this condition of "overeducation" had significantly increased, particularly for the college educated, forcing many to take jobs below the
skills level they would have found in the past. Added to this was a
general weakening of the economy in the late 1970s and early 1980s.
With slackened corporate earnings, the message coming from many
companies was particularly disheartening for the liberal-arts major.
Northwestern University's annual "Endicott Report" on the employment of college graduates, for instance, gave a bleak forecast in 1983
for hiring during the coming several years. Of the more than 260
companies responding to the annual Northwestern survey, 20% fore-
saw an increase in the hiring of liberal-arts graduates, while 40% expected a decrease. By contrast, 69% expected an increase in the hiring
of engineers, and only 4% a decrease. With the results of the Northwestern survey and similar reports widely circulated in the media,
many students turned to the security of undergraduate professional
majors such as business and engineering, viewed as more certain
avenues to employment than most liberal-arts majors.[7]

Employment prospects in areas of traditional strength for certain
kinds of liberal-arts majors—such as teachers—also sharply declined.
In 1963, according to a national study, humanities graduates from the
class of 1958 found ample opportunities in the then-expanding field
of teaching: of those employed full time 5 years after graduation,
a third of the male graduates in humanities (35%) and nearly two
thirds (64%) of the female graduates were teachers. By contrast, an
analogous study of humanities graduates in the late 1970s found
only 6% of male graduates and 17% of female graduates engaged in
teaching. With the renewed demand for teachers emerging in the
late 1980s, however, this trend could well reverse.[8]

The relative earnings value of a college education also slipped in
the latter part of the 1970s. While this affected all college graduates, its impact may have been most acutely felt by liberal-arts majors who already felt more vulnerable to the problems of securing
employment upon graduation. One traditional measure of the economic returns from higher education is the ratio of the earnings
of college graduates compared to high-school graduates who are in
the work force. As seen in Table 1.3, the earning power of the college degree declined in the late 1970s. Young male college graduates
who were working full time in 1975 had a 21% advantage over their
high-school-graduate contemporaries in 1975, but by 1979 this had
dropped to 15%. Young female college graduates working full time
had a 36% advantage in 1975, but this had also declined to 28% in

Table 1.3 Median Income of Year-Round Full-Time Employed College Graduates and High-School Graduates 25 to 34 Years Old

Year	Men			Women		
	College ($1000)	High school ($1000)	Ratio	College ($1000)	High school ($1000)	Ratio
1975	14.7	12.1	1.21	10.4	7.7	1.36
1976	15.3	12.6	1.21	10.8	8.2	1.32
1977	16.0	13.5	1.19	11.3	8.8	1.29
1978	17.3	15.0	1.15	12.1	9.4	1.28
1980	20.5	17.0	1.21	15.1	11.3	1.36
1981	22.8	18.1	1.32	16.7	12.0	1.39
1983	25.3	18.8	1.34	18.2	13.1	1.43
1984	26.5	20.3	1.30	19.9	14.0	1.43
1985	28.9	20.1	1.44	21.3	14.6	1.46

Source: U.S. Bureau of the Census (1987 and earlier years).

1978. However, during the early 1980s the advantage was more than fully restored for both genders, reaching 44% for men and 46% for women in 1985.

Indeed, this restoration of the earnings advantage of a college education is probably a critical contributing factor in the recovery of interest in the liberal arts among first-year college students recorded during the fall of 1986 and 1987 (see Table 1.1). If liberal-arts undergraduates felt more vulnerable than business and engineering undergraduates during the period of slack employment for college graduates in the late 1970s, their confidence may also have been more rapidly restored during the period of more robust employment prospects for college graduates in the mid-1980s.

B. Campus Culture

A more career-oriented and income-conscious culture on campus also skewed curricular choices away from liberal arts toward business and engineering, areas promising early access to well-paying positions. The political activism and concern with broader social issues of the 1960s and early 1970s gave way to the self-focused concern of "getting ahead." This reversal of the predominant cultural currents is perhaps no more starkly illustrated than by the opposite trends in two key barometers of college-freshmen values, their financial and philosophical goals. In 1970, 39% of the nation's entering students endorsed "being very well-off financially" as one of their primary life goals. By 1987, this had risen to 76%. Conversely, 80% of the freshmen in 1970 had endorsed "developing a meaningful philosophy in life" as a major goal, but by 1987 this had dropped to 39% (Figure 1.3).

Research on student values and occupational choice generally reveals that intensified concern with career values and diminished concern with reflective values encourage students to move toward careers in business. This is shown, for instance, in a detailed 4-year study of undergraduates in the graduating class of 1981 at Stanford University. The study designated as "careerists" those students who viewed the college experience primarily as an opportunity to prepare for a vocation; their values stood in sharp contrast to those who took great interest in learning for its own sake, designated "intellectuals." Careerists, the study found, were far more likely than the intellectuals to plan for a career in business.[9]

Campus currents became not only more career and less socially concerned in the 1970s and early 1980s, but student aspirations also became more explicitly oriented toward a future in the private sector. Comparing the outlook of first-year college students in 1987 with those in 1970 and at 5-year intervals between (Table 1.4), significantly higher proportions of college freshmen in 1985 and 1987 than in 1970 (1) intended to seek a career in business, (2) sought to have administrative responsibility for others, (3) looked to be successful

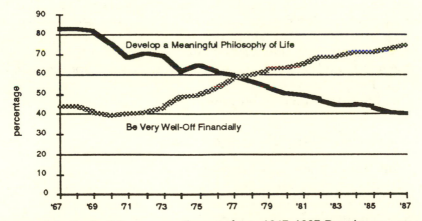

FIGURE 1.3. Goals of first-year college students, 1967–1987. Data in percentage of freshmen who identify goal as "essential" or "very important." *Source*: Astin *et al.* (1987b), reprinted by permission.

Table 1.4 Percentage of First-Year College Students Endorsing
Business-Related Career Goals, 1970–1987

Business-related goal	1970	1975	1980	1985	1987
Business is probable career occupation[a]	11	14	20	24	25
Having administrative responsibility for others is essential or very important	22	31	39	43	45
Being successful in business of one's own is essential or very important	44	44	49	52	51
Becoming an expert on finance and commerce is essential or very important	16	—	—	26	28
Being able to make more money was a very important reason for going to college[b]	50	54	63	70	71

[a]Includes business management, owner or proprietor, salesperson or buyer, and accountant or actuary.
[b]The figure in the 1970 column is for 1971 and in the 1975 column is for 1976; information was not collected on this issue in 1970 and 1975.
Source: Astin, Green, and Korn (1987); Astin *et al.* (1987b).

in a business of their own, and (4) aspired to be experts on finance and commerce. Also, consistent with the rise of financial well-being as a primary life goal, a higher proportion of freshmen stated that (5) being able to make more money was an important factor in their decision to attend college. College-student values, in short, markedly shifted during the 1970s and early 1980s toward goals far more oriented toward careers in business.

C. Academic Abilities of College Students

A third current that may have been responsible for the liberal-arts decline was a deterioration in the academic abilities of college-bound high-school graduates. The well-documented decline in student abilities during the 1970s, as measured in SAT scores and other standardized evaluations, left fewer students well prepared to enter certain liberal-arts disciplines. The national average SAT verbal score in

1970 was 460, but by 1980 this had dropped to 423; the average SAT mathematics score had declined from 488 to 467. The lowered verbal abilities among college entrants may have deterred some from entering English or foreign languages. The weakened mathematical abilities may have discouraged others from entering the quantitatively demanding fields of physics or chemistry.[10]

Graduating high-school seniors also brought a weaker foundation to college in many of the specific liberal-arts disciplines. The knowledge base of 17-year-olds has long been tracked by the National Assessment of Educational Progress, and knowledge in science and mathematics declined during the 1970s. Although time-series data are not available on the humanities and social sciences, a 1986 national assessment of the knowledge of 17-year-olds in the fields of history and literature found grave deficiencies in these areas as well. Chester E. Finn, Jr., one of the study's authors concluded: "We're raising a generation of historical and literary incompetents." Increased student hesitancy to enter college majors that presupposed certain levels of secondary-school preparation may have been one of the casualties.[11]

Liberal-arts colleges themselves were also partly to blame. The diverse and often weakly structured curriculum introduced or evolved by many institutions in the 1970s discouraged some students from pursuing the liberal arts, and perhaps even more parents from endorsing such study. The loss of "integrity in the college curriculum," noted an assessment offered by the Association of American Colleges, was among the most fundamental problems confronting higher education in the mid-1980s. How widespread public dissatisfaction with the overspecialized courses and understructured graduation requirements had become was evident in the mass public readership attracted to Allan Bloom's 1987 critique of the liberal-arts curriculum, *The Closing of the American Mind.*[12]

Sniping at the structureless curriculum found currency in other public forums as well. "At Princeton, they call it an education," but it amounts to a "total disintegration of Princeton's academic standards," said an author on the op-ed page in the *New York Times*. The target for his commentary was the publicly available transcript of a 1986 Princeton graduate with a degree in French, actress Brooke Shields. The critic noted that Princeton failed to require her to take any courses in history, mathematics, economics, world literature, or a science with laboratory experience. "If that adds up to a liberal arts education from a place like Princeton, there is no longer any danger that our society will ever suffer from elitism in any form," he concluded.[13]

III. Educational Reform

The ebbing of student interest in the liberal arts in the 1970s and early 1980s engendered a renewal of national interest in the mid-1980s. Alarmed at the declining numbers of liberal-arts graduates and limited exposure to the liberal arts by students in business, engineering, and other programs, public agencies and private associations initiated a range of efforts to revitalize the liberal-arts curriculum and restore public confidence in it (see Table 1.5). The initiatives focused on the quality of liberal education in itself, the importance of a liberal-arts foundation for undergraduate education in other fields, and the utilitarian value of liberal learning for professional and managerial careers.

Several federal-government agencies spearheaded the reform. The National Institute of Education charged a study group with reviewing the quality of higher education, and among its final recommendations in 1984 was a call for a vigorous strengthening of liberal learning on campus. The panel urged "what some might regard as a radical restructuring of undergraduate professional programs in fields ranging from agriculture, business administration, and engineering to music, nursing, pharmacy, and teacher education." The goal: students in all undergraduate fields—including management—should carry at least 2 years of liberal education, a change in requirements for many of the professionally oriented undergraduate disciplines that could mandate an undergraduate education extending beyond the customary 4 years.[14]

The National Endowment for the Humanities added its voice in 1984. Drawing on the findings of a special study group on the humanities, William J. Bennett, then chairman of the Endowment, called for the restoration of humanities to a central place in the college curriculum. The goal, he wrote, is for "all students to know a common culture rooted in civilization's lasting vision, its highest shared ideals and aspirations, and its heritage." This challenge was extended to secondary education as well in 1987 by the next chairman of the National Endowment for the Humanities, Lynne V. Cheney.[15]

Reform of the entire undergraduate curriculum was the objective of a far-reaching critique in 1985 by the Association of American Colleges (AAC). The AAC identified nine elements essential to any undergraduate education, ranging from instruction in critical inquiry and abstract reasoning to the study of science, arts, and a subject in depth. The elements define many of the generic components of a liberal education, and the AAC urged that they be part of every

Table 1.5 Recommendations for Educational Reform and Strengthening of the Liberal Arts

Organization (and author)	Year	Recommendations for liberal-arts education
National Institute of Education	1984	Require 2 years of liberal education for all undergraduate programs
National Endowment for the Humanities (William J. Bennett)	1984	Place study of humanities and Western civilization at the core of the college curriculum
Association of American Colleges	1985	Include nine elements basic to all undergraduate education, from critical inquiry to science, art, and international experience
Business–Higher Education Forum	1985	Broaden the curriculum in business programs to include social, political, and ethical issues
Carnegie Foundation for the Advancement of Teaching (Ernest L. Boyer)	1987	Integrate the liberal and useful arts in the undergraduate curriculum
National Governors' Association	1987	Expand international education and foreign-language requirements in undergraduate education
Professional Preparation Network	1988	More effectively integrate undergraduate liberal-arts and professional programs
American Association of Community and Junior Colleges	1988	Strengthen core curriculum and close gap between liberal and useful arts
Educational Leadership Project	1988	Provide a liberal-arts education for all high-school students

undergraduate experience, whether in the liberal arts, in business, or in engineering.[16]

Increasing the place of the liberal arts in enriching professionally oriented undergraduate training was among the goals for educational reform stressed by Ernest L. Boyer in his report, *College*, prepared for the Carnegie Foundation for the Advancement of Teaching. The challenge for undergraduate education, he concluded, "is to enlarge lives by bringing meaning to the world of work. And the special task of the undergraduate college is to relate the values of the liberal learning to vocation." He urged that college education combine the liberal arts and the "useful arts" throughout the undergraduate curriculum.[17]

Still other organizations urged additional emphasis on special elements of a liberal-arts education for those planning a career in the private sector. The Business–Higher Education Forum, a select group of corporate and university presidents, recommended in 1985 that the nation's business schools diversify their curricula to include more study of the social and political context of business and more emphasis on communication skills. Sharing similar concerns about national competitiveness, in 1987 the National Governors' Association called upon the states to increase their emphasis on international education. Colleges should raise or reinstate foreign-language requirements and courses should be more widely available on the history, geography, culture, and economics of other nations. "American businessmen involved in international trade have much to learn as they get started," observed the governors' report, and thus states "have an important role to play in educating businesses about the languages, cultures, and practices of foreign countries that are potential markets for American goods and services."[18]

Professional organizations also pressed for the strengthening of liberal education for undergraduate professional training in specific areas. The American Association of College Nursing recommended in 1986 a stronger liberal-arts experience for the undergraduate nursing curriculum. Observing that "liberally educated nurses make informed and responsible ethical choices and help shape the future of society," a national panel of the association asked for a vigorous exposure of nursing students to the liberal curriculum. In the field of teacher education, the Carnegie Forum on Education and the Economy urged in 1986 that the undergraduate preparation of teachers take place entirely in colleges of liberal arts—rather than in schools of education—and a similar reform was proposed in 1986 by the "Holmes Groups," and informal association of the leading graduate schools of education. To encourage the greater use of undergraduate liberal-arts programs that include teacher-training opportunities, the Association of American Colleges completed a study in 1988 of the approximately 1000 programs in the country offering such training. Many were found to be effective in attracting and training able students, suggesting that a national effort to more strongly base teacher training in liberal-arts programs could indeed improve the quality and supply of the next generation of schoolteachers.[19]

Even the undergraduate engineering curriculum felt the liberal-arts momentum. The Colorado School of Mines instituted a program stressing liberal learning as early as 1979, for instance, and the Massachusetts Institute of Technology moved to do the same in 1987. The MIT faculty adopted a new set of undergraduate requirements intended to significantly increase the exposure of its engineering students to the humanities and social sciences. A professional engineer "lives and operates in a social system, and he needs to understand cultural and human values," observed the president of MIT, Paul E. Gray. Among the goals was enhancing the engineering graduate's prospects for promotion into the managerial ranks of business. Said one Institute official: "Too many M.I.T. graduates end up working for too many Princeton and Harvard graduates." More generally, a study of the liberal-arts coursework of undergraduate engineering students at 18 institutions, completed by the Association of American Colleges of graduates in 1986, confirmed that many engineering students develop little depth or breadth in the humanities and social sciences. To improve the liberal-arts coursework of undergraduate engineering students, the association initiated efforts to enhance campus advising in this area.[20]

Focusing on all areas of undergraduate professional study, a group of educators called in 1988 for a general strengthening and integration of liberal arts and professional programs. Whether architecture, business, engineering, journalism, nursing, pharmacy, social work, or teacher education, the "Professional Preparation Network" urged that undergraduate teaching in these areas be more effectively integrated with traditional liberal-arts offerings. Among the proposals put forward by the educators, organized through the University of Michigan's School of Education, were the addition of courses jointly taught by faculty in liberal arts and professional programs and the creation of more joint faculty appointments across these disciplines.[21]

Still other groups urged a general strengthening of liberal education at levels of the American educational system where the liberal arts curriculum had generally received less attention. Focusing on the curriculum of community colleges, a commission created by the American Association of Community and Junior Colleges urged in 1988 that all 2-year colleges require a core curriculum "that provides historical perspective, an understanding of our social institutions, knowledge of science and technology, and an appreciation of the visual and performing arts." Headed by Ernest Boyer, the commission recommended that "community college faculty should take the lead in closing the gap between the so-called 'liberal' and 'useful' arts. Students in technical studies should be helped to discover the meaning of work," the panel wrote. "They should put their special skills in historical, social, and ethical perspective." Similarly, a group of more than 30 educators, brought together by the New York–based Educational Leadership Project, issued a call in 1988 for a liberal education for all high-school students, regardless of whether they are college bound. "Liberal arts and science courses should be established as the basis of the curriculum in all schools," recommended the group. All high-school "students deserve the opportunity that it affords to know what is possible for them in their lives."[22]

A range of agencies and organizations thus promoted a revitalization of liberal learning as a goal of American education. Liberal education was viewed as central to a variety of undergraduate programs, not just the liberal arts. But also at issue were the quality of liberal education and the underestimated value of liberal education for postgraduate careers.

IV. College Education and Corporate Employment

While educational reform is a deserving end in its own right, it acquires special power because of the strong linkage between college education and later occupational achievement. Moreover, the linkage between a college education and *corporate* employment is particularly strong, and both students looking to the private sector and employers in the private sector have a major stake in the outcome of the educational change.

The association between higher education and employment in America is well documented, and the critical event is completing college. Of those employed in 1986 who had completed a high-school education only, 17% held managerial and professional positions, and of those who had completed 1 to 3 years of college, 20% were so employed. But 60% of the college graduates were employed in managerial and professional positions.

The importance of having a college degree is also evident in individual earnings. This is starkly illustrated by a study of the graduates of one large Midwestern university: those who completed 3½ years of their undergraduate education with a solid "A" average—but then dropped out for personal reasons—earned *less* than those students with a "C" average who finished one additional term and graduated from the university. More generally, among full-time workers aged 25 to 34, college graduates have in recent years commanded salaries that are 30 to 45% higher on average than salaries of high-school graduates (Table 1.4). This income disparity increases as the employees grow older. Among those aged 45 to 54, the college educated are earning from 60 to 75% more than those with only a high-school education.[23]

The linkage between higher education and corporate management is also well established. A college education has become a virtual prerequisite for entry into a company's professional and managerial ranks. Surveys of middle and senior managers typically reveal that 80 to 90% hold college degrees. The present survey of company managers, for instance, finds that 88% had graduated from college. The nonmanagerial ranks of most companies, by contrast, include majorities who have not obtained a college degree.

Corporate employers use the college credential, according to a variety of studies, as a selection device for three interrelated reasons. The first and foremost acknowledged reason is the set of educated skills and abilities that the bachelor's degree confirms. Yet the specific skills and abilities of the college graduate are only part of the story. Employers also rely upon the college credential, second, as a measure of the social and personality skills that are required for exercising authority in a company setting. Maturity and drive are among the qualities often singled out by employers. Third, companies draw upon the college degree as a screening device, a measure of the holder's success in gaining entry into a competitive setting and in possessing the intelligence and self-discipline required to earn the 4-year degree.[24]

Within the corporate hierarchy, the college credential continues to exercise a commanding influence on promotion and salary. This is evident, for example, in detailed studies of employees within specific companies. An analysis of the career records of one well-established corporation with nearly 15,000 employees reveals that a BA degree provides a significant advantage to the holder's probability of promotion not only in the early years with the corporation, but also, for those who stay with the company for many years, throughout the career span. Moreover, earnings are sharply affected by the college degree as well. Focusing for analytic reasons on white males who had entered the firm during a 10-year period beginning in 1953, it is found that employees without a college degree earned on average about 42% less in 1962 than those with a college degree. Following the same cohort over a further 13-year period, the study revealed that the difference diminished some over time but never vanished, with the difference remaining about 25% in 1975. Additional education in the form of a MBA degree added modestly to the employees' earning power: MBA holders earned some 6% more than BA holders at the start of the period, and they retained a 3% advantage by the end (larger differences in MBA earnings may have been observed if the study had been conducted during the 1980s, an era in which the MBA acquired special salary advantages in many firms).[25]

Study of lower and middle-level managers in another large manufacturing corporation by two other analysts yields corroborating results. With a data base of over 8000 professionals and managers, they found that, even after taking preemployment and experience within the company into account, high-school graduates earned about 20% less than those with college degrees, and master's degree holders earned about 11% more. The introduction of performance ratings into the analysis reduces the direct effects of a college education on earnings, but even then a modest but statistically significant relationship remains.[26]

While a college degree thus has a substantial bearing on whether one enters the professional and managerial ranks of a company, and on promotion probabilities and earnings prospects long after hiring, we know that colleges differ in their capacity to deliver both. Certainly many students and their parents act on the assumption that the choice of a college does make a major difference. This is particularly true among parents who themselves have completed college. They are especially likely to encourage their children to take preparatory courses to maximize their SAT performance, to invest in the cost of applying to a number of institutions, and to take their children to visit a range of college campuses. While such steps are motivated in part by a search for a good "fit" between the student's abilities and the college's offerings, they are also intended in part to maximize the child's postgraduate opportunities.

Corroborating evidence comes from a market-research company whose clients include colleges and universities. With periodic surveys of high-school students intending to enter college and their parents, it found that a driving concern among students and parents in the mid-1980s had become the capacity of a college or university to assure good postgraduate opportunities. "What do students want? For what are they and their parents willing to pay?" asked the head of the market-research company: "There seems to be one answer—

status as embodied in programs that will lead to high-paying jobs or entrance to a prestigious professional school." Moreover, a college's capacity to deliver desirable postgraduate outcomes became more significant to students by the mid-1980s. Tracking college-bound-student assessments of the academic quality of colleges from the late 1970s to mid-1980s, the company found a steady increase in the proportions of students who emphasized the importance of the record of the college's graduates in gaining desirable positions in business and industry. In comparing two institutions with similar qualities in their academic faculties and teaching, graduating high-school seniors increasingly chose the institution with the superior track record in placing its matriculants after graduation.[27]

First-year college students confirm that future job opportunities are indeed a leading consideration in selecting their college of choice. In the fall of 1987, more than 200,000 freshmen at 390 colleges and universities were asked to rate 15 factors in their decision to attend the college in which they had enrolled. The institution's academic quality was the leading factor, but closely behind was its record of placing graduates into "good jobs." The five leading factors and the percentage of college freshmen selecting each are as follows:[28]

Percentage stating reason	Leading reason for attending this particular college
56	College has a very good academic reputation
48	*College's graduates get good jobs*
28	College's graduates gain admission to top graduate/professional schools
27	College has a good reputation for its social activities
22	College offers special educational programs

Research generally shows that a college's selectivity and reputation are indeed correlated with its graduates' career prospects in the private sector. One study examined the quality of the colleges from which nearly 1000 white male managers of Ford Motor Company had graduated, and the quality factor was found to enhance both earnings and the probability of promotion. Focusing only on graduates with grade-point averages of 3.5 or better, for instance, the study found that the annual probability of promotion was .53 for those from the most selective colleges, but .33 for those from the least selective colleges. The study of the 15,000-employee corporation described above also examined the impact of college selectivity on the likelihood of promotion, and it revealed that advantages do accrue from having attended a highly competitive institution, at least in the early years of employment. The probability of promotion averaged .63 among those from top-ranking colleges during the first 3 years of service, but it stood at .50 on average for those who had graduated from the least selective colleges. These promotion differences cannot, of course, be entirely attributed to the quality of the college or other intercollegiate differences, since students themselves bring important individual differences to college that are correlated with college selectivity and other institutional factors.[29]

The quality and reputation of a college can have lingering career effects on managers even after their arrival within the senior corporate ranks, according to a study of more than 2700 senior managers of 208 large American corporations. This research compared senior managers who held BA degrees from 11 top-rated institutions (such as Stanford University and Williams College) with those who held BAs from other colleges and universities. Both groups were far more likely than those without a college education to have reached their elevated status within senior management, but they also differed significantly from each other. The group of managers from top-ranked undergraduate colleges reached the vice-presidential level substantially earlier in their careers than the other college graduates; they were over 40% more likely to have reached the position of chief executive officer; and they were over 80% more likely to have been invited onto the boards of directors of several corporations. Differences in the managers' family origins and their "old-boy networks," the evidence suggests, explain some but far from all of these career disparities.[30]

The stature of the MBA institution also makes a difference, according to the same study. Graduates of the nation's top 11 MBA-granting institutions first acquired a vice-presidency at a significantly younger age than those from other MBA programs, and they were 25% more likely to have reached the chief-executive suite. In fact, holders of MBAs from institutions other than the top 11 were significantly less likely to reach the top of the corporate hierarchy than those who held BA degrees only from the top-ranked undergraduate colleges.[31]

It also should be noted that academic ability—as measured by college grades—has an independent effect on corporate employees' earnings and promotions. In the study of Ford managers cited above, the annual rate of salary increase among all managers was 4.5%, but, after taking the selectivity of the college into account, the college grade-point average accounted for as much as half-a-point difference in the percentage rate of salary increase above or below the average. Similarly, promotion rates among BA-degree holders with grade-point averages from 3.5 to 4.0 were a quarter to a third higher than among those with averages from 2.5 to 3.0, again taking into account the competitiveness of the college. Other studies of managers in specific companies (e.g., American Telephone and Telegraph), graduates of specific colleges and universities (e.g., Stanford and Michigan), and college graduates in cross sections of companies, often, though not always, find correlations between college grades and employee earnings.[32]

If a college education makes a difference in corporate careers, and if the quality of the college also makes a difference, logic would suggest that the field of the college degree should also make a difference in the careers of those who enter the private sector. We already know that the college major has a critical bearing on the likelihood of entering business and managerial fields. One study followed up college graduates from the class of 1958, for instance, focusing on their occupation 5 years later. It found that 59% of the male graduates in business and commerce were employed in business and managerial positions, while no more than 25% of the graduates of other fields were so employed; the analogous percentage for females graduates were 21 and 6%. Similar disparities are reported in other studies.[33]

While much of the divergence is obviously a product of differences in the career preferences of the graduates, there is ample evidence that employers place significant emphasis on college seniors' major field of study during campus recruitment. Michigan State University's placement services surveyed 648 employers, 80% in the private sector, in the fall of 1984. They were asked to rate the importance of 10 factors in prescreening candidates for campus interviews and 18 factors in inviting candidates to visit the company after the initial interview. Ratings were placed in five categories ranging from "no importance" to "extremely high" importance. The leading consideration at both the point of selecting candidates for interviews and the point of inviting them to visit the company was the academic major (Table 1.6). The field of study far outranked any other consideration in deciding who would be interviewed on campus; two thirds of the employers considered it extremely important—far ahead of such factors as grade-point average, work experience, extracurricular ac-

Table 1.6 Percentage of 648 Employers Highly Rating Criteria
in Selecting College Students for Campus Interviews
and for Visits to the Employer, 1984

Screening criteria	Percentage reporting extremely high importance
Campus interview	
Academic major	67
Degree level	21
Major grade-point average	16
Previous work experience	16
Expected date of graduation	14
Invitation to visit employer	
Academic major	45
Attitude toward work ethic	44
Oral communication skills	43
Enthusiasm and confidence	34
Motivation to achieve	34

Source: Shingleton and Scheetz (1984), pp. 34–35.

tivities, and communication skills. Academic major was still first in deciding who would come to visit the employer for a second round of interviewing, edging out work attitudes, confidence, and motivation.

With 9 out of 10 professional and managerial employees in most corporations now holding a college degree, having a BA degree has lost most of its power of distinction, other than to reinforce the divide between managerial and nonmanagerial employees. Within the managerial ranks, the quality of the college has become a new source of distinction, however, and the general area of study may have become a significant source of distinction as well.

The evidence that follows shows that companies do draw upon a college graduate's general field of study as a major consideration in their hiring and promotion practices. The decision to pursue undergraduate studies in the liberal arts, business, engineering, or other general area can therefore have a decisive bearing on how a graduate fares in the private-sector employment market. Yet the picture is a highly complex one. The general field of study influences many facets of hiring and promotion in the private sector. Liberal-arts graduates do not follow career paths identical to business and engineering graduates, the evidence indicates, but they do well. A college student's decision to major in the liberal arts or some other general area is thus found to be less one of whether to enter corporate employment and more one of orienting toward certain kinds of companies and specific areas of work within the corporation.

Notes

1. Chandler (1977); Levine (1986), p. 49.
2. Willis (1987); Hirsch (1987), p. 69.
3. Kanter (1983), p. 368.
4. Useem (1985); Keim (1985); Business–Higher Education Forum (1985), p. 13; Useem (1987); Directors and Boards (1987).
5. Fiske (1986).
6. Carnegie Foundation for the Advancement of Teaching (1987).
7. Rumberger (1981); Lindquist (1983).
8. Sharp (1970); Sharp and Weidman (1986).
9. Katchadourian and Boli (1985).
10. Astin, Green, and Korn (1987), p. 16; Austin and Garber (1982); E. Useem (1986).
11. Raizen and Jones (1985); National Assessment of Educational Progress (1978, 1983); Finn and Ravitch (1987); Fiske (1987b), p. B8; Cheney (1987).
12. Association of American Colleges (1985); Bloom (1987).
13. Koppett (1987).
14. National Institute of Education (1984).
15. Bennett (1984); Cheney (1987).
16. Association of American Colleges (1985).
17. Boyer (1987), pp. 110, 115.
18. Business–Higher Education Forum (1985); National Governors' Association (1987), p. 8.
19. American Association of Colleges of Nursing (1986), p. 5; Carnegie Task Force on Teaching as a Profession (1986); Holmes Group (1986).
20. M.I.T. School of Engineering (1986); Fiske (1987a); Johnston, Shaman, and Zemsky (1988).
21. Professional Preparation Network (1988).
22. American Association of Community and Junior Colleges (1988); Educational Leadership Project (1988).
23. U.S. Department of Education (1987a), p. 284; O'Neill and Sepielli (1985), pp. 39–42.
24. Gordon and Howell (1959), pp, 121–125; Collins (1979), pp. 31–48.
25. Rosenbaum (1984), p. 148–149.

25. Rosenbaum (1984), p. 148–149.
27. Krukowski (1985), p. 21.
28. Astin *et al.* (1987b).
29. Wise (1975a, 1975b); Rosenbaum (1984), p. 171; Klitgaard (1985), pp. 220–223.
30. Useem and Karabel (1986); the top 11 BA-granting institutions, as determined by a detailed study of their status in 1940, are Columbia University, Cornell University, Dartmouth College, Harvard University, Johns Hopkins University, Massachusetts Institute of Technology, University of Pennsylvania, Princeton University, Stanford University, Williams College, and Yale University.
31. Useem and Karabel (1986); the top 11 MBA institutions, as identified through several studies, are Columbia University, Dartmouth College, Harvard University, Massachusetts Institute of Technology, Northwestern University, Stanford University, University of California at Berkeley, University of California at Los Angeles, University of Chicago, University of Michigan, and University of Pennsylvania.
32. Wise (1975a, b); Bisconti (1978); Klitgaard (1985), pp. 220–223, provides a recent review.
33. Sharp (1970); Sharp and Weidman (1986); Freeman (1971); Calvert (1969).

2   Corporate Recruitment of Liberal-Arts Graduates

A college education has become the necessary credential for admittance to and advancement in corporate management. Its ascendance has followed the emergence of the professional manager at the top of the company. In the early part of the century when many firms were still led by their owner-founder, self-made men with little college education generally presided over their personally built organizations. The "managerial revolution," first characterized by Adolph Berle and Gardiner Means more than 50 years ago, increasingly swept owners from power, however. As new cadres of professional managers acquired control, they created a management culture which took it for granted that no professional manager could effectively rule without a college degree. By the 1950s, a college education had emerged as a requisite element for respectability within the world traveled by William H. Whyte's "organization man" and David Riesman's "other-directed" manager. Recent studies by economist Edward Herman confirm that the managerial revolution, whose start was chronicled by Berle and Means in the 1930s, was largely completed by the 1970s. It placed the professional manager firmly in control of most major companies.[1]

The rise of the college-educated professional manager at the helm of the nation's largest corporations can be seen in the evolving educational profiles of their chief executives. In 1900, about a quarter of the CEOs of the nation's large companies had completed college (Table 2.1). Yet by 1950 the proportion had reached nearly two thirds, and by the mid-1980s it was exceeding 9 out of 10. A study of the country's top 850 companies in 1987 thus found that 94% of their chief executives had been college educated, signifying what had become a universal expectation for corporate ascent. Postgraduate study came to replace the bachelor's degree as one of the new discriminators, though even here such study was no longer the province of a privileged few. Two thirds of the CEOs in one study of the mid-1980s had pursued at least some postgraduate study, primarily in business or engineering.[2]

Table 2.1 College Background of Top Company Managers,
            1900–1987

Year	Managerial group	Percentage with at least a bachelor's degree	Percentage with postbaccalaureate education
1987	CEOs of *Fortune's* 850 companies	94	—
1985	512 CEOs of *Fortune's* 1000 companies	89	63
1978	536 presidents and chairmen of *Fortune's* 1300 companies	93	58
1950	863 presidents and chairmen of largest companies	63	17
1925	319 presidents and chairmen of largest companies	41	15
1900	284 presidents and chairmen of largest companies	27	9

Source: See note 2.

While a college education has thus become the universal ticket
for entry into a managerial career, at least within the nation's largest
corporations, we found that companies discriminate sharply among
college-graduate applicants according to their majors. The industrial-
products firm we studied (Case C, see Appendix to Chapter 4) hired
nearly 500 college graduates in 1986, and a college degree was a
prerequisite for entry into its professional and managerial ranks.
Yet the firm's technology—it is one of the nation's leading makers
of electronic and related products—placed a premium on college
graduates with technical training, above all in engineering. Over half
of the nearly 500 college graduates hired in 1986 had earned degrees
in electrical engineering, and a large portion of the remainder had
graduated in engineering and, to a lesser extent, business fields.
Fewer than 20 had received liberal-arts degrees, and they were all
earned in mathematics or the natural sciences. By contrast, the

consumer-products company we studied (Case A, see Appendix to this chapter) had hired 32 new product managers in 1986, and the majority of these held a MBA with a liberal-arts undergraduate degree.[3]

American culture and lore are filled with accounts of where liberal-arts graduates purportedly do well or poorly. Managerial careers with one of New Jersey's largest employers are said to especially prosper if one possesses the four "Ps," with one of the "Ps" signifying the holding of an undergraduate liberal-arts degree from Princeton University. Careers at one of New York's major banks are presumed to be influenced as well by the possession of a Princeton degree, a presumption based on the presence of a bank officer on Princeton's board of trustees, the presence of a Princeton official on the bank's board of directors, and three Princeton graduates among the firm's seniormost officers.

Similarly, liberal-arts undergraduates at Williams College know that they are often sought by New York's financial firms who want the "best and brightest" regardless of field of study. A 1987 newsletter sent to prospective Williams College applicants was intended to reassure students-to-be and their parents who may have had any doubts: "One of the issues that you and your parents may be deliberating . . . is whether Williams, an undergraduate college of the liberal arts, or another institution offering career-oriented studies will do more to ensure better job opportunities after graduation. The answer . . . is that Williams graduates are capable of moving regularly—and unrelated to fluctuations in the U.S. economy—into all professional areas," including business. Among the highest earners in the recently graduated class of 1987, the report notes, was an art-history major working as a financial analyst with an investment bank. More generally, states the newsletter, business leads the careers areas in which Williams' 15,000 alumni are presently employed:[4]

Business	4164	Law	2024
Banking	918	Education	1809
Sales	620	Medicine	1238
Marketing	539	Research	635
Insurance	402	Government	438
Manufacturing	398		
Management consulting	349		
Other sectors	938		

Whatever the perceived advantage of a liberal-arts degree from an established college as a credential for entering banking, campus cultures also recognize that a liberal-arts degree will find little currency with companies in certain other sectors. Few opportunities are believed to exist, for example, among electronics and computer manufacturers. A manager of college recruitment for one of the nation's leading computer makers, Digital Equipment Corporation, confirms that "there isn't relatively a lot of opportunity for liberal arts majors," and although few students will have heard this directly, it is indirectly encoded in student opinion surrounding job hunting. Electrical equipment companies are not viewed as strong prospects for liberal-arts graduates.[5]

Yet numerous accounts do not a complete picture make, nor are the accounts always reliable guides in any case. While systematic general assessment cannot replace knowledge of whether a specific corporation is likely to hire a liberal-arts graduate, it can furnish a guide to the general context of opportunities within which individual choices are shaped. The present chapter is intended to develop that picture, focusing on where liberal-arts graduates are likely to find greatest opportunities as they enter the private-sector labor market. We are concerned with not only the type of corporation where opportunities may be greatest, but also the areas within the company where they may be most—and least—abundant.

I. Recruitment of Liberal-Arts Graduates

Support for the recruitment of liberal-arts graduates is substantial among the leadership of America's major corporations. Of critical concern is whether senior managers translate their general support for liberal education of future managers into explicit backing for the recruitment of liberal-arts graduates into their own managerial ranks.

The company survey revealed that senior managers in a quarter or more of the nation's corporations had indeed promoted the hiring of liberal-arts graduates in their own company. The responding company official was asked whether he or she and other senior managers had "encouraged or discouraged the hiring of liberal arts graduates for entry-level positions" during the past 5 years. Few were reported to have discouraged the recruitment of liberal-arts graduates, and significant proportions backed the hiring (liberal-arts graduates were defined as those completing 4-year degrees in the social sciences, natural sciences, and humanities). Encouragement most of-

Table 2.2 Percentage of Firms ($N = 535$) Reporting That Company Executives Encouraged or Discouraged the Hiring of Liberal-Arts Graduates for Entry-Level Positions During the Past 5 Years

Company executive	Encouraged	Discouraged
Chief executive officer	24	2
Chief financial officer	11	6
Responding human-resource executive	42	3
Other human-resource executives	37	3
Sales executives	22	5
Marketing executives	21	6
Manufacturing executives	6	9

ten came from human-resources executives—some two fifths had backed the hiring of liberal-arts graduates—but even a quarter of the chief executive officers were supportive (Table 2.2). In the case of a fifth of the companies, the sales and marketing executives had promoted the hiring of liberal-arts graduates as well. Manufacturing executives, however, expressed little interest.[6]

Company programs explicitly intended to recruit liberal-arts graduates are even more widespread. Almost half of the corporations recruited liberal-arts graduates on campus, and more than a quarter reported other efforts to recruit liberal-arts graduates (Table 2.3).

Table 2.3 Percentage of Firms ($N = 535$) Reporting Programs and Policies Related to the Recruitment and Training of College Graduates

Program or policy	Percentage
Recruitment	
On-campus recruitment of liberal-arts graduates	45
Other active efforts to recruit liberal-arts graduates	29
Training	
Training programs open to new employees with liberal-arts degrees	61
Internship or cooperative-education programs open to liberal-arts students	47

Moreover, nearly two thirds operated training programs for new employees that were open to liberal-arts graduates, and almost half provided internship or cooperative-education programs that were available to liberal-arts students.

Corporate recruitment of liberal-arts students on campus typically begins with the company contacting the college's or university's
placement office to arrange for a day or two of interviewing graduating seniors. The company indicates in advance the kinds of majors
it is seeking, and a list of forthcoming recruiter visits and the majors wanted is posted for student review. The recruiting calendar for
March 1988 for one major private university's general placement office, for instance, included 42 employers, most of which were large
companies. Among them were the following, along with the majors
they sought:

Company	Majors sought in recruitment
Northrop Corporation	Electrical, systems, computer, and mechanical engineering; computer science
Aetna Life and Casualty Company	Business; chemistry, physics, economics, mathematics; prelaw
GTE Inc.	Electrical, computer, and systems engineering; computer science; mathematics
Metropolitan Property and Liability	Liberal arts; communications; education
Osco Drugs	Any majors interested in retail

A few companies recruited liberal-arts graduates only, but more
commonly sought were liberal-arts graduates along with those in
business, engineering, and other fields. Some companies simply left
the major entirely open. Unexpressed company preferences may
surface when the companies prescreen student résumés to select
the interviewees, but this university requires that at least half of the
campus interviews be open to the first students who sign up, provided
that their majors fit the preannounced areas sought by the company.
Thus when companies report that they recruit liberal-arts graduates
on campus, they often mean that they include liberal arts among
the fields in which they seek candidates. Only occasionally do they

limit university recruitment to liberal-arts majors only, though many companies also recruit at liberal-arts colleges where that is all they will find.

The new liberal-arts graduates hired by major companies in 1986 still constituted a modest fraction of entry-level recruitment that year. Some companies hired no new employees, while a few brought several thousand onto the payroll. The average (median) number of new employees hired by a company was 71 (Table 2.4). The median figure for liberal-arts graduates hired was 9; for business graduates, 15; and engineering graduates, 2.

The trends were about the same for all groups: during the previous 3 years, one half to two thirds of the companies had increased or left unchanged the number of new graduates they hired annually. During the coming 2 years, the rate of hiring of liberal-arts graduates was expected to parallel that of all new hires as well. Two thirds to three quarters of the companies forecast no significant changes in hiring plans for either liberal-arts graduates or other entry-level hires. Fewer companies plan to increase their recruitment of liberal-arts graduates than do companies of other graduates (28 vs. 18%), but fewer companies also anticipate decreasing their hiring of liberal-arts graduates than do companies of other graduates (13 vs. 9%).

Table 2.4 Trends in Company Hiring ($N = 535$) at the Entry Level, 1983–1988

Type of new employee	Percentage of firms increasing or not changing the number of new hires, 1983–1986	Median number of new employees, 1986	Percentage of firms forecasting change or no change in number of new hires, 1987–1988		
			Increase	No change	Decrease
Liberal-arts graduates	64	9	18	73	9
Business graduates	68	15		n.a.	
Engineering graduates	53	2		n.a.	
All entry-level hires	61	71	28	60	13

The placement of liberal-arts graduates is skewed toward areas in corporations where communication and nontechnical skills are at a premium. Companies were asked to identify the two or three areas where the largest number of liberal-arts graduates have been placed during the past 3 years. At the top of the list were sales and marketing, followed by human resources and general management; at the bottom of the list were manufacturing, planning, and research and development (Table 2.5).[7]

More generally, marketing and sales are viewed as two of the areas where a liberal education has high payoff for managerial performance. The proportions of companies identifying the liberal arts as a useful background for a successful manager ranged from a high of 91% for human resources or personnel to 35% in manufacturing (Table 2.6). Marketing and sales were close to the top here as well, with 83% of the companies viewing them as areas where a liberal education would have substantial managerial value.[8]

The relative importance of this rank ordering is confirmed by the managers whom we directly surveyed. They were also asked to identify the areas of the company in which an undergraduate liberal-arts degree would prove to be a useful educational background. While slightly fewer managers generally felt that liberal arts would be useful for each of the areas than was the case for the companies, the relative assessments were closely parallel (Table 2.6). More than two thirds of the managers held that in human resources, public affairs, and marketing and sales liberal arts would be of value; manufacturing ranked at the bottom here as well.[9]

Table 2.5 Percentage of Firms (*N* = 535) Reporting Areas Where Largest Number of Liberal-Arts Graduates Have Been Placed During Past 3 Years

Area of company	Percentage of firms
Sales and marketing	53
Entry-level management	36
Human resources or personnel	37
Clerical/support staff	28
Public affairs or government relations	14
Manufacturing	8
Planning	7
Research and development	4

Table 2.6 Percentage of Corporations and Managers Reporting a Liberal-Arts Background as Useful to a Manager, by Manager's Area of Company

Manager's area of company	Percentage viewing liberal arts as useful for area	
	Corporations (N = 535)	Managers (N = 505)
Human resources or personnel	91	82
Public affairs or government relations	85	75
Marketing and sales	83	67
Planning	69	36
Finance	47	23
Plant or facilities management	40	23
Research and development	39	18
Manufacturing	35	23

Though this list is topped by human resources and public affairs as areas in the company where the liberal arts are most useful, marketing and sales employ far larger numbers. If there is a single area of opportunity within the corporation where substantial numbers of liberal-arts graduates will find optimal application, it is in corporate marketing and sales.

II. Market Factors in the Recruitment of Liberal-Arts Graduates

Companies differ in the extent to which they actively seek liberal-arts graduates. The distinguishing factors can be divided into those related to the company's market position and those associated with the leadership and organization of the company. The first are termed market factors and the second—institutional factors. The distinction is important not only for understanding the origins of company preferences for college graduates, but also for identifying what can be changed. While market factors are generally fixed, since they derive from the company's strategic position in the market, some institutional factors are less immutable. Self-conscious efforts at institutional change will not undermine the competitive position of the company, and may contribute to it. This section examines two critical market factors—a company's product sector and its general financial-health and employment picture. In the next section we turn to the institutional factors.

A. Product Sector

The demand for specific educational backgrounds is highly dependent on the product. Technology-oriented companies are likely to have a high demand for engineering graduates, while insurance companies tend to place a higher premium on liberally educated graduates. To assess the difference that sector makes, the companies are grouped by their major product area (the two-digit standard industrial classification code). Then we examine the proportion of companies within each area that meet four criteria signifying an interest in the recruitment of liberal-arts graduates: (1) have undertaken recruitment of liberal-arts graduates; (2) are led by a chief executive who has advocated the hiring of liberal-arts graduates; (3) have hired an above-average number of liberal-arts graduates in 1986 (defined as hiring a higher percentage of liberal-arts graduates than the average percentage hired by all firms); and (4) expect to increase the hiring of liberal-arts graduates in 1987 and 1988 compared to 1986.[10]

The sectoral breakdown in recruitment efforts and chief-executive attitudes reveals pronounced differences (Table 2.7). Service companies are generally more vigorous than manufacturing firms in seeking liberal-arts graduates. This difference can be seen in comparing the percentages of the manufacturing and service-sector companies recruiting liberal-arts graduates: 35% of the manufacturing companies do so, while 53% of the service-sector firms are active. (In this and other tables that include the number of companies or managers in a column within the table, percentages are to be read as the percentage of the companies or managers numbered to the left that fit the criterion identified at the top of the percentage column.)

Within the manufacturing and service sectors, however, the variation among specific product areas is large. Among companies in the service sector, nearly three quarters of the commercial banks and diversified financial companies sought liberal-arts graduates. (Since the grouping of diversified financial companies may not be generally familiar, the nation's 20 largest companies at the end of 1986 are identified in Table 2.8.) By contrast, fewer than one in five of the savings banks were so active. Similarly, within the manufacturing sector, three quarters of the pharmaceuticals recruited liberal-arts graduates, while fewer than one third of the petroleum-refining corporations and electronics companies did so.

Table 2.7 Percentage of Companies That Have Sought Liberal-Arts Graduates, by Product Sector[a]

Product sector	Number of companies	Active recruitment		CEO encourages recruitment
		On-campus	Other	
Manufacturing: total	253	35	24	21
Pharmaceuticals	12	75	58	75
Publishing and printing	12	50	33	42
Scientific and photographic equipment	10	50	40	0
Building materials	11	46	0	27
Paper and forest products	14	43	36	36
Chemicals	26	42	23	19
Aerospace	15	40	20	13
Food products	22	36	22	23
Motor vehicles and parts	12	33	50	25
Industrial and farm equipment	12	33	0	25
Computers	10	30	40	0
Petroleum refining	17	29	18	6
Electronics	31	13	13	13
Service: total	279	53	34	26
Commercial banks	63	73	48	38
Diversified financial	18	72	61	50
Insurance	38	58	40	21
Retail and wholesale	36	56	25	22
Diversified services	46	44	33	17
Transportation	54	43	19	20
Savings	23	17	17	17
All companies: total	532	45	29	24

[a]Manufacturing and service-sector totals include all companies, but detail on individual product sectors is given only if the sector includes at least 10 companies.

There is a parallel between the level of recruitment efforts and advocacy of liberal-arts recruitment by chief executives. Three quarters of the pharmaceutical CEOs had encouraged liberal-arts hiring, but only 13% of the electronics-company CEOs had so advocated. Similarly, more than a third to a half of the commercial-bank

Table 2.8 Twenty Largest Diversified Financial-Service
Companies, 1986[a]

Federal National Mortgage Association	Washington, D.C.	2,300
American Express	New York	78,700
Salomon	New York	7,800
Aetna Life & Casualty	Hartford	45,100
Merrill Lynch	New York	47,900
CIGNA	Philadelphia	50,100
First Boston	New York	4,500
Travelers Corp.	Hartford	33,400
Morgan Stanley Group	New York	5,300
Bear Stearns Co.	New York	5,700
E. F. Hutton Group	New York	18,900
American International Group	New York	28,000
Loews	New York	23,000
Student Loan Marketing Association	Washington, D.C.	1,000
Lincoln National	Fort Wayne	14,000
Transamerica	San Francisco	14,800
Paine Webber Group	New York	12,100
Continental	New York	17,000
Household International	Prospect Heights, IL	21,400
Fleet Financial Group	Providence, RI	8,400

[a]E. F. Hutton Group was acquired by Shearson, a unit of American Express, in 1987.
Source: See note 11.

and diversified-financial-company chief executives had encouraged liberal-arts hiring, while only 17% of the savings-bank CEOs had done so. It is notable, however, that the parallel is inexact, a divergence that we return to shortly.

The sectoral breakdown of actual hiring in 1986 and forecasts for 1987 and 1988 are shown in Table 2.9. We see again that the service-sector corporations are more likely than manufacturing firms to have been above average in hiring liberal-arts graduates in 1986, and service-sector companies are twice as likely to forecast an increase in liberal-arts hiring in 1987–1988. Diversified financial services are an area of particular opportunity for liberal-arts graduates—half expect to increase their liberal-arts hiring in 1987–1988—while far fewer

Table 2.9 Percentage of Corporations That Have Hired Above-Average Number of Liberal-Arts Graduates in 1986 and Expect to Increase Liberal-Arts Hiring in 1987 and 1988 Compared to 1986, by Product Sector[a]

Product Sector	Number of companies[b]	Above-average hiring in 1986 (%)	Increase in hiring in 1987–1988 (%)
Manufacturing: total	238/253	45	12
Pharmaceuticals	12	50	33
Publishing and printing	12	83	0
Scientific and photographic equipment	10	40	20
Building materials	10/11	50	9
Paper and forest products	14	50	7
Chemicals	24/26	58	12
Aerospace	12/15	27	13
Food products	20/22	60	9
Motor vehicles and parts	12	50	17
Industrial and farm equipment	11/12	54	8
Computers	9/10	—	10
Petroleum refining	16/17	13	12
Electronics	28/31	36	19
Service: total	262/279	53	22
Commercial banks	61/63	63	33
Diversified financial	18	89	50
Insurance	34/38	62	16
Retail and wholesale	33/36	49	25
Diversified services	43/46	54	11
Transportation	50/54	32	15
Savings	22/23	36	13
All companies: total	500	49	17

[a]Manufacturing and service-sector totals include all companies, but detail on individual product sector is included only if the sector has at least 10 companies.

[b]The first figure is the number of companies upon which above-average-hiring percentage is based; the second is the number of companies upon which the increase-in-hiring percentage is based. A single figure applies to both categories.

prospects are evident among savings institutions, where only one in eight anticipates expanded hiring of liberal-arts graduates.

The picture for manufacturing firms is less clear. While pharmaceutical companies hired liberal-arts graduates at near-average rates in 1986, relatively many expect increases in 1987–1988, reflecting the industry's continuing expansion; electronics companies hired liberal-arts graduates at below-average rates in 1986, but the forecasts for the next 2 years were above average. By contrast, publishing and printing had been hiring liberal-arts graduates at comparatively high rates, but none of the companies expect to increase their hiring in the immediate future.

If diversified financial services and several other industries are notable for their high level of interest in the liberal-arts graduate, one industry anchors the other end of the scale: mining. The mining sector is not shown separately in the tables because there are only nine firms, but not one of them recruits liberal-arts graduates; none are led by CEOs who have advocated their recruitment; they expect no increase in liberal-arts recruiting; and they recruited virtually no liberal-arts graduates in the recent past.

B. Work-Force Growth

The hiring of liberal-arts graduates is often viewed as a long-term strategy for managerial development. Liberal-arts graduates may require more training at the outset than graduates from business and engineering, and they may be more risky to hire. On the other hand, they may bring special strengths that make them strong prospects later in the career for entry into middle- and senior-management ranks (a subject to which we return in Chapter 4). A corporation's capacity to take the long-term view and to invest in liberal-arts graduates, however, may partly depend on the company's market position. Growing companies with high earnings might be expected to hire liberal-arts graduates more often. By contrast, stagnant or declining companies may of necessity focus on shorter-term agendas and hire comparatively fewer liberal-arts graduates.

Consistent with this expectation, many corporate managers believe that the hiring of liberal-arts graduates does correlate with the business cycle. Of the 505 executives in our managerial survey, a third agreed that liberal-arts hiring increases faster than the hiring of other college graduates during periods of expansion. And half of the managers concurred with the statement that the rate of liberal-arts hiring drops more rapidly during a period of decline (Table 2.10).

Table 2.10 Percentage of Managers (*N* = 505) Agreeing That the Relative Hiring of Liberal-Arts Graduates During Periods of Business Expansion or Contraction Exceeds That of Other College Graduates

Statement	Percentage agreeing
"During a period of work-force expansion, the hiring of liberal arts graduates is more positively affected than other graduates"	32
"During a period of work-force reduction, the hiring of liberal arts graduates is more adversely affected than other graduates"	54

The impact of a company's growth or contraction on the hiring of liberal-arts graduates is examined by looking at recruitment practices in relation to varying rates of employment growth. A company's employment growth is measured by comparing the size of its United States–based work force in 1986 with that in 1983. Companies are divided into three approximately equal groups—those with (1) a declining work force (20% or more decline), (2) a relatively stable work force, and (3) a growing work force (5% or more increase). These groups of companies were compared on the three measures of liberal-arts hiring used earlier: (1) the extent to which they recruited liberal-arts graduates, (2) whether they hired an above-average number of liberal-arts graduates, and (3) whether they forecast an increase in liberal-arts hiring during the 2 years ahead.

The findings, however, do not support the argument that liberal-arts hiring is relatively stronger in companies with an expanding employment force and comparatively weaker in those with a contracting work force. All three groups of companies displayed similar levels of recruitment of liberal-arts graduates. The same issue was examined for several subgroups of corporations whose general experiences are more uniform, including companies among the top 100 manufacturing firms and, separately, companies among the top 500 service companies. These subanalyses yield the same conclusion: the rate of liberal-arts hiring is relatively unrelated to whether a company is enlarging or reducing the size of its work force.

In cases of extremely large expansions or contractions of a company's work force, the hiring of liberal-arts graduates may be more sharply affected than is that of other college graduates. However, the general pattern found here is for liberal-arts graduates to fare about the same as do other college graduates. If a company is downsizing its work force, then, liberal-arts graduates would seem to be no less likely to find employment than are others, though of course the prospects of all college graduates would be adversely affected. Conversely, during a period in which a company's work force is expanding, liberal-arts graduates may have no special advantages over others, though again the opportunities facing all college graduates would be brighter.

To the extent that entire product sectors are expanding or contracting their employment, however, the prospects for liberal-arts graduates may be affected in the aggregate. We have seen that service-sector companies are generally more bullish on liberal-arts graduates than are manufacturing firms. Higher proportions of the service-sector corporations recruit liberal-arts graduates both on campus and off; they have hired at above-average rates during the past several years; and they anticipate above-average hiring in the 2 years to come. If service-sector employment in America is displaying long-term growth, then long-term prospects for liberal-arts graduates should be comparatively strong as well.

During the past decade, the service sector accounted for three quarters of all new jobs in the United States. Of the nonmilitary labor force in 1972, 43% were employed in the service sector; by 1986, the proportion had risen to 52%; and by 2000 it is projected by the Bureau of Labor Statistics to reach 57% (Table 2.11). However, many of these jobs are in small businesses where educational credentials are often relatively unimportant, especially in certain industries. Also, many of the jobs are at clerical levels where a college degree is not

Table 2.11 Sectoral Distribution of U.S. Jobs, 1972–2000 (Millions)

Sector	1972		1986		2000 (projected)	
	No.	%	No.	%	No.	%
Service	37	43	58	52	76	57
Manufacturing	24	28	25	22	25	19
Government	13	16	17	15	18	14
Other	11	13	13	11	14	10
Total	85	100	112	100	133	100

Source: Kutscher (1988).

a prerequisite in any case. Still, a number of the positions are with larger companies at responsible levels that presume a baccalaureate degree for entry, and, as they grow with the general service-business trends, so too should the demand for liberal-arts graduates.

III. Institutional Factors in the Recruitment of Liberal-Arts Graduates

Institutional factors differ from market factors in that they are characteristic of the corporation's organization rather than its relative position as an economic competitor. Two of the most critical institutional factors are examined here: the corporation's leadership and scale of operations. The leadership factor is particularly important—although market and some institutional factors are generally fixed, leadership is subject to intervention and change.

A. Company Leadership

The actions of top management have a decisive bearing on a company's financial performance, but they are also known to have leading influence on a range of other corporate characteristics not directly related to the company's annual earnings. Thus we know from studies of executive succession that companies perform significantly better in a period immediately following a forced change in top leadership. When a CEO is asked to step down, most often occasioned when earnings are in decline, a new chief executive is appointed, and corporate earnings often increase in the immediate aftermath of the change. Analogous effects are noted in studies of the impact of executive commitment to social programs. Case studies of five companies that adopted creative community-outreach programs, for example, reveal that the backing of top managers was critical to the initiation and implementation of the programs.[12]

Executive leadership is just as important, we find, in the recruitment of liberal-arts graduates. Indeed, the evidence indicates that the role of top management is more significant than any other single factor. Moreover, we find that the chief executive's stance on liberal-arts recruitment has a decisive bearing on the position taken by other top executives, and the aggregate impact of the stance taken by top management, in turn, has a major impact on the extent to which liberal-arts graduates are actively sought by the corporation.

If the chief executive has explicitly encouraged company hiring of liberal-arts graduates, as a quarter of the CEOs in the present study have done (Table 2.2), the company is found to be more aggressive in recruiting liberal-arts graduates. This can be seen by comparing companies led by CEOs who are active and passive on this front (Table 2.12). Of firms whose CEO has not encouraged the recruitment of liberal-arts graduates, 36% have recruited them on campus; by contrast, 71% of firms whose CEO has encouraged such action have done so. Thus firms whose CEOs have taken an explicit stand on the issue are nearly twice as likely to directly recruit liberal-arts graduates on campus. Similarly, they are twice as prone to recruit liberal-arts graduates through solicitation of résumés and other means. They are also nearly half more likely to be among companies with above-average recruitment rates of liberal-arts graduates (63 vs. 45%); and they are more than twice as likely to forecast an increase in liberal-arts hiring during the coming 2 years. These differences among companies are some of the largest observed in the study.

The chief executive not only has a direct impact on the likelihood of liberal-arts recruitment, but an indirect effect as well by setting a tenor for the organization. To the extent that other top managers come to share the CEO's beliefs in the value of liberal-arts recruitment, there is an additional cumulative effect on the company's policies and practices.

If the chief executive has explicitly encouraged the hiring of liberal-arts graduates, there is a high likelihood that other senior

Table 2.12 Percentage of Companies That Have Sought and Recruited Liberal-Arts Graduates, by Stance of the Chief Executive Officer[a]

CEO has encouraged the hiring of liberal arts- graduates	Number of companies	Company recruitment of liberal-arts graduates (%)			
		Active recruitment		Above-average hiring in 1986	Increase in hiring in 1987–1988
		On-campus	Other		
Yes	126	71	54	63	33
No	409	36	21	45	13

[a]The percentage differences for on-campus recruitment, other recruitment, hiring in 1986, and hiring in 1987–1988 are all significant at less than the .05 level. A percentage difference that is significant at less than the .05 level is very unlikely to have arisen from chance or sampling variations.

managers will have done the same. The correlation, a measure of
the strength of the relationship, between the CEO's stance and that of
the chief financial officer, the responding human-resource executive,
other human-resource executives, sales executives, marketing executives, and manufacturing executives ranges from .27 to .53. Probability ratios can also be calculated which reflect the likelihood that
a company's senior manager has endorsed such hiring if the CEO
has backed it. For the chief financial officer the ratio is 10.5, indicating that, if a CEO has backed the hiring of liberal-arts graduates, it
is over 10 times more likely that the chief financial officer will have
done so as well. The probability ratios for six senior managers and
groups are as follows:

Chief financial officer	10.5
Responding human-resource executive	3.4
Other human resource executives	3.2
Sales executives	4.1
Marketing executives	4.4
Manufacturing executives	7.6

That is, if the chief executive has publicly advocated the hiring of
liberal-arts graduates, the probability is increased by a factor of 3 to
10 that his senior managers have made the same public advocacy.

With the chief executive setting the pace, there is thus a pronounced tendency for other managers as well to endorse the recruitment of liberal-arts graduates. In concert, the simultaneous encouragement of liberal-arts recruitment from many senior quarters of the
company makes even a greater difference. The more widespread the
corporate commitment, the more extensive is the company's recruitment. This is evident if we divide the corporations into five groups,
ranging from those in which no managerial voice has urged the hiring of liberal-arts graduates to those in which four or more of the
managers or groups of managers have pushed for such hiring (Table
2.13).

We see that the more widespread the support for liberal-arts recruitment within the corporation, the more active is the corporation
in seeking liberal-arts graduates. For each increment in managerial
endorsement, there is a higher likelihood that the company recruits
liberal-arts graduates on campus and through other measures, hires
liberal-arts graduates at an above-average rate, and anticipates in-

Table 2.13 Percentage of Companies That Have Sought and Recruited Liberal-Arts Graduates, by Number of Senior Managers or Groups of Senior Managers in the Company Who Have Encouraged Hiring of Liberal-Arts Graduates[a]

Number of managers or groups of managers encouraging hiring	Number of companies	Company recruitment of liberal-arts graduates (%)			
		Active recruitment		Above-average hiring in 1986	Increase in hiring in 1987–1988
		On-campus	Other		
None	263	26	13	38	7
One	52	46	25	42	12
Two	59	58	32	53	20
Three	55	66	44	64	27
Four or more	106	73	60	66	39

[a]The percentage differences for on-campus recruitment, other recruitment, hiring in 1986, and hiring in 1987–1988 are all significant at less than the .05 level.

creasing liberal-arts hiring in 2 years to come. Thus the percentage of companies recruiting liberal-arts graduates on campus rises from 26% in corporations with no visible leadership to 46% in those with one senior managerial advocate, 58% with two advocates, 66% with three advocates, and 73% with four advocates. The role of the chief executive can be decisive in setting a tenor for top-management commitment, then, and that top-management commitment in turn has a significant additional impact. Encouragement by sales, manufacturing, finance, and human-resource executives can make a major difference in company practices in this area, a difference that goes significantly beyond that which is generated by the CEO alone.

The impact of such encouragement can be seen in the decision of the consumer-products company that we studied to increase its recruitment of liberal-arts graduates in the early 1980s. The initiative came from three individuals: the group vice-president for development and corporate marketing, the president, and the chairman and chief executive officer. They communicated their views directly to the manager of the company's college-relations unit, and, despite some resistance from the managerial ranks, particularly those who held MBA degrees, the college-relations manager successfully implemented a program to bring a stronger flow of liberal-arts graduates into entry-level management in product marketing.

Overall, it is evident that explicit managerial encouragement has a critical impact on liberal-arts recruitment. Moreover, while a fraction of this effect is due to sectoral differences, further analysis (not detailed here) reveals that managerial endorsement remains a driving force even within product sectors. Companies involved in the same product line, which generally have similar needs for education and training backgrounds in their work force, are thus far more apt to seek liberal-arts graduates if their top management presses for it to happen. If they do not, liberal-arts recruitment is far less likely.

B. Company Size

The second major institutional factor that shapes the hiring of liberal-arts graduates is the firm's scale of operation. Larger corporations establish more formalized and professionalized programs on a range of fronts. In the area of social and political outreach, for instance, larger companies have larger public-affairs staffs, more regularized procedures for making charitable contributions, and a broader array of forms of outreach, ranging from political-action committees to programs for loaning executives to public agencies. Larger corporations also generally have larger and more professionalized systems for recruiting college graduates and for tracking and managing career development among those hired.[13]

Regardless of need or interest, then, larger corporations would tend to maintain a larger staff and a more formalized process for recruiting all kinds of college graduates, including those in the liberal arts. And this is indeed found to be the case in the companies that we studied. It will be illustrated by comparing four groups of manufacturing corporations of highly variant size, as defined by their annual sales volume. In the first group are those among the top 100 manufacturing companies whose annual sales range from $3.8 to $103 billion. The second includes companies ranked from 101 to 250 on the Fortune 500 list, with annual sales varying from $1.3 to $3.7 billion. The third group consists of those ranked 251 to 500, with annual sales from $400 million to $1.3 billion. The fourth group of manufacturing companies have sales from $100 to $200 million per year.

We see from the information presented in Table 2.14 that larger manufacturers are indeed more active than smaller firms in recruiting liberal-arts graduates. Among the top 100 manufacturers, nearly half had sought liberal-arts graduates on campus; by contrast, only

Table 2.14 Percentage of Manufacturing Companies That Have Sought and Recruited Liberal Arts Graduates, by Size of Company[a]

| Size of company (annual sales) | Number of companies | Company recruitment of liberal-arts graduates (%) | | Above-average hiring in 1986 | Increase in hiring in 1987–1988 |
| | | Active recruitment | | | |
		On-campus	Other		
1. Fortune 1 to 100 ($3.8 to 103 billion)	75	47	32	42	17
2. Fortune 101 to 250 ($1.3 to 3.7 billion)	70	46	21	45	10
3. Fortune 251 to 500 ($400 million to 3.7 billion)	93	22	17	48	10
4. Middle-sized ($100 to 200 million)	26	12	19	46	19

[a]The percentage differences for on-campus recruitment are significant at less than the .05 level; the percentage differences for other recruitment are significant at the .06 level; the percentage differences for hiring in 1986 and hiring in 1987–1988 are not statistically significant.

one middle-sized manufacturer in eight had done so (column 2 in the table).

However, it is also evident that although the smaller companies are less active in recruitment, during the past year they had hired liberal-arts graduates at about the same rate as larger firms, and there were no consistent size differences in the projections for near-term future hiring (columns 3 and 4). Thus larger corporations are more vigorous in the formal recruitment of liberal-arts graduates, but they do not necessarily hire proportionally more of them.

Nor do large companies place more stress on a liberal-arts education in placement than do middle-sized companies. Those answering on behalf of the company in the corporate survey were asked: "When you consider hiring (or recommending hiring) a college graduate for an entry-level position, how important is it that the person" have a "liberal-arts degree?" The percentage of manufacturing companies asserting that it would be important were: 32% among the top manufacturers; 36% among the second tier; 41% among the third tier; and 38% among the middle-sized companies. A substantially higher proportion—53%—of the service-company representatives found special value in the liberal-arts background, which is consistent with the earlier finding that a liberal-arts education has particular appeal among service companies. Yet the interest in the manufacturing sector was also relatively widespread and by no means limited to the nation's largest employers.[14]

Larger companies thus follow more proactive policies in recruiting liberal-arts graduates, while middle-sized firms are less likely to actively seek them. Much of the difference can be traced, however, to the greater resources possessed by large firms for recruiting new employees, including liberal-arts graduates. Middle-sized companies display no less interest in liberal-arts graduates, just less initiative to actively find them on the college campus. College students, however, may mistakenly perceive the relative absence of middle-sized firms from campus-recruitment fairs and interviewing schedules as disinterest.

IV. Conclusion

A college education has become a prerequisite for entry into the senior levels of corporate management, and in many companies it is a starting prerequisite as well. Engineering and business graduates are now a major fraction—34%—of the nearly one million individuals receiving baccalaureates every year, and many are actively recruited for entry-level positions in major corporations. The results here, however, suggest that of the liberal-arts contingent—29% of the graduating seniors—a substantial proportion will be actively recruited as well.

Almost half of the surveyed companies seek liberal-arts graduates by coming to campus, and more than two fifths have managers who have encouraged the hiring of liberal-arts graduates for entry-level positions. The typical company hires nearly two business and engineering graduates for every liberal-arts graduate (the hiring ratio is 1.9:1). Yet there are also more new business and engineering graduates than liberal-arts graduates (the graduating ratio is about 1.2:1). Moreover, most business and engineering graduates plan to enter the private sector, while higher proportions of liberal-arts graduates seek employment in the public and nonprofit sectors. The aggregate numbers would thus suggest that liberal-arts students have ample opportunities to start careers with the nation's major private employers.

In looking at a future in the private sector, however, liberal-arts students should know where their opportunities are strongest. Management of the production side of an industrial firm is not an area of large prospect, although some companies, such as the health-products company studied more intensively (Case D, see Appendix to Chapter 4), report successful experience in assigning and training liberal-arts graduates for this area. But more generally, marketing and sales are areas of considerably brighter prospects than the management of production. "Boundary-spanning," communication skills, and analytic insights can be at a premium in these positions, and they are often among the fortes of the liberally educated college graduate.

Companies systematically differ in their demand for liberal-arts graduates, with both market and institutional factors accounting for much of the variation. Commercial banks and diversified financial-service companies are particularly good sources of opportunity; while savings banks and electronics firms, by contrast, provide far fewer prospects.

While the short-term employment opportunities for all college graduates with a company undergoing a work-force reduction will certainly not be good, the evidence suggests that liberal-arts graduates are not more adversely affected than others. On the other hand, liberal-arts graduates will not find that they have a privileged position in a period of expansion: their prospects at a corporation will rise at the same rate as for other graduates.

The most important single factor distinguishing companies, however, is the commitment of top management. Liberal-arts graduates will find their hiring chances considerably enhanced if the chief executive and other senior managers have taken steps to make it happen. If the company's top management has not done so, the prospects for liberal-arts graduates are considerably dimmed.

Employment opportunities for seniors in the liberal arts will appear to be greater at larger corporations, since these are significantly more likely to recruit on campus and through other formal means than are other companies. Moreover, the large size of their work force can inherently create a high volume of demand. Forty-six companies responding to the corporate survey, for example, hired at least 100 liberal-arts graduates in 1986, drawing a total of nearly 11,000 fresh liberal-arts graduates into their ranks.

It should also be kept in mind, however, that large and middle-sized companies hire liberal-arts graduates at about the same rate. The relative prospects for liberal-arts BA holders at middle-sized firms are as good as at the nation's largest and best known corporations. And while middle-sized companies each hire fewer persons, taken together they nonetheless constitute a large employment market for new college graduates. It is a market that may be underappreciated by college students and one that thus deserves more attention by both campus placement offices and students and graduates themselves.

Notes

1. Berle and Means (1967); Whyte (1956); Riesman (1950); Herman (1981).
2. *Wall Street Journal* (1987) for 1987 figures; McComas (1986) for 1985 information; Bonfield (1980) for 1978 data; Newcomer (1955) for 1950, 1925, and 1900 data.
3. Information from direct contact with the firms.
4. Williams College newsletter, "After Williams . . . What Next?" (1987).
5. Bowles (1987), p. 16.
6. Companies were asked: "During the past five years (that is, since 1981), which of the following individuals or groups in your company have formally or informally encouraged or discouraged the hiring of liberal arts graduates for entry-level positions?" The response categories are "encouraged the hiring," "neither encouraged nor discouraged the hiring," and "discouraged the hiring."
7. The question stated: "Of those liberal arts graduates hired at the entry-level within the past three years (that is, since 1983), identify the two or three areas where the largest numbers have been placed."
8. Firms were asked: "In your judgment, how useful is a liberal arts background to be a successful manager in the following levels and areas of the company?" The four response categories are

"highly useful," "somewhat useful," "not too useful," and "not at all useful." The first two categories are combined in the table.

9. The managers were queried: "In your judgment, in which of the following . . . areas of your company would an undergraduate liberal arts degree provide a useful educational background?"

10. The third criterion, the hiring of an above-average number of liberal-arts graduates, is evaluated as follows. The proportion of liberal-arts graduates hired in 1986 relative to all entry-level individuals hired during that year was calculated for each company; companies with an above-average level of liberal-arts hiring are defined as those whose proportion is above the median value for all companies. The fourth criterion, the expectation of an increase in the hiring of liberal-arts graduates in 1987 and 1988, is based on the question, "What forecast do you make regarding entry-level hiring [of liberal-arts graduates] in 1987 and 1988 compared to 1986?"

11. From *Fortune* magazine's annual compilation for 1986 (June 8, 1987).

12. Weiner and Mahoney (1981); Merenda (1981); Useem (1988).

13. Useem and Kutner (1986).

14. The question included four response categories: "very important," "somewhat important," "not too important," "not at all important." The first two categories were combined in the analysis.

Appendix to Chapter 2

Case A: Product Management and New Opportunities for Liberal-Arts Graduates in a Consumer-Products Corporation

With approximately $10 billion in annual sales in 1986, this consumer-products corporation is one of America's largest manufacturers. Many of its approximately 1000 products are familiar to virtually all consumers, and its products are the number one or two best-selling items in a majority of the product areas in which the company is active.

The corporation has a well-developed product-management system that assigns broad responsibilities for its products to individual product managers. In addition to developing a strategy for the product, including marketing plans and programs, the product manager is also the focal point for coordinating the internal and external resources necessary to carry out that strategy. A single manager thus carries responsibility for the promotion, advertising, marketing, and, ultimately, sales and success of a given product. Successful product management has been the primary avenue into general management at the company, and the hierarchy is clear: the entry-level assistant product manager moves up to associate product manager within about 18 months if first performance is successful, followed by movement to product manager, then senior product manager, group product or category manager, marketing manager, and, finally, general manager, the last rung on a successful climb toward the corporation's general-management system.

Although product management is the core of the organizational pyramid at the corporation, in recent years it had proved increasingly difficult to recruit able MBA graduates to fill open entry-level positions. Management-consulting firms remained the first choice of a large number of the top MBA graduates, and the high starting salaries of many firms on Wall Street were an intensified source of competition as well (though the stock-market decline in the fall of 1987 weakened some of this competitive pressure).

To ensure a steady flow of new talent into the product-management career chain, the firm moved to partially solve the problem by seeking good college graduates, including those with liberal-arts degrees. It was not an action that was favored by some middle-level product managers. They generally held MBA degrees and, in the words of one inside observer, they "want their own kind. The frame of reference here is the MBA." But the business reasons for seeking liberal-arts and other college graduates were nonetheless viewed as compelling by top management.

BA holders were, first of all, considerably less expensive. In 1987, new MBA hires in product management commanded salaries of approximately $45,000, while new college graduates received salaries closer to $30,000. Second, the MBAs and BAs performed nearly the same functions when they started, and from limited past experience it was already known that the BAs tended to quickly acquire the specific business skills needed to move ahead. Finally, liberal-arts hires often brought the positive advantage of strong qualitative capacities for understanding trends and preferences in consumer markets.

Despite some middle-management resistance, top management established a policy in 1981 of recruiting more bachelor-degree holders into the product-management system, with an informal goal of at least a fifth of the new hires coming from among new college graduates (with the balance remaining MBAs). Three individuals were the driving force behind the change. Most directly involved was the company's group vice-president for development and corporate marketing, who himself holds a liberal-arts degree from Princeton and no MBA degree. Also forceful were the company's president who served as the chief operating officer, and the chairman who was the CEO. All three had communicated their views directly to the manager of college relations. The president, for example, had expressed his belief that the "best and the brightest can come from liberal arts colleges just as well as MBA programs," and that it was the company's objective to hire the best, regardless of degree.

The message registered. After establishing the goal in 1981 of recruiting more BA holders including liberal-arts graduates for its product-management system, the company placed as many as seven in a given year. The operational definition of the best and brightest among liberal-arts graduates is a blend of characteristics, starting with a grade-point average of at least 3.0 and preferably 3.5. But equally important were signs of leadership potential as manifested in extracurricular activities on campus and signs of analytic potential as evidenced in both quantitative and qualitative reasoning. Original thinking was important as well, and so too were signs of entrepreneurial or creative business experience, practical intelligence, and personal drive.

The recruitment experience to date, however, has not been encouraging. Performance has not been at issue, but longevity has been. Of the 13 new BA holders hired for product-management positions between 1981 and 1983, for example, only two remained with the company by 1987. Most had worked successfully for several years with the corporation, but then, perhaps because of the MBA-oriented culture that still prevailed, left to enter full-time graduate programs in management and did not subsequently rejoin the company. The firm found that retaining the BA holder can be significantly harder than the MBA recipient whose schooling has been completed.

The BA holders who have remained, however, have prospered in their careers. The experience of one is illustrative. She had joined the company in 1981 as an assistant product manager, fresh out of a strong liberal-arts college with a BA in economics. She progressed steadily up the product-management line and within 6 years had become a senior product manager for a major cereal product. At the age of 27 she was already overseeing an annual marketing budget of more than $30 million. She observed, "The stars at this company are those who can communicate and think, and this has nothing to do with business education per se. I don't care if a person took no economics, but if they carried English, history, or French literature where they had to absorb a lot of knowledge, that is what they need for what we do here."

This product manager had learned from her own experience in the company that other liberal-arts skills were critical as well. "You have to be flexible here," she found, and effective communication skills were essential as well. The importance of writing skills for product management was underscored, for example, by her own success in managing the process of budget development. As a product manager, she annually submits a budget proposal for all aspects of marketing her product, and the final level of funding is dependent on the persuasiveness of the document. The budget allocation is set by a senior marketing manager who will read and evaluate the proposal but otherwise have no direct contact with her. Her previous budget requests had been consistently well received, and, emboldened by the track record, she submitted a request in 1987 for a budget near $40 million. The manager of college relations confirms the general importance of the product manager's background. "Liberal arts students have better communication skills," she concludes from hundreds of recruiting contacts. "I've seen their papers, and they really know how to write. They are very creative and original, and they are able to take in a broad array of information and integrate it."

Breadth of perspective and a capacity to think in different ways

are valued at the consumer-products corporation, particularly because of the premium placed on finding new areas for expansion in a mature industry. Here, too, liberal-arts graduates are perceived to have an advantage, since their schooling has more often
stressed such diversity. So important is this emphasis that the company has introduced a major humanities component in its 18-month
executive-development program. For senior managers with or without a liberal-arts background, the humanities agenda is intended to
stimulate creativity and better understanding of the culture of the
company and the environment in which it operates. The purpose, in
the words of one manager, is to expand their horizons: some "general managers are focused on the business 10 hours a day. You take
company reports home at night, and in your spare time you read
Business Week and *Fortune* and *Harvard Business Review*. So we
want people to broaden out."

Whatever the new emphasis on hiring liberal-arts and other college
graduates, the fact remains that the company's product management
has long depended on the MBA holder. The firm hired 38 new assistant product managers in 1977, and all but one of these held MBA
degrees (see Table 2.15). During the 5-year hiring period from 1982

Table 2.15 Number of New Product Managers Hired by the
Consumer-Products Corporation in 1977–1986 and
Senior Product Managers Employed by the Company in
1987, by Educational Background

		Educational background		
Year	Total	MBA and liberal arts degree	MBA and business or engineering degree	Other
New product managers hired				
1977	38	27	10	1
1982	23	15	2	5
1983	33	17	5	10
1984	36	23	7	6
1985	38	21	11	6
1986	32	17	10	5
Senior product managers employed				
1987	38	24	7	7

to 1986, between 23 and 38 new assistant product managers were brought annually into the company, and two thirds or more of these held MBA degrees during each of the 5 years.

Further examination of the product managers' educational background, however, reveals that the majority of the MBA holders are also liberal-arts graduates. The educational profiles of two new assistant product managers hired in 1982 are typical of many:

First new product manager	Second new product manager
BA, psychology, 1974, Wesleyan University	BA, international affairs, 1979, University of North Carolina
MBA, marketing, 1982, Harvard University	MBA, marketing, 1982, Columbia University

For every MBA hired who held a business or engineering undergraduate degree, two or more MBAs were hired who held a liberal-arts degree. As a result, more than half of the new product managers who joined the corporation in 1977 and between 1982 and 1986 were liberal-arts graduates with a postgraduate business degree.

Like most corporations, the company experiences a relatively high turnover among its new managerial hires. A majority of the "class" of 1982, for example, had since left the firm: of the 23 individuals hired in 1982, only 6 remained with the company in 1987. Similarly, of the 38 individuals recruited in 1977, only 5 were still with the company in 1987. What is educationally distinctive about these 11 managers retained by the company is that all held MBA *and* liberal-arts degrees (among the 11 managers are the two individuals whose educational credentials are profiled above). While two thirds of the new recruits in 1977 and 1982 held this combination of degrees, 100% of those who were still with the company in 1987 were holders of both an MBA and a liberal-arts degree.

The senior ranks of the corporation's product-management lines are thus predominantly recipients of MBA and liberal-arts degrees. Of those with ranks of group product manager and above, two thirds were so educated (see the table's bottom row). The primary educational route into product management and up the company's organizational ladder is a postgraduate degree in management, and more often than not one that is preceded by undergraduate study in the liberal arts.

Case B: A College Education and Communications Skills in a High-Technology Company

While many high-technology companies can boast of an existence little more than a decade or two long, some have matured over a half-century or more, including one major manufacturer of consumer and industrial products. With annual sales of more than $1.5 billion and over 13,000 employees, the company uses a variety of innovative chemical and related processes to manufacture a broad range of products widely known to both the public and to institutional buyers. Its hiring policies and corporate culture are oriented toward science and engineering. Yet even here a liberal education can serve as an important and recognized asset.

The orientation toward science and engineering is overwhelmingly evident in the company's annual recruitment of entry-level college graduates. It is a rigorous winnowing process in a highly competitive environment, with a comparatively small number of select candidates finally joining the company's employ. In fiscal 1987, the company interviewed more than 1200 students on campus. Of these, approximately 400 were invited to visit the company for further interviewing, 106 received offers, and 65—only 5% of those originally interviewed on campus—accepted offers and joined the company. Even this figure underestimates student interest in working for the company. Many campus applicants do not make it to the first stage of interviewing, and there is a large flow of unsolicited résumés arriving at company headquarters as well. Some 300 to 500 résumés are received "over the transom" every week, and additional unsolicited inquiries come as referrals from employees within the company.

Among the stimulants of the strong unsolicited applicant flow is the household familiarity with some of the company's products and its appearance in a widely read reference book on the nation's best employers. The bulk of the hiring, however, comes from solicited campus interviews, with about 70% of new managerial and professional employees secured through this avenue. The unsolicited contact is not without some success—20 to 25% of new recruits are obtained that way. The remainder come from in-house referrals.

To initiate the corporation's annual campus-recruitment cycle, the source of most of its new college-educated employees, the corporate staffing office requests information from the company's many divisions on the type of college graduates that they will be requiring. From this information, the staffing manager assembles a consolidated college-recruitment handbook. The 70 entries for the

1987–1988 recruitment cycle predominantly require degrees in engineering and scientific fields (Table 2.16). Several entries require MBA degrees, and one calls for a liberal-arts degree outside of the natural sciences.

The college-recruitment handbook includes a history of previous hiring for each of the approximately 34 colleges and universities that will be visited in the spring of 1988. With this information

Table 2.16 College-Recruitment Plans of a High-Technology Company, 1987–1988

Division	Title	Degree	Major field
Finance	General analyst	BS/BMA	Accounting; finance
Personnel	Personnel administrator	MS	Industrial relations
Marketing	(To be announced)	MBA	Business
Product	Environmental affairs coordinator	BA, BS, or MS	Liberal arts
Industrial Engineering	Industrial engineer	BS/MS	Industrial engineering or technical degree
Engineering	Product R&D, product design (16 openings)	BS/MS/ PhD	Electrical, mechanical, chemical, and electrical engineering; physics
Manufacturing	Engineer, product supervisor, and other titles (31 openings)	BS/MS	Various engineering fields; computer science; materials science
Other	Various titles (18 openings)	BA, MS, PhD	Various science and engineering fields

in hand, the company recruiters look for relatively well-rounded individuals among the pools of candidates with appropriate college majors. A grade-point average of at least 3.0 in the core field of study is considered essential. A relevant summer job, research project, or internship in an area related to the field of study is also viewed as important, particularly for a student whose academic record is not outstanding. Such experiences are seen as important for clarifying and affirming career interests and for introducing the student to the language and culture of the corporate setting. The company employs a standard form for appraising applicants, and the form's contents are indicative of the criteria applied. In addition to the applicant's grades, class rank, and list of coursework relevant to the company's opening, each candidate is rated on a 5-point scale (from "unsatisfactory" to "outstanding") on 10 major factors:

- Clarity of career goals
- Work experience
- Communication skills
- On-campus involvement
- Leadership experience
- Enthusiasm (drive/spark)
- Personal presentation
- Knowledge of the company
- Interest in the company
- Willingness to relocate

While an applicant's preparedness in engineering and scientific fields is paramount, it is far from being a sufficient condition for recruitment. The company's founder and former longtime chief executive had stressed the importance of broad vision, and he was a "great believer" in the humanities even though he had received little formal training in the area. He had set a tenor in which managers were expected to be literate communicators and innovative thinkers. Lists of great books were circulated among senior managers, and the company enrolled some executives in the management-development programs stressing the humanities that are operated by Aspen Institute and by Dartmouth and Williams. The current president and CEO himself had attended one of the Aspen seminars. The company's philosophy had permeated its high-technology recruitment as well. "We are by nature and culture an internal communications company," stated the manager of the college recruitment program. It is thus "so important for our technical people to communicate."

On occasion, this has translated into the explicit recruitment of a liberal-arts graduate without a science major because of the presumed possession of exceptional communication skills. The 1987–1988 college-recruitment roster summarized above sought a liberal-arts graduate as an "environmental affairs coordinator" for one of the company's product divisions. The reason, according to the college recruitment manager who guided the development of the position requirements, went to the heart of liberal-arts training. For this position, he said, "we want a person with good analytic abilities and writing skills to work with state, local, and federal government. The person must be an excellent communicator with an ability to gather data and communicate its meaning."

The absence of communications skills among many of the engineers hired by the corporation was recognized by the division responsible for human-resource development, and a number of internal short-term courses had been designed to overcome the limitations. The manager of the division explained: "Engineers want everything to fit into an objective format that is predictable with clear cause and effect. When they get into people situations, they can't understand individuals who deviate from the model. They think they can tell people what to do, and they will always do it. But you have to have a lot of tolerance for ambiguity here."

The possession of exceptional skills in communicating and human understanding can thus be as critical in a high-technology manufacturing company as anywhere else. Evidence for the importance can be seen in the career of one individual who was responsible for all human-resource and personnel affairs for the company's North American marketing arm. His father had been a marketing executive for another major manufacturer, and he had been urged by his father to acquire a liberal-arts degree as the best preparation for entering business if one were not sure which function or company one intended to pursue after college. He therefore earned an undergraduate degree in history and after graduation, with only a single business course on his record, joined a transportation company as a regional sales representative. His college-honed writing abilities soon came to the attention of management, and he was invited to become district editor of a company magazine. "My history degree gave me a head start on writing. I could write great news stories that were logical, grammatical, and well summarized," he observed. As is often the case in the evolution of company careers, this opportunity led to a subsequent transition into human resources, since the magazine was managed by the personnel department. He was soon involved in a range of personnel issues and, capitalizing on this on-the-job training, later became general personnel manager for another smaller company. With 7 years of wide-ranging experience there, he was invited to join the manufacturing corporation.

Despite the manager's various career moves and the passage of many years, his undergraduate degree in history continued to inform his daily experience. "The thing that has always stayed with me is the idea that there are many ways of going about solving a problem. After studying [in college history courses] how decisions were made in the [White House] Oval Office and how creative they were, I can better appreciate the same kinds of issues in business decisions."

The liberal-arts background also has continuing impact on his decisions as a personnel manager. His first position in the company discussed here included general college-recruitment responsibilities for one of the firm's major plants. Most of those he hired from campus were newly minted chemical engineers, but he looked for evidence in their records that they had had humanities and social-science courses as well, since, in his view, "it would broaden their horizons and let them see the big picture." He directed questions at such coursework during his campus interviews as a useful device for "looking for their creativity, inquisitiveness, and adaptability."

Whatever the personal values or experiences that a corporate recruiter may bring to the dialogue with a prospective employee, the broader policy parameters are typically set by senior management. The present company is no exception, and the hiring policies of one of its units illustrate how senior management can decisively influence the kinds of entry-level employees who are brought into the company by setting forth a clear policy about the educational background required for hiring. The information-systems group's entry-level hiring is not done on the college campus, since its applicants generally must have 3 to 5 years of experience in programming. While such experience is by far the most significant credential, a college degree nonetheless remains a nearly absolute formal prerequisite for hiring. This standard is maintained even though it has at times excluded applicants who were very much wanted by those for whom they would be working. "The immediate need is to hire somebody who can get the job done," said the group's primary recruiter, and that is the worry of the immediate supervisor. "But higher up in the company, they worry about whether the person" will contribute to "general management."

The vice-president for personnel had insisted that anybody coming into the firm have the potential for being promoted twice. And the convenient proxy for the likelihood of that occurring was whether the candidate held a college degree. The general manager of the systems group had therefore required that all new hires have a college education, whatever the field of study. Even though middle managers from time to time had recommended candidates without college credentials because "they can get the job done," the senior manager generally held the line, making their appointment far more difficult.

One of the indirect consequences is that a number of liberal-arts graduates had been recruited into this division of the company. They had acquired programming and applications experience after college, and they brought the necessary educational credential. And, in the view of the chief recruiter, they often made better employees as well. He was presently dealing with one technically able programmer, for example, whose communication and organizational skills were so poor that most of the division managers were no longer willing to assign tasks to her. "She is a computer science professional through and through, but she does not appreciate how to get people to accept her ideas for change," he said. By contrast, according to the recruiter, liberal-arts graduates often came with the interpersonal and political skills that were essential for effective negotiation and teamwork within the organization.

Discussion with this recruiter broke off as he left for a scheduled meeting with his general manager to review the dossiers of three systems programmers whose hiring he was recommending. Taking out his files, he offered a spontaneous test of what he'd been stressing for over an hour. All three of his candidates had indeed had substantial postgraduate work experience in the information-systems field. All three were also college graduates, but none in computer science or related fields. One held a BA in business, and two had earned liberal-arts baccalaureates—one in political science, the other in philosophy (followed by a master's degree from a divinity school). His parting word: "See!"

3

What Companies Want in Liberal-Arts Graduates

Corporations that hire many liberal-arts graduates look for specific accomplishments. Hiring decisions are no less fine-honed than for MBA or engineering graduates. The special skills a company wants in liberal-arts recruits for entry-level management positions depend in part on the specific position. Yet companies also look for more generic skills and experiences that would have prepared liberal-arts graduates for effective entry into employment whatever the specific position in the company.

This chapter focuses on the general criteria used in screening liberal-arts applicants. It assesses the strengths and weaknesses that companies find among liberal-arts graduates and discusses the recommendations that companies would make to college students planning a career in the private sector and to university administrators designing courses of study for their students. If there is an overriding theme to what the companies want, it is a preference for a combination of the liberal and practical skills. The analytical and communication skills of a liberal education are viewed as invaluable, but graduates looking for a place in the corporate world should also leave college, suggest many companies, with an appreciation for the language of business, the nature of work in a corporate setting, and the practical skills for coping with a company environment.

I. The Liberal Arts and the Useful Arts

What emerges from this study is a picture of contrasts—a corporate stress on liberal learning, but also an emphasis on practical skills. The view of a large number of companies is closely akin to Ernest L. Boyer's position in his 1987 report on higher education for the Carnegie Foundation for the Advancement of Teaching. At present, he suggests, the "unhealthy separation between the liberal and the useful arts, which the curriculum and the faculty too often reinforce, tends to leave students poorly served and the college a weak and divided institution." He argues, however, that the "liberal and the useful arts can be brought together in the curriculum just as they inevitably must be brought together during life. Such linkage should be cultivated in all disciplines, and be exemplified in the lives of those who teach them." The "challenge then is to enlarge lives by bringing meaning to the world of work. And the special task of the undergraduate college is to relate the values of liberal learning to vocation."[1]

Such an integration is not without its tensions, as Earl F. Cheit documented in his 1975 report, *The Useful Arts and the Liberal Tradition.* He concluded in his report to the Carnegie Commission on Higher Education that a creative synthesis of methods and subjects must be found, if students majoring in the liberal arts are to be effectively exposed to the "useful arts" and, conversely, if students majoring in the latter are to be effectively exposed to the former. Yet whatever the particular integrative solutions, the corporations surveyed in the present study widely subscribe to the conviction that a priority for campus administrators and college students alike is to create the means for combining both.

Companies generally look for some combination of both liberal education and practical training in the liberal-arts graduates they hire. They do not dismiss the value of the liberal learning, seizing on only the immediate practical skills that the liberal-arts graduate may have acquired. At the same time, they do not fail to search for signs that the liberal-arts graduate possesses at least some of the useful skills and practical outlooks required for the work-a-day world of the corporation. The stress on both the liberal and the useful arts can be seen in the assessments by company representatives of what their firms seek in college graduates.

Companies were asked to assess the importance that they placed on coursework, undergraduate performance, and off-campus experiences in evaluating a college graduate for entry-level work. At the top of their list are courses in business, finance, and accounting, closely followed by courses engendering quantitative skills (Table 3.1). Humanities and other courses are viewed as significant by far fewer companies. Even more important than specific courses are high academic achievement, an internship or work experience in business, and evidence of energy and initiative as manifested in campus, athletic, and community activities. The major financial-services company we studied (Case E, see Appendix to Chapter 4) preferred college graduates with a grade-point average of 3.5 or better and placed emphasis on signs of personal drive and at least some business-related

Table 3.1 Percentage of Companies ($N = 535$) Reporting Factors in a College-Graduate's Record as Important in the Hiring Decision

Factor	Percentage stating that factor is important
Undergraduate coursework	
Business, finance, accounting	88
Computer science, mathematics	81
Psychology, industrial relations	53
Humanities (e.g., literature, philosophy, language)	45
History, political science	24
Undergraduate performance	
Strong academic record on campus	96
Undergraduate experience	
Involvement in student, athletic, or community activities	88
Internship or work experience	85
Study abroad	9
Undergraduate institution	
Graduated from a high-quality institution	80

experience. Also highly important is the quality of the undergraduate institution from which the applicant is graduating, an emphasis consistent with the findings of other studies reported in Chapter 1. It is also an emphasis consonant with the common practice among major corporate recruiters of visiting only a select set of campuses in seeking college graduates.[2]

Companies want candidates for entry-level positions to have strong academic records, but they also want clear evidence of exposure to business, through either coursework or direct experience in the business setting. The cross-sectional survey of middle and senior managers yields corroborating evidence on the importance of the latter. The managers were asked about the qualifications that were important to them in the hiring of a college graduate. At the top of the list, stressed by nearly three quarters of the managers, was an "internship or work experience in business."[3]

Direct discussions with managers reveal that the preference for some exposure of the college graduate to business practices reflects a convergence of several concerns. One is that candidates need to know at least a modicum of the vocabulary and concepts of the business setting. Another is that they should have some familiarity with the day-to-day practices and culture of corporate life. A manager in one large consumer-products company that hires many liberal-arts students complained that "the liberal arts student is not liberally educated"—that such students too often know too little about the organization and operation of one of the nation's most central institutions, the private sector.

A third concern is attitude. Those we interviewed at several companies reported that liberal-arts graduates were occasionally ambivalent about working for the private sector at best and at times even overtly anti-business in attitude. While not a major factor, it was of some concern, as can be seen in the written comments of one of the managers responding to the corporate survey:

> I look very closely at the motivation of the young person in seeking a liberal arts degree. Is it preparation for the professions—law, medicine, teaching? Is it to delay embarking on a specific career? Or is it because, for whatever reason, the business world is alien and perhaps considered somewhat crass by the young person?

The general importance of attitude toward business is evident in a comparative study of liberal-arts graduates from institutions that offer an undergraduate business major (as do many of the nation's major universities) and graduates from liberal-arts colleges that do not offer business studies. As perceived by employers, reports that study, the latter are less risky hires than the former. Their reasoning: liberal-arts students attending an institution without a business concentration had no choice but to major in the liberal arts, while liberal-arts students at an institution with a business major could have chosen it, but opted not to do so. Company recruiters tended to infer that students who could have majored in business but did not may be ambivalent about business values.[4]

Many corporations actively seek a large number of liberal-arts graduates, as we know from evidence presented in the preceding chapter. But in recruiting liberal-arts graduates, we find, they are looking for evidence not only of a liberal education, but also of a useful education. Above all, this means some exposure to the culture and experience of the corporate workplace, whether through coursework, internships, or actual work sponsored by the college, such as cooperative education programs (in which students intermittently attend college and take paying jobs in work settings arranged by the college).

II. The Strengths and Weaknesses of Liberal-Arts Graduates

Contrary to impressionistic observations, many liberal-arts students, regardless of their practical business experience, are recruited by companies because of, not in spite of, their liberal education. Liberal-arts graduates often have strong learning, leadership, and other capacities that are vital to effective managerial work.

Systematic study of student development confirms that liberal education is particularly effective at developing learning and leadership abilities. Psychologists David Winter, David McClelland, and Abigail Stewart compared the college experiences of students at three institutions: a private liberal-arts college, a public college with a range of general and career programs, and a community college emphasizing career curricula. The greatest changes were observed in the students fully immersed in the liberal-arts curriculum. They made significantly greater gains than other students in their (1) analytical and critical thinking, (2) independence of thought, (3) self-assurance and leadership abilities, and (4) maturity of judgment. Confirming the importance of these qualities for lifelong experience and performance, the researchers also found that the qualities were good predictors of managerial and professional success a decade later.[5]

While possessing strengths in several areas important for the corporate workplace, many liberal-arts graduates leave college with significant shortcomings that a liberal education should not have permitted. The absence of quantitative-reasoning ability, most pronounced among humanities and, to a lesser degree, social-science graduates, is among the most important of these weaknesses. This is evident, for instance, in a study of the college transcripts of a large national sample of students in the high-school class of 1972 who went on to earn a bachelor's degree by 1984. Of those who graduated in the humanities, only 8% had course credits in quantitatively based courses (mathematics, natural sciences, and engineering). Social-science graduates did little better—13%. By contrast, graduates in the natural sciences had 62% of their coursework in quantitative areas.[6]

To assess the relative qualities of liberal-arts graduates in the corporate work setting, the companies in our study were asked to evaluate the characteristics and skills of liberal-arts graduates in 13 areas. With ratings from 1 (significantly above average) to 5 (significantly below average), we see in Table 3.2 that companies generally viewed liberal-arts graduates as bringing above-average abilities in communication, understanding people, appreciating ethical concerns, and leadership skills. At the bottom of the list, by contrast, are their quan-

Table 3.2 Company Rating of Qualities of Liberal-Arts
Graduates

Personal qualities	Mean rating[a]
Communication (oral and written) skills	1.79
Understanding people	2.07
Appreciating ethical concerns	2.11
Leadership skills	2.31
Innovativeness	2.36
Ability to organize and prioritize	2.50
Analytic skills	2.66
Understanding the company's environment	2.65
Understanding the company's internal world	2.69
Disposition toward business	3.02
Quantitative skills	3.06
General business knowledge and skills	3.18
Technical knowledge and skills	3.49

[a]Rating scale: 1—significantly above average, 3—average, 5—significantly below average. Number of companies—385 to 391.

titative skills, disposition toward business, and general and technical business knowledge and skills.

It is notable that liberal-arts graduates are viewed as above average (above 3.0) compared to all new employees in 9 of the 13 areas. These include generic capacities that should be useful in any professional or organizational setting, such as communication, leadership, and analytic skills, abilities that are the hallmarks of a liberal education. Liberal-arts graduates are assessed as being below average in only four areas, all of which relate to attitudes and skills that are relatively specific to the business setting. Thus business gives above-average marks to liberal-arts graduates for their general and managerial abilities, but finds them undereducated in the specific abilities needed for business performance at the start.

It would appear, then, that liberally educated entry-level managers are better trained for the leadership responsibilities that they may assume later in a career and less well prepared in the technical skills required at the outset of a career. The effect may be to slow the early advancement of liberal-arts graduates compared to those with more technical training and then perhaps equalize the relative advancement rates later in the career.

III. Company Advice to College Students and Educational Administrators

America's major companies find special value in the liberal-arts experience of the college graduates they hire, and many are making special efforts to recruit able graduates of arts and science. While this is an era of substantial opportunity in the private sector for liberal-arts students, business wants more than liberal-arts from the graduates it hires, which is more than many graduates can offer.

If there is a singular concern, it is that liberal-arts majors considering careers in the private sector should have more management-oriented training and business-related experiences. The thrust of the corporate advice is not so much to reduce areas of the liberal curriculum as to add opportunities for liberal-arts students to learn about business and to acquire greater exposure to the quantitative, financial, and other skills that are viewed as being essential for a career in the corporate world.

At the present time, liberal-arts students have virtually no direct exposure to business or management coursework of any kind during their undergraduate years. This is starkly evident in the national study of the transcripts of college graduates from the high-school class of 1972. The study examined the proportion of course credits that liberal-arts students carried in business. As can be seen in Table 3.3, the proportions were minuscule. Less than 2% of liberal-arts students' course credits were in the business curriculum, and less than 1% in engineering. On average, liberal-arts undergraduates had less than one course in either business or engineering during their entire undergraduate career.

By contrast, it is notable that many of the course credits of students in business and engineering are in the liberal arts. While the bulk of the engineering graduates' liberal-arts courses are in the natural sciences, still nearly a fifth of their undergraduate coursework is in the humanities and social sciences. For business graduates the balance is more even, with relatively similar proportions of course credits in the natural sciences (16%), humanities (14%), and social sciences (24%).

Though undergraduate business and engineering students take a substantial fraction of their coursework in the social sciences and humanities, detailed study of the actual course distribution reveals significant limitations. The Association of American Colleges (AAC) examined the transcripts of engineering students completing their programs in 18 undergraduate programs across the nation in the

Table 3.3 Percentage of Course Credits in Liberal Arts, Business, and Engineering Completed for Bachelor's Degree, by Graduate's Field of Study[a]

	Percentage of course credits in field						
	Liberal arts						
Field of study	Social sciences	Humanities	Natural sciences	Total	Business	Engineering	Other
Liberal arts							
Social science	49	23	13	85	2	0	13
Humanities	18	60	8	86	1	0	13
Natural sciences	14	18	58	90	1	1	8
Business	24	14	16	54	35	0	11
Engineering	9	9	31	49	1	38	12

[a]Natural sciences include life and physical science, mathematics, and computer science.
Source: U.S. Department of Education (1986).

spring of 1986. The typical institution requires engineering students to take five or six courses in the social sciences and humanities, consistent with the policy of the national accrediting organization, the Accrediting Board for Engineering and Technology, which requires that at least 12.5% of engineering-degree coursework be in the social sciences and humanities. The AAC's analysis of the composition of the coursework reveals, however, that only about half of the engineering students achieved *breadth*—defined as taking at least one course in the social sciences and one in the humanities; only half achieved *depth*—defined as carrying at least one advanced, nonintroductory course in the social sciences or humanities.[7]

Thus business and engineering graduates have usually had a more diverse repertoire of courses than liberal-arts graduates, but their coursework in the liberal arts in many cases is still somewhat restricted. Cognizant of such limitations, companies and managers are also calling for greater emphasis on the liberal-arts curriculum for those students outside of the liberal arts who intend to pursue careers in management. Companies want more of both the liberal-arts graduate and the professional-undergraduate-degree holder. This is evident in both of our surveys. Two thirds of the 505 surveyed managers endorsed the view that liberal education should include more business and technical courses (Table 3.4). At the same time, a similar majority also thought that business and engineering programs should include additional liberal-arts courses. And more than three quarters shared the position that future business leaders should have at least some exposure to liberal learning. Perhaps symptomatic of the lim-

Table 3.4 Percentage of Managers ($N = 505$) Agreeing That Additional Coursework in Liberal Arts, Business, and Engineering Should Be Required of College Students

Statement	Percentage agreeing
"Liberal arts education should include more business and technical courses"	64
"Business and engineering education should include more liberal arts courses"	65
"Future business leaders in America should have at least some liberal arts education"	77
"Future political leaders in America should have at least some liberal arts education"	68

ited vision that business sometimes ascribes to political leaders and the power of liberal learning for broadening that vision, more than two thirds of the managers endorsed the value of liberal learning for future political leaders as well.[8]

The dual emphasis on both liberal learning and business study can also be seen in commentary by the 535 surveyed corporations on what college students should do to prepare for careers in the private sector and what colleges should do to prepare liberal-arts students for such a future. The responding managers were asked, "If you were to address a college audience, what course of study and set of educational experiences would you recommend to today's students who wish to enter the business world?" With no preset areas of response, a large proportion of the managers spontaneously suggested liberal-arts *or* business studies. However, most recommended a strong emphasis on both liberal arts and business. A representative sample of their commentary appears in the tables that follow. Table 3.5 presents a cross section of recommendations focusing entirely on the liberal arts, Table 3.6 samples the recommendations for more business studies, and Table 3.7 includes commentary stressing a combination of liberal arts and business. While some company representatives promoted only the liberal arts and others only management and technical subjects, the predominant thrust was to urge students to acquire elements from both.

For students intent on finding corporate employment upon graduation, the advice may be well taken. Yet in many instances it is difficult to follow, since their academic institution may not provide the needed opportunities, encouragement, or incentives. Liberal-arts students appear to face the stiffest barriers. While undergraduate business and engineering programs typically require matriculants to carry at least some liberal-arts coursework, virtually no liberal-arts programs maintain a reciprocal requirement for coursework in business and engineering. The result, as we have already seen, is that although business and engineering students will take a number of liberal-arts courses before graduation, rare is the liberal-arts student who will have had even a single business or engineering course. This disparity may have diminished in recent years when a number of institutions instituted minors in business administration for liberal-arts students and opened other opportunities for cross-disciplinary studies in this direction. Yet the predominant pattern is still for most liberal-arts graduates to have never had a single course in a business-related field.

This limitation in the background of liberal-arts students is acutely appreciated by the companies that we surveyed. It is amply evident in

Table 3.5 Company Recommendations to College Students Intending to Enter the Business World: Representative Commentary Stressing a *Liberal Education* from the Corporate Survey

Avoid business courses at the undergraduate level—take classics, languages, art, writing.

In my opinion, the actual course of study is less important than the level of commitment, achievement, and maturity of the graduate. Liberal arts graduates are generally prepared to get more out of life and contribute more as citizens.

Major in a physical science or engineering, learn another language, travel overseas, study economics, history, rhetoric, and expository writing, learn how to use a computer. Be active in extracurriculars that develop communication, interacting skills, and organizational ability. Study philosophy, including logic and ethics.

(1) Select a major based on the body of *knowledge* that is most important to you; (2) use electives for "rounding" and exploration; variety is the key here; (3) concentrate on developing the following *skills*: written and oral communications, research and analytical reasoning, conceptualizing, planning, and organizing; (4) utilize classroom and extracurricular opportunities to develop leadership and teamwork skills as well as an understanding of human behavior.

Liberal arts—emphasis on language and other communication skills, together with ability to think conceptually and analytically.

A liberal-arts education generally provides a wider knowledge base from which to draw upon and thereby enables one to view matters from a larger perspective than can someone whose focus had been primarily groomed in one specific field of study. It is for this reason that I would recommend a liberal-arts education.

It is my judgment that regardless of the field one is entering, a strong liberal-arts background is essential in order to be an effective employee.

Reading poetry; studying German or Japanese.

the responses of the company representatives to a question on what policy changes higher education should introduce into the liberal-arts curriculum. The firms were asked: "What could colleges do to better prepare liberal arts graduates for careers in your company and the business world?" The most dominant theme in their assessments was

Table 3.6 Company Recommendations to College Students
Intending to Enter the Business World: Representative
Commentary Stressing *Management and Technical*
Education from the Company Survey

Our managers do not have any orientation toward liberal-arts graduates
for recruiting and placement in our company. We always look for people
who have been educated in a specific field, i.e., accounting, law,
engineering. If you plan to enter the business world, study business.

For our highly technical organization, the dominant need and development
opportunities lie with the engineering disciplines, computer technology,
etc. Business graduates should pick majors in accounting, marketing, or
finance.

Business management—strong emphasis on written communication skills,
computers, accounting, and finance.

If you feel you must engage in a liberal-arts education, don't plan on a
career in manufacturing unless you prepare yourself with some useful
skills via choice of electives and summer-work experience.

Technical fields: engineering, computer science, artificial intelligence,
telecommunications, human-factors engineering, public relations,
organizational management, or behavior.

Finance, accounting, and *computers*!!

the need for colleges to give liberal-arts students more exposure to
an education in management.

The critical emphasis, spontaneously suggested by 135 corporations, was to urge colleges to open more business coursework to liberal-arts students. This emphasis is consistent with the
near-universal stress that corporations place on business-related
coursework for the college graduates they hire, whatever their field
of study. The companies' specific suggestions were richly diverse.
The common principle was more exposure to business studies, but
the means of implementation were as varied as the curricular structures to which they were applied. The suggestions ranged from
increasing business electives to instituting minors in management,
adding business issues to existing liberal-arts courses, and introducing training in business skills. The recommendations generally spoke
of either (1) encouraging more business courses for liberal-arts students or (2) bringing business-related issues directly into liberal-arts

Table 3.7 Company Recommendations to College Students Intending to Enter the Business World: Representative Commentary Stressing *Liberal and Management Education* from the Corporate Survey

I would recommend that they balance their educational background with liberal arts, business-related, computer science, and mathematics. Analytical thinking abilities are key to survival in the business world today.

Any course of study which would strengthen oral and written skills, the ability to think independently and creatively, along with some exposure to business careers.

Get a broad education, but definitely acquire practical business skills, such as accounting or management information systems.

An economics degree, plenty of computer science, some accounting, and lots of philosophy and English lit.

Get a good solid foundation in the arts and humanities, but at the same time take courses that would create an understanding of business.

A liberal-arts curriculum provides an excellent, well-rounded foundation for career growth. However, to enter the business world, particularly financial services, one must demonstrate the ability to handle quantitative information such as accounting and finance. The suggestion is to take at least one or two courses in these areas and do them well.

Ideal: Undergraduate degree in a demanding academic environment requiring all humanities plus accounting, economics, finance, computer science, and extensive writing and speaking work; international and foreign-language experience; work experience (internships and part-time work); leadership and volunteer work in extracurricular and sports activities

We recommend that students focus on acquiring a broad liberal-arts education that encourages intellectual curiosity and strengthens verbal and written communication skills. Furthermore, they should participate in as many extracurricular activities and internships as possible that encourage familiarity with the business world, the development of necessary technical skills, and the savvy to deal effectively and communicate well with other people.

Get a combination of business and liberal arts, and try plenty of internships.

courses. A cross section of company recommendations that more business-related coursework be made mandatory or at least elective for liberal-arts students is as follows:

- Give them more business and quantitatively oriented courses as part of the curriculum.
- Require them to take more business-oriented courses; require engineering and business students to take more liberal-arts courses.
- (1) Make basic business courses available for liberal-arts majors; (2) provide summer institutes for business-oriented liberal-arts majors; (3) provide noncredit seminars and/or workshops on business management, basic accounting principles, business law, etc.
- Provide some basic business courses for the liberal-arts major. They need to be made aware that they need more than a college degree these days to get into the corporate world as the competition is tough.
- Encourage liberal-arts graduates to take business courses and prepare themselves for the reality of the business world through internship programs.
- Prepare students to handle specific skills required by business *while* they are being educated and trained in the "arts."
- Colleges should encourage liberal-arts graduates to take courses such as statistics, computer science, accounting, and marketing in order to broaden career options.
- Require a business minor.

A 1987 survey of the human-resource directors of companies in the New York metropolitan area provides corroborating evidence. Of the 85 responding firms, three quarters affirmed that liberal-arts graduates would make more appealing applicants if their curricula had included business courses. Courses in business writing, business communication, and decision making were at the top of the list; computer literacy and marketing as well drew substantial favor. The study also reaffirmed the overriding importance of communication skills. When asked what criteria the human resource directors use to evaluate college-graduate applicants, writing and oral skills were almost universally identified as the leading considerations; by contrast, the particular major, whether in a business or liberal-arts field, was considered to be less important.[9]

A number of company representatives went even further to suggest that liberal-arts courses themselves could be more creatively structured to include a stress on issues related to business. For undergraduate liberal-arts colleges without companion undergraduate business schools, these suggestions may be particularly apt. Although the colleges may have little inclination to introduce courses in business administration, they do have the capacity to broaden their own liberal-arts curriculum. But even liberal-arts colleges based in universities with existing undergraduate business colleges, say the companies, could usefully reexamine their curricula with these suggestions in mind. Cross-registration of their liberal-arts students in business courses is to be encouraged, but many companies recommended that an equally strong if not stronger means of reaching the largest number of liberal-arts students is to bring the changes "home":

- Include more business issues in coursework. A great deal about business and economics can be included in traditional liberal-arts courses.
- [Add] more case-study work to bring some semblance of reality to the courses taught.
- First, provide a very challenging and demanding liberal-arts curriculum, and *do not* graduate those who fail to master it. Second, expose students to business, government, and foreign culture as part of their study of "the whole."
- Integrate liberal-arts and business courses so that graduates would be better equipped to theorize, conceptualize, and organize themselves within a business environment.
- In every one hour of class, the final 10 minutes should be devoted to the reality of the postcollegiate world.

A second theme in the recommendations of the company representatives to college administrators concerned with the liberal-arts is a stress on the creation of business internships, cooperative-education opportunities, and other means of bringing liberal-arts students into direct contact with the business world. This theme, spontaneously mentioned by 72 of the 535 corporations, is symptomatic of a widespread corporate stress on internship and work experience for the college graduates they hire. We saw that 85% of the firms in the corporate survey stated that "internship or work experience" was an important consideration in hiring college graduates.

Liberal-arts programs should cultivate internship and cooperative-education opportunities for their students, say the companies, to ensure that they acquire a more realistic appraisal of the corporate work environment before seeking full-time entry into it. Such an understanding is important for stepping effectively into a first company position, and there are few ways for a liberal-arts student to acquire it except through direct placement in a work setting. In the direct commentary of the responding managers:

- Provide actual hands-on experience (internships). Explain *profit* and how you make dollars through effective utilization of time and talent.
- Be sure that they require some small number of courses or internships in the business world so that when the liberal-arts graduate enters the business world, it is not completely foreign to him.
- Offer more opportunities to supplement coursework with (1) business areas—finance and accounting, and (2) cooperative work-study programs to allow students to apply theory learned in class to real-world settings, to get acclimated to corporate environments.
- Encourage cooperative-education or internships programs. Develop realistic expectations regarding starting salaries, the level of work (it can't always be challenging), and the pace of progression (don't expect promotion in the first few months; you have to prove yourself).
- Expose them to the business world in one way or another.

A third theme in company suggestions to college and university administrators, less pervasively expressed but more far-reaching than the first two, is to reconsider the underlying tenor of the liberal-arts curriculum vis-à-vis the private sector. A number of company representatives suggested that the liberal-arts curriculum leaves many students either ignorant of or hostile to the culture of the corporation, the economic principles around which business is organized, and the role of the private sector in American life. Among the "most significant failures of entry-level graduates," commented one company representative, was "very little understanding of the fact that profit is not only the very small difference between revenue and cost—but the *only* reason why business exists."

The themes of political complaint parallel those observed in the 1970s by Leonard Silk and David Vogel in their study of top corporate executives. Listening to informal discussions among chief executives and others that were organized by the Conference Board, they found a widespread belief among top managers that America's media and educational institutions were turning much of the public and tomorrow's college graduates against business by either leaving them ignorant of the main tenets of economic life or, worse, when the knowledge gap was filled, instilling them with antibusiness ideologies.[10] Though this is a less pervasive view of the shortcomings of the educational system now, the critical assessment lingers:

- Business courses should be included with a balanced view of the contribution of corporations to society. Too often business is viewed as the enemy!
- Refrain from "bad-mouthing" business as the greatest evil of the USA, teach that it's because of the free enterprise system we can provide the human and social programs that do exist today in the USA. . . . I feel that a large percentage of the liberal-arts graduates lean too far in support of social programs and don't understand that *individual* hard work built this country.
- Above all, *do not* preach antibusiness sentiments.

College and university administrators are not likely to agree either that such imbalances exist or that they can readily intervene to alter those that do exist. The principles of academic freedom are strong in protecting faculty from administrative interference in the tenor or the interpretations offered in their teaching. Many of the managers are aware of such constraints and would be loath to suggest any abrogation of the principles of academic freedom. Yet they did formulate suggestions that could indirectly alter the underlying tenor of liberal-arts teaching as it relates to conceptions and interpretations of the private sector. The most commonly recommended strategy was to create a two-way flow of personnel and communication between higher education and business, a recommendation built on the premise that lack of familiarity is the chief barrier to appreciation. Faculty members should have some direct exposure to the corporate environment, a number of companies suggested, and business managers should be brought to campus:

- Professors should have a better understanding of how and what business contributes to our society and a more positive orientation toward it. Their ignorance and prejudice is often appalling.
- Staff liberal-arts departments with educators who do not possess an antibusiness bias.
- Have professors involve themselves in programs that would create an understanding of today's business climate and the needs of business today. Structure curricula that reflect today's [business] environment and problems.
- Bring business people in to speak on career experiences and their own application of educational background.

- Too many courses are theoretical and too idealistic. I would recommend using the resources of the local business community for seminars on corporate culture and the realities of the business world.

A few responding managers discouraged liberal-arts graduates from even considering a future in their company, regardless of any changes in the college curricula. Said one manager: "Tell them not to be liberal-arts majors to get into our organization." But despite the sometimes difficult entry process faced by liberal-arts graduates, another manager urged that colleges train in persistence: "Teach them to apply endlessly to us until we finally let them in." Still another could offer no guidance for altering the liberal-arts undergraduate curriculum or student experience and simply urged appropriate postgraduate training of liberal-arts graduates seeking careers in business: After the liberal-arts degree, "send them to get MBAs."

IV. Combining the Liberal and the Useful Arts

We have seen that many of America's major companies find special value in the liberal-arts experience of the college graduates they hire. Employees educated in the liberal arts bring communication and leadership skills to the corporate workplace. They are comparatively undereducated, however, in the principles and concepts of business practices, and they tend to have fewer of the specialized skills that corporate recruiters often seek for entry-level positions.

Business wants more from the liberal-arts graduates it intends to hire. This has been evident in many signals, each focused on a different facet, which, taken together, offer a clear message. Among the leading signals in the present study are these findings:

- Two thirds of the 505 surveyed managers supported the view that liberal education should include more business and technical courses.
- More than four fifths of the 535 surveyed companies stress an internship or work experience for the college graduates they hired.
- The surveyed companies give liberal-arts graduates comparatively good ratings for their general leadership, creativity, communication and organizational skills, but poor ratings for their specific business and quantitative skills.

Many companies, then, consider it a priority that the principles of business and management be introduced into the liberal-arts curriculum, at least for students who intend to work in the private sector. How this would affect the learning experiences of liberal-arts students who are not leaning toward a career in business is a question unaddressed. It is one, however, that would require careful attention by college administrators if the changes proposed by the companies studied here are considered for introduction.

While the focus has been on the liberal-arts curriculum, it should be noted again that many companies and managers urge change in the undergraduate business curriculum as well. Convergence of the two is a central theme. If liberal education should be broadened to include management courses, a view shared by most company managers, so too should management and education be broadened to include more liberal-arts courses, a view also shared by a majority of the surveyed managers. Some combination of the liberal and the useful arts would be the college curriculum of the future if business had input into its design.

Undergraduate management education has incorporated liberal-education requirements into its curriculum, but undergraduate liberal-arts education still only rarely finds a place for management courses in its curriculum. A number of institutions, however, have already moved in the direction of providing some management training to interested liberal-arts students by way of such options as minors and certification in business administration and internships for credit in business settings. Also, both higher-education institutions and companies are moving to reduce the gulf between their two cultures. Such companies as CBS and Shell Oil developed programs to bring college and university faculty into contact with their managers in company settings. Colleges and universities have established programs for bridging the culture gap the other way, such as the University of Maryland's Program in Business and the Humanities and the State of New Jersey's Business/Humanities Project, which bring managers onto campus.[11]

Given the intensified student interest in the private sector, the private sector's increased interest in liberal-arts students, and the fact that liberal-arts graduates are relatively well prepared for organizational life but underprepared for the corporate setting, it is an opportune moment for reexamination of the undergraduate curriculum. With educational reform of the liberal-arts curriculum already on the American political agenda, attention should be directed at a range of new options in the undergraduate curriculum that will permit the interested student to prepare more effectively for a career in the private sector. For the liberal-arts student, this means increased opportunities for exposure to business issues—in and beyond the classroom. For the business and engineering student, this also signifies additional opportunities for exposure to liberal learning. From the standpoint of many corporations, a convergence of educational opportunities in the liberal arts and the useful arts would be a welcome change in American higher education.

Notes

1. Boyer (1987), pp. 102, 110, 112.
2. Companies were asked: "When you consider hiring (or recommending hiring) a college graduate for an entry level position, how important is it that the person had or did any of the following?" The four response categories are "very important," "somewhat important," "not too important," and "not at all important"; the first two responses are combined in the table data.
3. The question asked of managers was: "'When you consider hiring (or recommending hiring) a college graduate for an entry level position, which of the following experiences, qualifications or achievements are most important to you in evaluating the candidate?"
4. Collins (1971); Garis, Hess, and Marron (1985); Unger (1985).
5. Winter, McClelland, and Stewart (1981); other studies and research on this question are reviewed in Useem (1986).
6. Center for Educational Statistics (1986).
7. Johnston, Shaman, and Zemsky (1988).
8. Similar results emerge from a 1985 survey of 213 managers of major Canadian companies (Rush and Evers, 1986). The study reported that more than three quarters of the managers felt that university students majoring in technical fields should carry more courses in the liberal arts. In evaluating recent university graduates already working in industry, the managers ranked their communication and leadership skills as the lowest of 13 skill areas (technical and quantitative skills were ranked at the top).
9. Queens College (1987).
10. Silk and Vogel (1976).
11. The steps that some colleges and universities are taking in this area are described in Mohrman and Hirsch (1986) and Rice (1983).

Appendix to Chapter 3

Case C: An Engineering Culture at an Industrial-Products Company

The industrial-products company is among the nation's top 100 manufacturing corporations, with annual sales of more than $5 billion and a work force of more than 65,000. Its products range from electronic systems to industrial and consumer appliances. In this technology-driven corporation engineers hold key positions in many parts of the company. Business and liberal-arts graduates, by contrast, find limited opportunities.

Both the chairman and the president of the company had earned degrees in engineering, and engineering is the most common background in the corporation's managerial and professional ranks. The annual recruitment of recent college graduates focuses primarily on engineers, above all electrical engineers. Nearly 500 new college graduates were hired in 1986; more than half were electrical engineers and a quarter were other engineering graduates (Table 3.8). Fewer than 1 in 10 were business graduates, and fewer than 1 in 20 were liberal-arts graduates, all of whom had degrees in mathematics or physics.

The company generally looks inward for its managerial talent. Most of its officers and senior managers are "homegrown" individuals who began with the company as entry-level engineers years ago and gradually rose into the more senior ranks. Without a technical background and intimate familiarity with the company's technology and products, advancement is not likely. This is partly due to the complex technical features of many of the company's major products and a corresponding technical expertise among its buyers. "The customer is a highly sophisticated technical buyer," commented the director of the company's research, and "you have to be able to interact on a technical peer basis. You have to know the technical details to get and retain their respect."

Relatively few business graduates are recruited into the firm, and most of those who are hired are concentrated in the accounting and financial operations. Nor does the company seek many MBA degree holders. For entry-level hiring, it usually prefers those who

Table 3.8 Degree Areas of College Graduates
Recruited by an Industrial-Products
Firm in 1986

Area	College graduates recruited
Engineering	376
Electrical	269
Mechanical	46
Engineering technology	28
Industrial manufacturing	29
Aeronautical	2
Chemical	2
Computer science	69
Business and accounting	35
Liberal arts	16
Mathematics	13
Physics	3
Total	496

have recently earned their bachelor's degree, and, in any case, a technical background rather than the MBA is considered to be the prerequisite for movement into general management. In the phrasing of the employment director for the company, "we don't hire a lot of MBAs here. . . . If you are to assume a leadership role, you have to have a technology base." While few new MBAs are hired by the company, some managers return to school part time to acquire an MBA degree from business colleges located in their area.

Since engineers have rarely taken business courses in college and only a fraction have added an MBA degree to their credentials, the company has built its own internal management-development programs. Both middle-management and advanced-management programs are available for engineers who might assume general responsibilities for the firm's operation. The working philosophy is to rely on the company's own resources for cultivating future managerial cadres. Both engineering and manufacturing topics are included on the agendas of the management-development courses and programs.

Similarly, there are limited opportunities for liberal-arts graduates. A handful of mathematics and physics graduates are hired by the company, but there are few other openings for which a liberal-arts background would be suitable. Accredited engineering programs generally require half a dozen courses in humanities and social sciences for graduation, and thus most engineers will have had some exposure to a liberal-arts education. Company officials expressed concern about the course load of engineering students if they must also continue to complete essential science and engineering courses. "If you want trained engineers, you have to give them courses in science and engineering," said the employment director. On the other hand, company officials recognized the need for their engineers to have writing, communication, and other skills that are well learned through a diverse liberal education.

Despite the concentrated focus on a technical grounding in engineering, the corporation seeks far more than just technical proficiency during its college-recruitment efforts. Company recruiters looked closely at the candidate's breadth of interests, communication skills, and signs of leadership potential. The ability to apply the technical knowledge in the company setting was as important as the knowledge itself. College recruiters sought individuals with strong academic records—an undergraduate grade-point average of at least 3.0 in the engineering curriculum was expected—but they also looked for evidence of "well-roundedness." Extracurricular activities, internships and cooperative-education experiences, and research projects with faculty were among the major indicators used to measure such breadth. Of particular value were also the applicant's expressive abilities during the campus interview and subsequent visits to the firm. Persuasive communication skills, especially an ability to articulate technical issues clearly, were considered essential for success in the company.

Liberal-arts (and business) graduates thus find few opportunities for employment with this engineering-oriented corporation. The technology used in producing electronic-based and other industrial products places a premium on the hiring and promotion of well-trained engineering graduates. Business education does find limited demand in the financial areas of the company. So does liberal-arts education in a few positions open to science and mathematics majors. It should be added, however, that communication skills and related abilities are actively sought in the engineers recruited by the company.

Case D: Opportunities for Liberal-Arts Graduates with Postgraduate Experience in a Health-Products Corporation

The health-products corporation offers a broad range of health and health-related products to the general consumer and to the medical field. With a worldwide workforce of 70,000 and sales of more than $8 billion annually, it is organized as a family of more than 150 companies that operate under a corporate umbrella. Many of the companies hire liberal-arts graduates, though they are a small minority of the college graduates brought into the corporation as a whole.

During the past 8 years, approximately 200 college and university graduates have been hired each year by the corporation, with 203 recruited during the 1986–1987 school year. The new employees represented 104 institutions, but half came from 33 colleges and universities where the company's recruiting efforts have been concentrated. Most of those hired held undergraduate degrees only: 72% had BAs or BSs and no postgraduate training, 22% had MBAs, and the remainder had other postgraduate degrees.

Nearly half of the baccalaureate holders had majored in a business subject, with accounting being the largest field (Table 3.9). The next largest group—liberal-arts majors—constituted about one sixth of the college-graduate hiring. Most of them held science degrees, particularly in biology (14 of the 27 hired). A small number of social-science majors were recruited, but no humanities graduates were hired in 1986.

In hiring college graduates at the entry level, the corporation is generally looking for highly specific skills that have immediate application. One of the companies reports, for example, that it seeks people with technical skills and a basic understanding of business. It recognizes that the kinds of skills associated with a liberal-arts education, including the ability to look at "the big picture," are required at higher-level positions. But since such skills are not sought at the entry level, they are given little attention in the recruitment process.

Liberal-arts graduates without work experience are often perceived to be more naive about business than are other graduates, and this hurts their hiring prospects as well. One company's employment manager reports that although a new liberal-arts degree holder may be competent for a position, he would find it difficult to place the graduate because of a "poor cosmetic fit." From experience the

Table 3.9 Distribution of Field of Study of New Employees Hired by a Health-Products Corporation Who Held Undergraduate Degree Only, 1986–1987

| | New employees hired | |
Field of study	Number	Percentage
Business	67	46
Accounting	32	
Business administration/management	13	
Marketing	6	
Other	16	
Liberal Arts	27	18
Natural science	21	
Social science	6	
Engineering	25	17
Industrial	7	
General	6	
Mechanical	5	
Electrical	3	
Other	4	
Computer science	12	8
Pharmacy	8	5
Communications and journalism	4	3
Other	3	2
Total	146	

company's human-resource managers know that it could take a year or two for a liberal-arts graduate to adapt to the language and culture of the business and that it would therefore be difficult, though not impossible, to convince the hiring supervisor to take a liberal-arts graduate.

Another company confirms that it faces a similar problem in recruiting recent liberal-arts graduates. The company feels that they often have "no feel for business." They frequently require more orientation time than do other graduates to learn which products are likely to sell and what is compatible with corporate culture. Moreover, liberal-arts graduates sometimes bring with them biases about business that can initially limit their effectiveness.

To overcome these shortcomings and to improve the prospects of liberal-arts graduates, officials responsible for this particular company's hiring—the vice-president for human resources, the director of sales administration and training, and the director of the employment office—urge that colleges (1) require courses in business, technology, and economics for all liberal-arts majors and (2) create stronger linkages between liberal-arts colleges and the business community to alter the climate on campus toward business.

The corporation's overall director of college relations offers parallel advice: campuses should provide liberal-arts students with more opportunities to take business courses and to develop their leadership and communication skills for a business environment. In essence, liberal-arts graduates need more context and perspective on the role and function of business if they are to work effectively in that environment.

Marketing, sales, and supervisory roles in operations and manufacturing can provide some opportunities for liberal-arts graduates. These jobs require an ability to work with a range of people, leadership and confidence, communication and coordination, and a capacity to get things done. Liberal-arts graduates often bring such qualities. Particularly successful in operations and manufacturing have been liberal-arts graduates who served in the military after graduation, because they bring energy and identifiable organizational and leadership skills to the corporate setting.

Recruitment for entry-level positions in product management of consumer goods has focused on MBAs, especially those from top-ranked schools. Many of the MBA holders had earned undergraduate degrees in liberal arts, however, and this has been one of the primary indirect means for liberal-arts graduates to enter the company. Moreover, this combination is viewed by several executives as having special strengths. The MBA training overcomes the unfamiliarity with business culture that is the weakness of many newly minted liberal-arts graduates, and the liberal-arts education provides an intellectual foundation that can prove invaluable for further upward movement. MBA holders with liberal-arts degrees, according to the impressions of the vice-president for personnel at corporate headquarters, may bring a greater creativity and intellectual curiosity to their position than do MBAs with an undergraduate business degree. They are not notably better at working with other people in entry-level positions, he found, but in more senior positions they do appear to work very effectively.

One of the companies reports that liberal-arts graduates are generally able to handle a variety of tasks well, are exceptionally flexible, and possess good information-processing skills. In 1986–1987 it hired four liberal-arts graduates as sales personnel (they held BA degrees in anthropology, biology, psychology, and sociology). However, all four had worked for several years after college and were already very familiar with business culture. The requisite skills for sales include an ability to master the technical features of products; to communicate effectively; to motivate others to use the products, especially pharmacists and physicians; and to be a well-organized self-starter.

In the past the technical features of the product led to an emphasis on graduates with science backgrounds. More recently, however, while the college degree is still considered a prerequisite for entry, a specific major is not. The company's national sales manager notes that he does not care what the majors may have been, so long as the individuals are college graduates with substantial sales experience and talent.

In sum, business graduates are the major source of new employees at this health-products company. Some liberal-arts graduates are hired directly from college as well, but more common is their recruitment after they have acquired work, military, or MBA experience. Without that postgraduate experience, however, those involved in hiring and managing personnel would generally urge liberal-arts students to acquire more exposure to marketing, management, and other basic business courses while still in college.

4 Liberal-Arts Graduates in Corporate Careers

A large proportion of this generation's college students, including many in the liberal arts, are preparing for occupational careers in the private sector. When they enter the corporate world, some skills and abilities they are now acquiring will find immediate application, while others will prove more valuable as work experience and responsibilities expand. Liberal-arts education has traditionally emphasized the lifelong elements, such as intellectual flexibility and independence of thought, while undergraduate professional programs in business, engineering, and other areas have stressed skills of more immediate utility. There are tradeoffs in the mix of these elements for the college student intent on entering the private sector. One must have the skills necessary to perform first-level responsibilities, but one must also have the capacities necessary later to assume higher-level responsibilities. Lacking one or the other may prove to be problematic for a corporate career.

It can be expected, then, that liberal-arts graduates often begin comparatively slowly in the corporate workplace, but frequently move up the corporate ladder quickly and finish well. This chapter examines the experience of companies and their managers in the promotion of liberal-arts graduates and their momentum toward career success within the corporate hierarchy. We also focus on the horizontal differences, identifying the various areas of the company into which senior managers of varying educational backgrounds tend to concentrate. Finally, we examine the value of liberal-arts education for managers in representing the corporation to external communities.

I. Early Advancement of Liberal-Arts Graduates

College placement offices and various research studies generally indicate that liberal-arts graduates do less well than business

and engineering graduates in obtaining their first job in the corporate world. Corporate employers list proportionally fewer openings
for liberal-arts graduates, and starting salaries are often lower as
well. Liberal-arts graduates possess fewer technical skills, the evidence indicates, around which entry-level business positions are often defined.[1]

If slow to start in the private sector, liberal-arts graduates can be
expected nevertheless to do well after the start. Studies of the criteria
used by companies in managerial promotion indicate that many of
the objectives of liberal-arts education are the skills upon which
managerial advancement is later achieved. A survey of 113 officers of
large American corporations in 1982, for example, asked the officers
to identify the factors that "become important to success as a college
graduate employee progresses to middle and top positions in your
company." The traits most often singled out are, in rank order: (1)
verbal communication skills, (2) ability to identify and formulate
problems, (3) willingness to assume responsibility, (4) interpersonal
skills, (5) reasoning ability, (6) creativity, and (7) ability to function
independently.[2]

We saw in the preceding chapter that liberal-arts graduates are
highly rated by companies in areas closely akin to many of these
characteristics. Liberal-arts graduates received above-average marks
from the surveyed companies in communication skills, leadership
skills, innovativeness, and analytic abilities. Liberal-arts graduates
should therefore have a relative advantage in progressing through
the middle and senior ranks of the companies.

Direct study of the careers of college graduates confirm that the
need for technical skills declines and the demand for general talents increases as graduates acquire greater experience. Following
two groups of college graduates who had been working for 3 to 9
years, one study found that alumni who had taken English courses
reported more application of such coursework with the passage of
time, while those who had had engineering courses found less application for that specialty. Similarly, social-science degrees were found
to increase in value over time, as measured by the graduates' earnings, while engineering degrees, starting higher, lost some relative
value. The latency effect was not limited, however, to liberal-arts
courses. The value of business courses and a business major were
also found to increase with time.[3]

Similar conclusions were reached by a study of more than 4000
bachelor's degree holders who had acquired no postgraduate train-

ing and who were working in company management a decade after completing college. Among those who started their careers in finance, marketing, accounting, personnel, research and development, or engineering, fewer than one in three reported that they had needed planning, writing, speaking or general managerial capabilities on their first job (Table 4.1). After a decade of work experience, 45% of the engineers, 73% of the finance specialists, and over 75% of those working in other areas reported that general management competencies were essential to their work. There is a parallel growth in demand for planning and budgeting abilities.[4]

This study revealed as well that the demand for communication skills also increases with career development. Of the marketing specialists, for instance, 26% reported that they were required to draw on writing skills in their first position, but 63% needed such skills a decade later (Table 4.1). While only 4% of the accountants and 3% of the engineers led meetings and spoke before groups when their career began, well over half were doing so 10 years later.

The importance of technical skills for starting and continuing a managerial career, however, should not be underestimated. A longitudinal study of the graduates in the late 1970s of the MBA programs of Stanford University, University of California of Los Angeles and Berkeley, and University of Southern California confirms that the technical content of their education was considered important. Two thirds of the graduates found that the technical knowledge they had acquired was needed for effective performance in their first job, and half found that this was still true 5 years later. But this study also confirmed that general, nontechnical skills increase in importance over time. Analytical abilities were required by 60% during the first year after graduation, but by 75% after 5 years on the job. Interpersonal skills such as communication and teamwork were deemed essential at first by 67% of the MBA holders, but by 93% after five years.[5]

Consistent with the comparatively strong emphasis on more specific skills at the entry level and just above, companies studied in the present research generally estimate that liberal-arts graduates advance somewhat more slowly than do other college graduates with business-related undergraduate professional training. Companies were asked to assess the rate of advancement of five groups of graduates during their first 10 years with the company (Table 4.2). Among those with undergraduate degrees only, business graduates received the highest rating, followed by engineering and then liberal arts. MBA holders with liberal-arts degrees advanced on a par with

Table 4.1 Percentage of College Graduates in Business in Mid-1960s Requiring Major Skills on First Job and a Decade After Graduation, by Functional Area in Company

Major competency		Functional area					
	Finance	Marketing	Accounting	Personnel	R&D management	Engineering
Management						
First job	27	22	4	20	18	3
After decade	73	78	93	85	93	45
Planning and budgeting						
First job	13	7	19	2	17	3
After decade	40	56	67	46	86	52
Writing and editing						
First job	20	26	22	34	43	28
After decade	53	63	81	78	71	38
Leading meeting, speaking to groups						
First job	27	22	4	32	25	3
After decade	73	59	67	78	77	52

Source: Bisconti and Kessler (1980), pp. 12–14.

Table 4.2 Company Rating of Advancement of College Graduates
During First 10 Years, by Type of Degree

Type of degree	Number of companies	Mean rating[a]	Percentage of firms stating "above average"
Liberal-arts graduates	467	2.89	23
Business graduates	476	2.39	56
Engineering graduates	393	2.61	46
MBAs with liberal-arts degrees	440	2.38	56
MBAs with other undergraduate degrees	419	2.20	71

[a]Rating scale: 1, significantly above average; 3, average; 5, significantly
below average.

the business undergraduates, and MBAs with degrees in business,
engineering, and other nonliberal-arts fields did best of all.[6]

II. Liberal-Arts Graduates in Senior-Management Levels

While liberal-arts graduates are rated as doing less well than other
graduates during the first decade in company management, other evidence points to their accelerating prospects. This is illustrated by a
long-term research project on managers working for American Telephone and Telegraph (AT&T), the nation's largest private employer
until its breakup in 1983. Liberal-arts graduates hired as managers
by AT&T in both the mid-1950s and late 1970s, the two groups most
intensively studied, were found to score higher on average than those
with undergraduate professional degrees (largely in business and engineering) in such critical areas as creativity, leadership, communication, and problem-solving.[7]

AT&T also periodically evaluated the actual performance and advancement of a management group first hired in the mid-1950s. The
results, which have been widely reported, showed that those with
humanities and social-science degrees moved up the corporate ladder in the early years nearly on a par with business and engineering
graduates. Significant differences began to appear after a decade,
however, and after two decades they became even stronger: while

21% of the engineering graduates and 32% of the business graduates had reached at least the top levels of middle management, 45%
of the humanities and social-science majors had done so.[8]

Though the AT&T study is telling, particularly since it is a relatively
technologically oriented company where liberal-arts students might
not be expected to do especially well, the present study indicates
that the pattern may prevail more generally. This can be seen, first
of all, in assessments of the value of liberal arts for performance
at various levels of management. Companies were asked to evaluate
the usefulness of a liberal-arts background for effective performance
in entry-level, middle, and top corporate management. Two in three
of the company representatives reported that such a background
was useful for entry-level management, but more than four in five
concurred that it was also of value for the middle- and senior-
management ranks. Even sharper differences were evident in the
fractions asserting that a liberal-arts background was highly useful
for these three levels (Table 4.3). Viewed differently, 34% of the
companies rated the value of a liberal-arts background more highly
for top corporate management than for entry-level management, and
only 8% of the firms rated it less highly.[9]

If this delayed payoff for liberal education generally prevails, the
higher the managerial rank in a company, the higher should be the
proportion of liberal-arts graduates found in that rank. In one of the
only publicly available studies performed on this question, Illinois
Bell Telephone Company analyzed the educational background of
its managers in 1984. It divided the managers into seven standard
levels, ranging from more than 5000 managers in the lowest layer to
only 10 who occupied the two upper rungs. Although the higher-level
managers had been with the company somewhat longer than lower-
level managers, ranging from 19 to 27 years, the differences were

Table 4.3 Percentage of Companies (*N* = 535)
That Rate a Liberal-Arts Background
as Highly Useful for Managerial
Performance, by Level of Management

Level of management	Percentage rating highly
Entry-level	13
Middle-level	18
Top corporate	30

Table 4.4 Number and Educational Background of Managers of
Illinois Bell Telephone Company, by Management
Level, 1984

Management level	Number of managers	Average years with company	Percentage with liberal-arts degrees
1 (lowest)	5,376	19	6
2	1,330	23	14
3	255	25	18
4	67	26	27
5	19	26	32
6 and 7	10	27	60

Source: See note 10.

not great, particularly among those in the second tier and above (Table 4.4). The educational differences, however, were systematic and pronounced: While 6% of the lowest-level managers held liberal-arts degrees, 27% of the fourth level and 60% of the top-level officers had been liberal-arts majors.[10]

The results of the studies of AT&T and Illinois Bell, however, are not necessarily generalizable. The accelerating prospects of liberal-arts graduates observed in these company settings may not prevail at large, and the present study indeed indicates that liberal-arts graduates on average do well—but no better—than business and engineering graduates in reaching into middle- and senior-management ranks of a cross section of American companies.

This pattern is evident when we examine the educational background and managerial position of the 505 individuals in the managerial survey. The great majority of the managers had graduated from college; 40% had obtained an undergraduate degree in business, 32% had earned a liberal-arts degree, and 16% held an engineering degree (Table 4.5). About one in four of the managers had gone on to earn an MBA degree after college (Table 4.6). The rates of completing postgraduate training were about the same for liberal-arts and business graduates, while engineering graduates were somewhat more likely to have acquired MBA training. If we reverse the calculation and ask about the undergraduate background of those who hold MBAs, we find that business graduates were most common but liberal-arts and engineering graduates were not far behind. Of the MBA holders, 37% had majored in business while in college,

Table 4.5 Educational Background of Company Managers
($N = 505$) in Managerial Survey

Educational background	Percentage holding degree
Undergraduate education	
Did not attend college	2
Attended college, no degree	9
Business degree	40
Liberal-arts degree	32
Engineering degree	16
Graduate education	
MBA degree	24
MA or PhD in liberal-arts field	8
Engineering degree	4
Law degree	2

31% had concentrated on the liberal arts, and 21% had a degree in engineering.

While the managers are not a full cross section of the managerial ranks, since entry-level positions are not represented, there is nonetheless substantial variation in their responsibilities. Company officers, ranging from chief executive to senior vice-president and treasurer, constitute 44% of the 505 managers; managers reporting to officers, with titles such as plant manager and director of sales, are 39%; and managers reporting to nonofficers are another 17%.

The proportions of liberal-arts graduates at these three ranks, however, do not differ significantly. Among the officers, 30% hold

Table 4.6 Percentage of Business, Liberal-Arts, and Engineering
Graduates Among Company Managers Who Earned
MBA and Other Postgraduate Degrees

Undergraduate degree	Number of managers	Postgraduate degree			
		MBA	MA or PhD	Engineering	Other
Business	202	22	2	0	6
Liberal arts	159	24	18	1	11
Engineering	81	32	0	19	4

liberal-arts degrees; among the managers reporting to officers, 34% had earned liberal-arts degrees; and among the managers reporting to nonofficers, 31% were liberal-arts graduates (Table 4.7). A breakdown of the firms by sector and size reveals that liberal-arts degree holders are moderately overrepresented among service-sector companies and among the largest manufacturing corporations. Subanalyses of the educational background of managers of varying ranks within these groups of firms, however, shows little correlation between background and rank. Thus, while a liberal-arts degree heightens the prospect that a manager will be working with a service-sector firm or large manufacturing company, it does not appear to make a major difference in the likelihood of reaching the upper ranks of business management.

The AT&T and Bell Illinois studies suggest that liberal-arts graduates fare better than other graduates in some companies. But the present research indicates that those findings may be more the exception than the general rule. On average, liberal-arts graduates are neither more nor less likely to reach the higher managerial ranks

Table 4.7 Percentage of Managers Holding Liberal-Arts Degrees, by Managerial Rank and by Company Sector and Size[a]

Type of manager	Number of managers	Percentage with liberal-arts degree
Managerial rank		
Officer	156	30
Managers reporting to officers	195	34
Managers reporting to nonofficers	88	31
Company sector and size[b]		
Service sector	168	39
Large manufacturing	100	32
Medium manufacturing	126	25
Small manufacturing	107	26

[a]The percentage differences among managerial ranks are not statistically significant; the percentage differences among manufacturing firms of varying size are also not statistically significant.

[b]Large manufacturing firms include those ranked by sales from 1 to 339; medium firms are those ranked from 340 to 679; and small manufacturing firms are ranked from 680 to 1000.

than are other graduates. An undergraduate's decision to major in the liberal arts rather than business or engineering has a bearing on the kind of company in which a career is likely to evolve, but overall it will have little general bearing on the likelihood of reaching upper corporate ranks. It should be stressed, however, that the overall pattern masks important differences from company to company. In some corporations, liberal-arts graduates hold the edge for accelerating advancement, as suggested by experiences of graduates in AT&T and Bell Illinois. In other companies, such as the industrial-products corporation described at the end of Chapter 3, liberal-arts graduates may, by contrast, find their prospects for reaching top management less promising than do those with engineering or business backgrounds.

While the overall pattern reveals little more concentration of liberal-arts graduates in the very highest managerial ranks than somewhat below, there is evidence that liberal-arts graduates in the senior-managerial ranks find their educational background to be particularly applicable in communication, leadership, and other areas of performance. We compare the surveyed managers' assessment of the areas in which their undergraduate education has proved to be particularly valuable. For this comparison, the managers are divided into three groups: those holding undergraduate liberal-arts degree, those with undergraduate business degrees, and those who earned undergraduate engineering degrees. Despite the passage of two decades or more since their college days (nearly three quarters of the managers are 40 years of age or older), large proportions of all three groups of managers report continuing utility of their undergraduate education in a number of areas (Table 4.8). Approximately half of the liberal-arts, business, and engineering graduates, for instance, find that their bachelor's training, whatever the field, still has value in helping them to organize their work and set priorities.[11]

The three groups differ significantly, however, in their assessment of where the undergraduate degree has had greatest payoff. Business and engineering baccalaureates report far higher utility of their degree than do liberal-arts graduates in mastering the technical knowledge and procedures of the firm (differences of 10 and 55 percentage points, respectively). Engineering graduates hold large quantitative and analytical advantages over liberal-arts graduates as well (38- and 24-point differences).

The liberal-arts degree, however, brings competitive advantages in a number of other areas. Compared with both business and engineering graduates, liberal-arts graduates report far greater application of

Table 4.8 Areas of Application of Undergraduate Education Among Company Managers, by Undergraduate Degree of Manager

| Area of useful application | Undergraduate degree of manager | | | | |
| | Liberal arts (N = 159) (1) | Business (N = 202) | | Engineering (N = 81) | |
		(2)	(1)–(2)[a]	(3)	(1)–(3)[a]
Communication skills	85%	80%		63%	19
General knowledge and information	85	82		65	20
Understanding people	66	46	20	27	39
Analytic skills	62	63		86	−24
Appreciating ethical concerns	62	37	25	28	34
Ability to organize and prioritize	59	52		58	
Leadership skills	49	34	15	33	16
Innovativeness	38	21	17	44	
Quantitative skills	37	46		75	−38
Technical knowledge and procedures	33	43	−10	78	−55
Understanding company's environment	24	15		27	
Understanding company's internal world	13	10		13	

[a]Only differences of 10 or more points are shown. All of the percentage differences of 10 or more points are statistically significant at less than the .05 level.

their undergraduate learning to their present job in (1) understanding people, (2) appreciating ethical concerns, and (3) leadership skills. In addition, liberal-arts graduates report a stronger payoff value of their degree than do business graduates in (4) innovativeness, and stronger value than do engineering graduates in (5) communication skills and (6) general knowledge.

The areas of managerial work where a liberal-arts education appears to have particular value are not limited to those in which liberal-arts graduates tend to concentrate. Rather, the applications are to issues of concern to virtually all managers: managing people, exercising leadership, and understanding ethical issues. The concerns are generic, and, with the exception of technical and quantitative skills, liberal-arts graduates generally find significantly greater payoff of their undergraduate experience in a number of areas at the top levels of management than do business and engineering graduates.

III. Men, Women, and the Liberal-Arts Degree

Business, engineering, and liberal-arts graduates are all found in ample numbers among the upper echelons of the nation's major corporations. All of these educational avenues offer a suitable start up the career ladders of firms. There is, however, a strong gender disparity in the avenues employed, as manifested in the divergent educational backgrounds of men and women in the corporation.

A survey in the early 1980s of recently promoted company executives, for instance, found that the male executives had come in nearly equal proportions from business, engineering, and liberal-arts undergraduate majors (32, 28, and 35%, respectively). The female executives had come, by contrast, disproportionately from the liberal arts. While 9% had majored in business as an undergraduate and 2% in engineering, 78% had acquired a liberal-arts degree. The present study confirms a similar though less pronounced disparity.[12]

Among the middle and senior managers surveyed, business administration was the single largest area of undergraduate concentration for the men and liberal arts for the women (Table 4.9). Of the male managers, 41% had graduated with a business degree; of the female managers, 44% had received a liberal-arts degree. The male managers were also more likely to have obtained a MBA degree (held by 25% of the men and 14% of the women).

The disparate educational backgrounds of men and women in company management are largely a product of their differing undergraduate interests. Among first-year college students in 1970, men were nearly twice as likely to intend to major in business as were women, and women were substantially more likely than men to ma-

Table 4.9 Undergraduate-Degree Area of Company Managers and Percentage of Entering Freshmen Intending to Major in Liberal Arts, Business, or Engineering in 1970 and 1986, by Gender

Respondents	Liberal arts	Business	Engineering
Company managers, 1987			
Men	31	41	18
Women	45	33	0
College freshmen, 1970			
Men	35	20	16
Women	44	12	0.4
College freshmen, 1986			
Men	20	27	20
Women	26	27	3

Source: Company manager survey; Astin, Green, and Korn (1987), pp. 18–19, 36–37; Astin *et al.* (1987a), pp. 42, 46.

jor in liberal arts (Table 4.9). This difference, however, nearly vanished by the mid-1980s. Among entering college freshmen in 1986, equal proportions of men and women intended to major in business.

The relative distribution of bachelor's degrees in business among men and women during the past three decades confirms the same. Of those graduating with undergraduate business degrees in 1960, near the time when many of those participating in the survey of company managers were completing college, 7% were women. By contrast, of the business graduates in 1986, 46% were women. Similar trends are evident among MBA recipients: of the 4814 master's degrees in business in 1960, 4% were earned by women, but of the 67,137 degrees in 1986, 31% were obtained by women.[13]

The fact that more women than men with liberal-arts degrees have found their way into company management is thus probably an artifact of the era in which they had attended college. Comparatively few women majored in business, and virtually none concentrated in the engineering disciplines. Liberal arts was then the preferred route for women (a close second was a major in education). Now, however, large proportions of women undergraduates are majoring in business as well. In 1986, a slightly higher fraction of female first-year students intended to major in business than in liberal-arts, and the general distribution is far closer to that of male students than before. In time, therefore, the educational background of women in corporate management can be expected to converge with that of men. Moreover, since educational background correlates with the kinds of positions within the firm where a manager is likely to prosper, as we see in the next section, the distribution of women inside the company is also likely to become more similar to that of men.

IV. Undergraduate Studies and Areas of Employment

The field of undergraduate degree study displays little overall correlation with the level of corporate responsibility. Liberal-arts graduates generally do about as well as business and engineering graduates. The field of undergraduate study can be expected, however, to make a major difference in the areas within a firm in which middle and senior managers are working. We have seen in Chapters 1 and 2 that the college major is viewed by companies as an important criterion in selecting applicants for a campus interview and for a visit to the company. Company recruiting plans for college graduates typically specify the general field of study as one of the first considerations. This was evident, for instance, in the college-recruitment plans of the high-technology firm we described (Case B, see Appendix to Chapter 2). The company's 70 openings for the 1987–1988 recruitment season were all defined by the field of study that applicants would be expected to have: business for one opening, for example; industrial engineering for another, and liberal arts for still another.

Liberal-arts graduates should be expected to concentrate disproportionately in the two major areas of marketing/sales and human resources/personnel. When companies and managers were asked to identify the functional areas in which a liberal-arts background would be most useful, they placed these two areas near the top, along with public affairs/government relations (see Table 2.6). Similarly, when companies were asked to specify the areas in which the largest number of liberal-arts graduates have been placed during the preceding 3 years, more firms singled out marketing/sales and human resources/personnel than any other area (Table 2.5). These two areas are thus viewed as particularly likely fields of employment for those with a liberal-arts education.

Table 4.10 Area of Primary Responsibility of Company Managers, by Undergraduate Degree of Manager[a]

Percentage of managers with area of primary responsibility	Undergraduate degree of manager		
	Liberal arts (N = 159)	Business (N = 184)	Engineering (N = 75)
Marketing and sales	28	21	25
Human resources and personnel	20	14	1
Finance and accounting	10	36	3
R&D, technical, and engineering	10	0	20
Information and data processing	8	7	4
General management and administration	8	9	24
Plant and production management	3	3	16
Other	13	10	7
Total	100	100	100

[a]The percentage differences among managers with varying educational backgrounds are significant at less than the .05 level.

The areas of the managers' primary responsibility are divided into seven major fields: (1) marketing and sales; (2) human resources and personnel; (3) finance and accounting; (4) plant and production management; (5) information and data processing; (6) general management and administration; and (7) research, development, engineering, and technical. The distribution of the managers among these areas as a function of their undergraduate field of study is shown in Table 4.10. We see that nearly half (48%) of the managers with liberal-arts degrees are concentrated in marketing, sales, human resources, and personnel. The largest area of concentration for business graduates is finance and accounting (36%), followed by marketing and sales. Engineering graduates are notable for their disproportionate presence in R&D, plant and production management, general management and administration, and sales and marketing. The top three areas that liberal-arts, business, and engineering graduates most often enter are as follows[14]:

Liberal arts	Business	Engineering
Marketing and sales	Finance/accounting	Marketing and sales
Human resources/ personnel	Marketing and sales	General management/ administration
Finance/accounting	Human resources/ personnel	R&D, technical, engineering
(69% of all liberal arts graduates)	(71% of all business graduates)	(69% of all engineering graduates)

The sharply differing career paths likely to be followed as a function of the undergraduate experience should result in distinctive educational profiles of those in the varying areas of responsibility. The college background of managers in the seven major areas is shown in Table 4.11; for clarity, only those figures are presented for which managers with a given undergraduate degree constitute at least a quarter of those in the area. We see sharp differences in the educational composition in the varying areas of responsibility. Nearly three quarters of those employed in finance and accounting had earned undergraduate degrees in business; almost half of those in human resources and personnel were liberal-arts graduates; and over half of those in the R&D, technical, and engineering areas of the company held undergraduate degrees in engineering. In sum, the top three areas in which liberal-arts, business, and engineering graduates are most predominant are:

Liberal arts	Business	Engineering
Human resources/ personnel	Finance/accounting	R&D, technical, engineering
R&D, technical, engineering	General management/ administration	Plant and production management
Marketing and sales	Marketing and sales	General management/ administration

Table 4.11 Undergraduate Field of Study of Company Managers, by Area of Primary Responsibility[a]

Area of primary responsibility	Number of managers	Undergraduate degree of manager (%)[b]				
		Liberal arts	Business	Engineering	Other	Total
Marketing and sales	121	32	36			100
Human resources and personnel	69	45	39			100
Finance and accounting	98		72			100
R&D, technical, and engineering	35	37		51		100
Information and data processing	50		28		42	100
General management and administration	50		42	32		100
Plant and production management	27			44		100
Other	55	36	35			100

[a]The percentage differences among managers with varying areas of responsibilities are significant at less than the .05 level.

[b]Only figures of at least 25% are displayed.

A third (34%) of the managers included in tables above had gone on to earn a postgraduate degree, primarily an MBA (acquired by 24%). Completing a postgraduate training program can significantly alter the career course, particularly if one earns the MBA degree. Though reliable analysis is not possible for all of the subgroups because of their small size, the impact of postgraduate training in business can be seen if we compare the experience of four subgroups: liberal-arts graduates with and without an MBA degree and business graduates with and without an MBA. We assess the relative probabilities of entering the three main areas in which business and liberal-arts-and-business undergraduates most often find employment: marketing and sales, finance and accounting, and human resources and personnel.

Table 4.12 reveals that BA holders in liberal arts who go on to acquire the MBA degree modestly increase the likelihood of reaching middle and senior management in marketing and sales (by a factor of 1.24); sharply increase the probability for finance and accounting (by 4.61); sharply decrease the chance of entering human resources and personnel (by a factor of 0.32); and modestly decrease the likelihood of entering other areas of the company (by 0.75). Similar patterns are evident among the BA holders with degrees in business. If they subsequently acquired an MBA degree as well, they enhanced their likelihood of entering and remaining in finance/accounting and mar-

Table 4.12 Probability of Entering Three Areas of Responsibility Among Managers Holding an MBA Degree Compared to Those Holding No Postgraduate Degree, by Undergraduate Degree of Managers[a]

	Undergraduate degree of manager[b]	
Areas of responsibility	Liberal arts	Business
Marketing and sales	1.24	1.11
Human resources and personnel	0.32	0.41
Finance and accounting	4.61	1.62
Other	0.75	0.63

[a]The probability differences among liberal-arts graduates are significant at less than the .05 level; the probability differences among business graduates are significant at the .06 level.

[b]Number of managers: liberal-arts bachelor's degree only, 105; liberal-arts BA and MBA, 38; business bachelor's degree, 146; business BA and MBA, 45.

keting/sales, but decreased their likelihood of remaining in human resources/personnel and other areas of the company.

We see again, then, that the field of study can make a major difference in the areas within the company in which a career is pursued. While there is little discernible overall impact of the field of study on vertical mobility, as we have seen earlier, there is a pronounced effect on horizontal tracking of managers among the major functional areas within the firm.

The field of study should also have a major bearing on the type of corporation in which the managers are pursuing their careers. This too is expected from our earlier data in Chapter 2, which indicated, for instance, that service-sector firms are generally more likely to recruit liberal-arts graduates than are manufacturing firms. Confirmation of this supposition is evident if we examine the distribution of the managers between service and manufacturing firms as a function of their college background. Table 4.13 reveals a strong skew: of the liberal-arts graduates, 42% are now working in a service-sector firm; of the business graduates, the proportion is 34%; and of the engineering graduates, only 17%.

Even greater disparities are evident if we divide the managers according to whether their company activities are primarily concerned with consumer or industrial goods and services. This division reflects

Table 4.13 Primary Product Areas of Company and of Managers, by Undergraduate Degree of Manager[a]

Primary product area or responsibility	Undergraduate degree of manager (%)		
	Liberal arts ($N = 158$)	Business ($N = 184$)	Engineering ($N = 75$)
Primary product area of company			
Manufacturing	59	66	83
Service	42	34	17
Primary product responsibility of manager			
Industrial goods and services	40	47	79
Consumer goods and services	46	41	12
Other	14	13	10

[a]The percentage differences by primary product areas of the company are significant at less than the .05 level; the percentage differences by primary product responsibility of manager are significant at less than the .05 level.

both the type of company in which the manager is employed and the area of the manager's responsibility within the firm. We see in Table 4.13 that liberal-arts graduates are more likely to be concerned with consumer than industrial goods and services (by a ratio of 1.16:1); business graduates are slightly more likely to have responsibility for industrial than consumer products (1.15:1); and engineering graduates are far more likely to be concerned with industrial products (6.55:1).[15]

The field of undergraduate study thus has an important bearing on the area of responsibility in which a graduate is likely to become engaged, and on the kind of firm in which a corporate career is pursued. As students choose a field of undergraduate study, then, the decision is not one of whether or not to enter the private sector. Nor will the choice among fields have a major bearing on their likelihood of movement to the upper ranks of corporate management. But it will influence the paths that they are likely to follow within the company world, leading them toward certain kinds of positions and companies and away from others. Liberal-arts graduates are more prone than other graduates to find their way into sales and marketing positions, to work for service companies, and to acquire responsibility for consumer goods and services. Business graduates, by contrast, are more likely to move into finance and accounting, and engineering graduates are far more prone to move onto the front lines of industrial goods and services.

V. Corporate Outreach

The expanding public role of the corporation has intensified the need for more managers, not only those in public affairs, to take direct part in political and social outreach on behalf of the firm. The complex environments with which many line managers must now cope place special premium on their capacities to acquire and analyze highly diverse and often fragmentary sources of information.

Many companies, as a result, stress social and political awareness among their employees. A Conference Board survey of 149 large firms during the 1980 election found that four out of five firms had at least one program for developing political awareness, most commonly including courses on politics, voting drives, sponsorship of political clubs, and forums for candidates and elected officials to speak within the company. Social and political performance has also become an element in managerial promotion. Another study of 176 major corporations in 1979–1980 shows that a majority of the companies stressed external experience in appointing plant and divisional managers.[16]

At the senior levels, management development for external affairs has been among the leading concerns of major firms. A survey of 432 chief executives in 1981 asked, "When it comes to the top management group, . . . what are the key challenges you believe your company will face during the next five years?" Developing a "strategic business-planning perspective" ranked first, but political affairs was close behind, with half of the CEOs specifying that "improving top management's grasp of emerging political, social, and economic issues" was a key challenge, and half giving high priority to "building top management effectiveness in dealing with governments and other external forces and groups."[17]

An early education in the interpretation of the social and political forces shaping the company's environment may thus have become an important asset for managerial effectiveness. If so, a college education, particularly when built on a liberal-arts foundation, may well be valuable not only for more effective internal managerial performance, but also for more effective management of the firm's environment. Mastering the social and political forces that constitute a company's environment depends on an appreciation of issues ranging from urban politics to American history and cultural trends. Exposure to substantively relevant coursework is also likely to increase a personal interest in public affairs. Whatever the written or unwritten company policies toward encouraging managerial external involvement, a liberal education can thus be an important motivator and facilitator of community engagement.

To gauge the relationship of a liberal-arts background to a manager's involvement in public affairs, the managerial survey acquired information on the manager's outside engagement in five areas. Two involve the manager's direct representation of the company (1) to a community organization or in a community setting and (2) to a government agency or unit. Three are voluntary involvements that usually reflect on the company and the manager's performance: service as (3) a trustee or advisor to a nonprofit organization, (4) a volunteer or fund raiser for a nonprofit organization, and (5) advisor or consultant to a government agency. Though these outside engagements are voluntary activities, they are normally cleared by the company if they involve company officers and are often reviewed by the company for other senior managers.

The outside involvement of officers must be distinguished from that of nonofficers. Company representation is typically expected of officers, while it is useful but more discretionary among managers of a lesser rank. Thus if educational background makes a difference in the likelihood of external involvement, the difference should be greater among the nonofficer ranks. It is here that a manager's prior familiarity with the language and culture of institutions outside of business may best facilitate his or her involvement. Those with less understanding are less likely to voluntarily become involved in these diverse and complex settings.

Assessment of the manager's external involvements is made for the officers and nonofficers separately. Managers with liberal-arts backgrounds are compared with those holding undergraduate business degrees (Table 4.14). Ratios of the rate of involvement of liberal-arts graduates compared to business graduates are calculated. They reveal that liberal-arts graduates are generally more active on the outside of the company. With the exception of representation of the company to government agencies by officers, the ratios all exceed 1.0, and they range as high as 2.0.[18]

Moreover, the differences between the liberal-arts and business graduates are consistently larger among nonofficers than officers. While company officers with liberal-arts degrees are 3% (a ratio of 1.03) more likely to be involved in representing the company to community organizations than are officers with business degrees, among nonofficers the probability difference is 24%. Similarly, officers with liberal-arts degrees are 31% more likely to serve as a trustee of a nonprofit organization than are officers with business degrees, but the probability difference increases to 42% among nonofficers.

Another way to view the differences is to compare the rates of external involvement of nonofficers who hold liberal arts degrees with officers who hold business degrees. In all areas save one (representation of the company to the government), the liberal-arts nonofficer is more actively engaged outside the company than the officer with a business degree.

While the external involvement of nonofficers is considered important for promoting the goals of the firm, effective outside work can also add to an individual's general managerial reputation. It signifies that a rising middle manager possesses public affairs capacities, which become even more essential with movement into a firm's senior ranks.

The career-development value of external involvement may be a key factor in the experience of one manager in a high-technology manufacturing firm, an experience that is typical of many. The indi-

Table 4.14 Involvement of Company Managers in External Affairs, by Educational Background and Position of Manager

Area of external involvement	Educational background and position of manager							
	Officers			Nonofficers				
	Liberal arts (N = 66) (1)	Business (N = 96) (2)	Ratio (1):(2)	Liberal arts (N = 93) (1)	Business (N = 106) (2)	Ratio (1):(2)		
Representation of company to								
Local community	74%	72%	1.03	73%	59%	1.24		
Government	65	69	0.94	48	44	1.09		
Voluntary service as								
Trustee of nonprofit organization	68	52	1.31	54	38	1.42		
Fund raiser for nonprofit organization	67	60	1.12	77	61	1.26		
Advisor to government	15	10	1.50	12	6	2.00		

vidual was recognized as a highly effective manager, and, consistent with the company's policy of encouraging public involvement, the manager had joined the board of trustees of a prominent community organization. The organization underwent a major internal crisis, so wrenching and visible that the board by necessity became directly involved in seeking a solution. The company manager came to play a highly effective and prominent role in bringing the crisis to a satisfactory conclusion. Soon thereafter the company's chief executive called the manager in for a discussion of the crisis and his successful role in resolving it, a rare and highly valued experience for a middle manager. Six months later, the manager received a promotion to a company vice-presidency.

Successful involvement in national affairs, not just local organizations and community issues, can also be important for a managerial career. This can be seen in the experience of a manager working for a producer of metal products. The individual held bachelor's and master's degrees in industrial engineering, and he began with the company as the manager of computer information for one of its plants. He was soon identified as a "high-potential" manager, and, as an investment in his growth, the company encouraged his application to become a White House Fellow in one of the executive agencies. He was accepted and worked for a year as a program manager for a high-ranking federal official. Upon return to the manufacturer, he subsequently moved quickly through the firm's ranks—first as a plant comptroller, next as the plant business manager, and finally as a general manager at company headquarters. The Washington opportunity and the diverse experience within the company itself provided the pubic-affairs exposure and broadening deemed by this company to be essential for an upper-level position.

Successful external experience can thus enhance further upward movement within the firm. Entry-level managers are rarely if ever recruited because of their ability to operate in the public domain on behalf of the company. Public-affairs involvement typically evolves only when a manager has reached a relatively elevated level after a number of years with the corporation. Still, the evidence presented here indicates that a latent advantage brought by the liberally educated manager is an exceptional ability to represent the company to its various public constituencies.

VI. Conclusion

If liberal-arts graduates begin their careers in the private sector somewhat more slowly than other college graduates, they finish relatively well. Evidence presented here reveals that companies generally rate the early advancement of business and engineering graduates ahead of liberal-arts graduates. It also shows that companies rate a liberal education as particularly useful for performance in the top managerial ranks.

In the top echelons of some companies liberal-arts graduates predominate. But this is more the exception than the rule, according to the information presented here on a cross section of American companies. Comparing officers, managers reporting to officers, and managers reporting to nonofficers, we find little difference in the overall proportion of liberal-arts graduates. Still, there are wide variations among companies, often in the same industry, in the educational profiles of their middle and senior managers. Much of this difference may be attributable to unique educational cultures within companies that have evolved over decades of experience and recruitment, an issue taken up in the next chapter.

While there is little difference in the vertical distribution of managers as a function of their college background, major differences exist in the horizontal distribution among areas of responsibility within the firm. Liberal-arts graduates are significantly more likely to enter marketing and sales than other areas, while business graduates are substantially more prone to enter finance and accounting. Postgraduate-management training further shapes the differences: liberal-arts graduates who later acquire an MBA degree are even more likely to enter marketing and sales and less likely to enter human resources and personnel.

The evidence indicates that liberal-arts graduates are often competitively advantaged in their performance both within and outside the company. Compared with business and engineering graduates, managers with liberal-arts backgrounds report underpreparation in technical and quantitative skills, but better preparation in other areas critical for company performance, such as leadership, innovativeness, and an appreciation for ethical concerns. Moreover, liberal-arts graduates report higher rates of external involvement on behalf of the company and in voluntary community affairs, with the differences most pronounced among nonofficers.

Just as the advantages of leadership, innovativeness, and other skills that liberal-arts graduates bring to their jobs can have a direct bearing on a company's performance, liberal-arts graduates' advantages in external representation of the company may also have a favorable impact on company goals. Managing the external environment can be important for growth and income, particularly among companies whose public reputation may have a bearing on their opportunities for performance. Many insurance companies, for example, must work with a range of government regulations and agencies. The author of a study of the industry concludes that effective management of the external constituencies can be critical to industry prosperity. He writes: "Failure to establish and maintain effective long-term relationships with industry peers and agents of the public interest and to effectively manage industry-specific, social and political contingencies is directly associated with both unsatisfactory market performance and corporate strategies of flight and avoidance."[19]

Similarly, a study of corporate relations with the nonprofit community in Minneapolis–St. Paul finds that public involvement improves a company's reputation not only for being socially responsible but also for being an effectively managed enterprise. In the concluding words of the researcher, "a reputation as a successful business appears to have been a function of either how much a company earned or how much it gave away" to the local community. The tangible payoff of such a reputation is illustrated by the local response to an attempted hostile takeover of one of the major Minneapolis contributors and corporate citizens, the Dayton-Hudson Corporation, the nation's eleventh largest retail company. When Dayton-Hudson's local ownership was threatened by an out-of-state acquirer in 1987, a number of the nonprofit organizations and local officials in Minneapolis rallied support for state legislation to deter the company's acquisition. The community organizations feared that an absentee owner would compromise the company's exceptional record of community involvement. When its corporate identity was at stake, Dayton-Hudson found an immediate and vigorous ally in the local community that it had supported over a number of years.[20]

Many senior managers of large firms are committed to building enduring relationships with agents of the public interest. Because of the "ever-more complex and time-consuming relationship between business and government in the United States," observed two analysts of company decision making, "senior managers have found themselves increasingly involved in dealing with various government agencies . . . to influence legislation and policy." What is relatively new is the emphasis placed on the role that all managers, not just the chief executive and public-affairs specialists, can play in this influence process. Preparation of a manager for external involvement is facilitated by liberal learning, suggests the present evidence, and thus a manager's liberal education, whether acquired as a liberal-arts major or by exposure to liberal-arts coursework as a business or engineering student, can be an important asset in the long-range development of a firm's human resources.[21]

Notes

1. See, for example, the annual "Northwestern Endicott-Lindquist Report" (published by Northwestern University); the annual "Recruiting Trends" report by the Placement Service of Michigan State University; Sharp and Weidman (1986); and studies cited in Useem (1986).
2. Warren (1983).
3. Solmon (1981).
4. Bisconti and Kessler (1980).
5. Louis (1985).
6. Companies were asked: "How would you assess the rates of advancement of the following groups during their first ten years with your company?" The company assessment that young MBAs with liberal-arts degrees have lower advancement rates than MBA graduates with other degrees meets potentially contrary evidence in an early study of MBA graduates. The study surveyed more than 5000 MBA holders who had graduated from one of 12 leading graduate business programs between 1965 and 1968. The survey was conducted in 1970, and it thus captures only very early career differences. Overall, the MBAs were earning a little more than $17,000 on average in 1970. The typical MBA graduate with an undergraduate business degree, however, earned nearly $600 less than the overall average, while the typical MBA graduate with a liberal-arts major earned over $750 more than the average. The MBA holder with an undergraduate engineering degree received about $350 more than the average (De Pasquale and Lange, 1971).
7. Howard (1984, 1986); Howard and Bray (1988).
8. Howard (1986).
9. Firms were asked: "In your judgment, how useful is a liberal arts background to be a successful manager in the following levels . . . of the company?" The four response categories are: "highly useful," "somewhat useful," "not too useful," and "not at all useful."
10. Wade (1984) and personal communication with Illinois Bell Telephone Company.
11. The full question asked of the managers: "In which areas of your work do you find that your undergraduate college education is particularly useful?"
12. Hildebrandt (1985), pp. 11–12.
13. U.S. Department of Education (1987), p. 202.
14. The area of the managers' primary responsibility are drawn from

their own identification of what "best describes your main area of responsibility" from a list of 15 areas, grouped here in the 8 areas used for the present analysis:

- *Marketing and sales.* Marketing planning: market analysis, market development, market planning, market research, product development. Sales: customer relations, customer services, field sales. Sales support: art direction, merchandising, packaging, promotions, advertising.
- *Human resources and personnel.* Personnel: pension administration, industrial relations, recruiting.
- *Finance and accounting.* Finance, accounting, cost control.
- *R&D, technical, and engineering.* Research and development; engineering and technical.
- *Information and data processing.* Data processing.
- *General management and administration.* Corporate and subsidiary general management and administration.
- *Plant and production management.* Plant management: manager, director, superintendent of plant, mill, refinery, works. Production management: maintenance, manufacturing, operations, quality control, material control, inspection.
- *Other.* Distribution management: export management, traffic, warehousing. Purchasing. Corporate planning. Other function.

15. The primary product area of the company was determined from the manufacturing vs. service classification of companies utilized in constructing the sampling frame for the Executive Caravan Survey. The primary area of product responsibility of the manager was assessed from the question, "Are the company activities that you are concerned with mainly related to *consumer* goods or services or *industrial* goods or services?" The category of "other" in the table includes "both about equally" and "neither of these."
16. McGrath (1980); Lusterman (1981). For more general background on the corporate social and political outreach, see Shepard and Hougland (1984); Mills (1987); Ryan *et al.* (1987); Zeithaml *et al.* (1988).
17. Schaeffer (1982).
18. The number of managers with undergraduate engineering de-

grees is too small for reliable analysis when the groups are sub-
divided in the analysis here.
19. Mills (1987).
20. Galaskiewicz (1985); *Minneapolis Star and Tribune*, June 20
    (1987), p. 1A; June 21 (1987), p. 26A; *St. Paul Pioneer Press Dis-
    patch*, June 21 (1987), p. 1.
21. Donaldson and Lorsch (1983), p. 13.

Appendix to Chapter 4

Case E: A Fast-Paced Culture at a Diversified Financial Corporation

We focus here on a rapidly growing division of a financial-services company. The division has a staff of more than 40,000 and, like the other divisions of the company, operates relatively autonomously.

The division has an aggressive leadership style in which the company takes pride. A fast-paced, risk-taking management approach defines the division's culture, and it is reflected in the hiring process. A recruitment brochure for the division stresses assertiveness, strong interpersonal skills, decisiveness, adaptability to change, high energy level, personal maturity, and excellent communication skills. Intelligence is critical as well for mastering the pace of change within the company.

Jobs must be learned quickly, since people move through them at a rapid rate. Entry-level professional and managerial jobs are immediately demanding, and new college graduates have little time to learn on the job. The director of staffing describes the organization as having a "think and do" rather than a "look and learn" culture. Although liberal-arts graduates may bring the requisite personal qualities, they are often at a disadvantage in marketing and finance assignments, since they lack the work experience and skills to take charge of an entire project at the outset.

Recruitment policies place a premium on hiring people who are, and can present themselves as, the "best and brightest." Academic qualifications must be strong, with grade-point averages of 3.5 or higher often sought. But the candidate's persuasive skills must also be highly effective. In the job interview, division recruiters often ask about the candidate's best and worst experiences in life. The vice-president for human resources observed, "If you yawn, you know you don't have a hot ticket." A third important criterion is the candidate's versatility, as manifest in the range of campus and summer experiences. The company has found, however, that although many liberal-arts graduates have had diverse extracurricular and work opportunities, they are often poorly skilled at reporting how nonbusiness experiences in organizing, managing projects, and negotiating are germane to the business setting. A fourth criterion is communication skills. Surveys of line managers in the division find that strong writing and verbal skills are among their first priorities in hiring. Perhaps reflecting a universal view in management life, the managers also say that their bosses should have stronger interpersonal and people-management skills, while they themselves would mainly benefit from additional technical and general management training.

Because of the rapidly changing nature of the business, the division places special stress on hiring those who can learn and change quickly. "You have to master the job fast," observed the division's director of management development, "since you move out of it in eighteen months." "What is increasingly important here, is the speed of getting up to speed on new ideas," commented another manager. The division recognizes that a general educational foundation that helps a person place different experiences in a broader context will facilitate the person's capacity to change. There is thus a stress on a broad educational background in recruiting college graduates. However, a broad education is not enough—one's background must also include a set of "finite skills," focusing on business and management abilities.

As a result, the division has maintained a preference for MBA holders, with 50 to 60 fresh MBA graduates hired every year. About a third to half are placed in marketing, a third in finance and planning, and the remainder in operations, human resources, systems, and strategic planning. The division's culture esteems the MBA degree, and it is seen as an invaluable credential for upward movement on the division's management ladder. MBAs with liberal-arts undergraduate degrees and 2 to 5 years of work experience are especially valued.

While working in their first assignments, new MBAs pass through an elite graduate management program, a 1-year experience in which they are exposed to a range of functions within the company and are introduced to the way in which the division conducts its business. Generally, BA holders have been excluded because they are not expected to meet the targets for rapid advancement that the division has set for this group. Of the more than 600 participants in the program during the past 10 years, nearly 60% are still with the company, and more than 100 have already reached the company's most-senior management levels.

The division does have a limited undergraduate recruiting effort, focusing specifically on BS degrees in accounting and computer science. "Bright undergraduates" with a degree in finance can also move into positions normally reserved for those with MBAs as they gain company experience. College graduates without advanced training have become more attractive in the finance area as competition in the MBA market has intensified.

Similarly, while the strategic-planning unit also seeks MBA holders, competition with management-consulting firms for them has become vigorous. This past year the unit hired a handful of good under-graduates who could be quickly trained, and it hired several with liberal-arts degrees. Marketing has also hired some BA holders, and since it is relatively unconcerned with the specific major, a propor-tion of those hired brought a liberal-arts degree as well. The division is now considering broadening the kinds of experiences and train-ing given to the BA holders, possibly instituting a program to rotate them through various positions and functional areas of the division in much the way it does for new MBAs slated for general manage-ment careers.

The division is concerned about the shortcomings of college and university training available to those it expects to hire into profes-sional and managerial positions. It has begun to work on curricular change with several graduate business programs from which it most often recruits, especially in moving courses and case materials to focus more on the financial-services industry. It has also initiated ef-forts to enhance ethics training in the business curriculum. Much of the division's involvement in the redesign of graduate business programs has come from the initiative of specific business schools, which have invited division executives to serve in advisory capacities. Would the division also be willing to work with undergraduate busi-ness and liberal-arts programs to suggest ways of improving their curricula and of providing the kinds of "finite skills" now required by this company and other firms in the service industry? "Yes," said the division's vice-president for human resources, "the division would be ready to do so, but so far it had not been asked."

5　Educational Cultures in Corporate Management

Business, engineering, and liberal-arts degrees are well represented in a cross section of American corporate management. Yet in certain firms the proportion of managers with one or another of these degrees is exceptionally high or low. In some companies the skew is toward engineering; in others, business and MBA degrees predominate; and in still others, liberal-arts graduates prevail.

The variation deserves special attention. If the variation is a result of a company's product area and the need for particular technical skills, there is little room for change. But if it is due also to socially constructed but technically unnecessary preferences, there is opportunity for intervention. Constructed preferences are cultural products that have little basis in the company's technology or organization. They represent powerful traditions, but, like many traditions that are not rooted in technical imperatives, they can be reexamined and altered if they are no longer serving the organization well.

The evidence suggests that some of the variation in educational preferences from company to company is in fact socially constructed. The variation can be traced to the influence of distinctive "educational cultures" that have evolved within companies, cultural attitudes and preferences that place one kind of managers' educational background above others. The preferences usually have, or may have once had, at least some relation to the company's products and required skills but often go far beyond the current technical needs of the company.[1]

The influence of distinctive educational cultures within companies on managerial promotion is well illustrated by the findings of a detailed study of one large corporation by researcher James Rosenbaum. Analyzing personnel records of nearly two decades, he found that two neighboring colleges were the source of an exceptionally high number of managers. Not only were the two institutions major sources of hiring, but their graduates were significantly advantaged in receiving promotions within the firm, even when taking the quality of the institution into account.

During the first 3 years of employment with this corporation, for instance, the probability of promotion among white male managers from one of the two institutions—a nearby state university—was .83, while the probability of promotion of managers who had graduated from other universities of equivalent selectivity was only .57. Similarly, the probability of promotion of the graduates of the second nearby institution, a highly selective private university, was .74, while the probability for graduates of equivalent selective institutions located elsewhere in the country stood at only .63. Expressed differently, graduates of the favored state university were 45% more likely to receive a promotion in the first 3 years of their career than graduates of other colleges and universities of comparable quality; and graduates of the favored private university were 17% more likely to be promoted. Moreover, the differences in promotion probabilities continue nearly throughout the careers of the managers, looming just as large or even larger after managers had been with the company for 25 years or more. The graduates of the two area universities may have been far superior to those recruited from other institutions, but the gaps are so large that a unique preferential culture within the firm is a more plausible explanation. Managers from the two area universities, dominating in number from the start, established an informal ambiance in which managers with similar educational credentials were viewed more favorably and were thus more often promoted. While the field of study was not analyzed in this research, the results illustrate the importance of educational traditions within a firm in shaping managerial careers for reasons that are largely unrelated to managerial qualifications.[2]

I. The Power of Educational Cultures in Corporate Management

The power of prevailing educational preferences within a corporation for certain fields of college study was repeatedly evident in our case studies. The managers we interviewed, for example, made frequent reference to the importance of such preferences in hiring and promoting in the corporation. A senior human-resources manager in the high-technology manufacturing company described at the conclusion of Chapter 2 (Case B), for example, observed that at one of the main production facilities managers without a chemical-engineering degree were viewed with some skepticism. Virtually all of those in senior positions had such a degree, and one's career prospects were considered to be limited without this background, even though knowledge of chemical engineering was not essential for performance in some of the more senior positions. The human-resources manager had served for a period at the facility, and he had formed an informal luncheon group of those who, like himself, were without such a background. The members of his "Society for the Preservation of the Non-Technical Degree" met occasionally to discuss their common awareness that, in the words of the founder, "they wouldn't make it in that environment."

In other companies, the "MBA culture" dominates. Middle-level product managers at the consumer-products company studied, for example, usually held MBA degrees. In the words of one inside observer, they "want their own kind. The frame of reference here is the MBA." It is a refrain heard frequently in the corridors of many corporations, and an important factor in the return of many working college graduates to business schools after several years of experience in companies where the MBA culture prevails.

The more general influence of educational culture can be seen in an analysis drawing on the information about the educational backgrounds of senior managers in the companies in the corporate survey. Information was acquired on the higher education of the chief executive officer, the chief operating officer, and the responding manager, generally a vice-president or director of human resources or personnel. The correlation among their undergraduate-degree areas is strong. If the chief executive held a liberal-arts degree, for instance, the contingent likelihood that the chief operating officer held the same degree was raised from .11 to .45. That is, in only 11% of the companies where the chief executive did *not* have a liberal-arts degree did the chief operating officer (COO) hold a liberal-arts degree. But in 45% of the corporations where the CEO did hold a liberal-arts degree, the COO also had a liberal-arts degree. The ratio of these two percentages is a "probability ratio" of 4.09. This indicates that if the CEO held a liberal-arts degree, there is a more than fourfold increase in the probability that the COO will also have graduated in the liberal arts. On the other hand, if the chief executive held an MBA degree, the chief operating officer is 2.06 times more likely to have an MBA as well (Table 5.1). Comparing the educational backgrounds of the CEO and the responding manager, probability ratios that exceed 1.0 are found here as well, also indicating a correlation between their backgrounds.

Thus if the chief executive held a liberal-arts degree, the probability was sharply increased that both of his or her two senior managers

Table 5.1. Likelihood That Chief Operating Officer and Responding
Manager Held the Same College Degree as the Chief
Executive Officer, by Type of Degree[a,b]

Type of college degree of chief executive officer	Chief operating officer		Responding manager	
	Probability	Probability ratio (yes/no)	Probability	Probability ratio (yes/no)
Undergraduate degree				
Liberal arts				
No	.11	4.09	.42	1.72
Yes	.45		.72	
Business				
No	.22	2.37	.26	1.58
Yes	.51		.42	
Engineering				
No	.13	3.91	.02	7.09
Yes	.52		.16	
Graduate degree: MBA				
No	.23	2.06	.23	1.24
Yes	.47		.28	

[a]Number of companies = 412.
[b]All probability differences are significant at less than the .05 level, except for a nonsignificant probability difference for the MBA comparison for responding managers.

were liberal-arts graduates as well. Analogous patterns of contingent educational probabilities also hold for undergraduate business and engineering degrees.

The relationship among the educational backgrounds of the chief executive officer and two other executives is partly an indirect product of variant technical requirements among industries. Liberal-arts and MBA degrees are more expected in the service sector, and business and engineering educational backgrounds are more prevalent in manufacturing firms. Yet the observed correlation among the educational backgrounds of the top managers remain even when company sector and size are taken into account. The results of an analysis of the background of top executives in large service-sector firms alone (firms in the top 500) and in large manufacturing firms alone (companies among the top 200, with annual sales of at least $1.78 billion) are shown in Table 5.2. The results reveal that the probability ratios, though altered somewhat, are generally still far above 1.0. In comparing the likelihood ratios for a liberal-arts degree, for example, in all firms taken together the probability is increased by 4.09 that the chief operating officer will hold this degree if the chief executive is a liberal-arts graduate. When large manufacturing firms and large service firms are taken separately, the ratios are 3.11 and 3.49, respectively, still far larger than unity, which implies a strong correlation among the educational backgrounds of senior managers regardless of the firm's size and sector.

A parallel pattern is evident in the preferences of company managers when hiring new college graduates. Managers were asked which college degrees they viewed as being important "when you

Table 5.2. Probability Ratios for Company Executives to Have Same College Degree as the Chief Executive Officer, by Type of Degree and Company Sector[a, b]

Type of college degree of chief executive officer	Probability ratio of same degree held by	
	Chief operating officer	Responding manager
Undergraduate degree		
Liberal arts		
All companies	4.09	1.72
Large manufacturing	3.12	1.79
Large service	3.49	1.50
Business		
All companies	2.37	1.58
Large manufacturing	1.41	2.04
Large service	2.44	1.35
Engineering		
All companies	3.91	7.09
Large manufacturing	1.72	—[c]
Large service	6.72	2.84
Graduate degree: MBA		
All companies	2.06	1.24
Large manufacturing	1.90	1.51
Large service	2.24	0.84

[a]Number of firms: all companies, 412; large manufacturing companies, 90; large service companies, 188.

[b]All probability differences are significant at less than the .05 level, except for nonsignificant probability differences for the business degree/manufacturing comparison for chief operating officers; the business degree/service comparison for responding managers; the engineering degree/service comparison for responding managers; and the MBA degree/service comparison for responding managers.

[c]Ratio cannot be calculated because of a zero denominator.

consider hiring (or recommending hiring) a college graduate for an entry-level position." The correlation between the manager's own degree area and the recommended area was found to be very high. If the manager held a liberal-arts degree, he or she was more than twice as likely to rate a liberal-arts degree as an important asset (51 vs. 23%). If the manager possessed a business degree, the probability was substantially higher that he or she would rate a business degree highly (83 vs. 50%). If the manager held a MBA degree, the likelihood was nearly doubled that the MBA degree was viewed favorably (41 vs. 23%). Again, reanalysis of these results for managers in large service and manufacturing firms taken separately reveals that the basic pattern remains even in firms of similar technical requirements.[3]

It is evident, then, that "educational cultures" vary considerably from company to company, with liberal-arts graduates prevailing at the top of some, MBAs at the helm of others, and engineering graduates at the apex of still others. In corporations where one of the educational cultures is relatively dominant, the data reported here indicate that managers tend to reproduce their own educational profiles in those whom they hire and bring into the senior ranks, part of a general process of the perpetuation of social homogeneity among managerial cadres that Rosabeth Kanter characterized in her *Men and Women of the Corporation*. What we see here is that the process of educational perpetuation carries down to the preference not only that one have a college degree, but that it be earned in a particular subject area. Once established, the management educational culture is relatively self-perpetuating, whether or not it is specifically required for managing the particular production process and products of the corporation in question.[4]

The importance of the corporate culture for the recruitment of liberal-arts graduates can be seen in the comparison of companies led by chief executives with varying educational backgrounds. CEOs with a liberal-arts background are far more likely to have encouraged the hiring of liberal-arts graduates than CEOs without a liberal education (the likelihood ratio is 2.6). This can have a decisive bearing on company practices, judging by evidence presented in Chapter 2. The college recruitment profiles of companies led by chief executives who had advocated increased hiring of liberal-arts graduates were compared with companies whose CEO had remained silent on the topic. Firms headed by CEOs encouraging the hiring of liberal arts graduates are:

• Twice as likely to have actively recruited liberal-arts graduates on campus (71 vs. 36%).

- Twice as prone to have also recruited liberal-arts graduates through other avenues (54 vs. 21%).
- Half again more likely to have recruited an above-average proportion of liberal-arts graduates (63 vs. 45%).
- Twice as prone to forecast an increase in liberal-arts hiring during the coming 2 years (33 vs. 13%).

Moreover, the stance of the chief executive, it was found, has a critical bearing on the position taken by other senior managers. If the CEO advocated the hiring of liberal-arts graduates, the probability is increased by factors of 3 to 10 that the chief financial officer, manufacturing executives, marketing managers, and others had also promoted the hiring of liberal-arts graduates. The chief executive's action can therefore be crucial in establishing an educational culture shared by others in the firm. That culture, in turn, has a decisive influence on company recruitment practices. Thus in firms with no visible leadership position on seeking liberal-arts graduates, 26% actively recruited liberal-arts graduates on campus; when there are two advocates of liberal arts among the top managers, 58% of the companies seek liberal-arts graduates; with four or more senior advocates, 73% of the firms do so.

Since a major factor in the chief executive's likelihood of advocating the hiring of liberal-arts graduates is his or her own educational background, the CEO's education is itself a strong predictor of company practices. Knowing nothing about the inside culture of a firm or the views of top management on hiring liberal-arts graduates, the hiring practices of a firm can nonetheless be predicted with some accuracy by simply knowing the educational background of the chief executive officer. Compared to firms whose CEO does not hold a liberal-arts degree, corporations whose CEO has a liberal-arts education are (1) 1.4 times more likely to have recruited liberal-arts graduates on campus; (2) 1.7 times more likely to have recruited liberal-arts graduates through other avenues; (3) 1.5 times more likely to have recruited an above-average proportion of liberal-arts graduates; and (4) 2.0 times more likely to forecast an increase in hiring of liberal-arts graduates.

A managerial educational culture thus has a powerful self-perpetuating momentum of its own and a major influence on hiring policies. To the extent that that culture is not entirely related to the technical requirements of the industry, however, self-conscious change in the emphasis placed on educational requirements for college graduates can make a difference in who is hired without undercutting the company's competitive position.

II. Educational Cultures and Corporate Recruitment

The role of top management in changing the company's culture and recruitment policies can be particularly critical, since the impetus for change is far more likely to come from above than below. Moreover, senior managers and front-line supervisors bring different sets of concerns to the hiring process. Upper-level management is more receptive to liberal-arts recruitment, and lower-level management is less receptive.

The differences are evident in the widely noted tendency for senior managers to extol the virtues of a liberal education while their own college recruiters are stressing technical specialization. The chief executive of one manufacturing firm, for instance, was a strong believer in the liberal arts and had written and spoken as an advocate of liberal education in several public forums. At the same time one of his company's chief college recruiters was urging students at campus forums to pursue studies in business and technical areas rather than the liberal arts. College placement directors report the same seemingly contradictory tendency. One director reported: "Prospective employers are primarily interviewing for graduating seniors with majors in business and engineering. In other words, employers express an interest in liberal arts graduates, but in actuality, they most often interview graduating seniors with majors in technical fields." The placement officer reported that recruiters are typically looking for individuals to fill a slot within the organization that requires specific skills, but they seldom seem interested in whether candidates possess additional skills that might be utilized for the next step upward.

It is a widespread and deeply rooted conflict, then, between senior managers who speak favorably of liberal learning and college recruiters in their companies who are seeking those with specific technical and business degrees. Moreover, the difference has been observed by analysts going back several decades. In a major study of business education in the late 1950s supported by the Carnegie Corporation of New York, for example, author Frank Pierson observed that "actual recruitment among college graduates does not accord with the pronouncements of top business leaders." It "is often stated," he found, that "top management stresses the advantage of having a broad educational background for most types of business but that company recruiters tend to hire students with specific training needs to fill specific jobs." A parallel study at the same time sponsored by the Ford Foundation recorded the same conflict. On the basis of interviews with managers at a number of firms, researchers Robert A. Gordon and James E. Howell found that a "certain schizophrenic tendency was apparent in a number of our respondents. A good many stated that ideally the best preparation for business was . . . an undergraduate program in liberal arts or engineering followed by graduate business studies. Yet the recruiting policies of their companies reflected the view to only a very limited extent." Still another assessment in 1963 urges a closing of the gap:[5]

> [O]ur most important recommendation is that an attempt should be made, once and for all, to "pin down" the executives and personnel recruiters who reportedly say one thing and do another with respect to liberal education for business. To paraphrase William H. Whyte, American business leaders keep crying out for well-rounded, liberally-trained graduates—generalists rather than specialists—and their recruiters go right on doing what they have been doing: demanding and hiring more specialists.

The contradiction between top-management preferences and college-recruitment policies is still evident today. The gap is not an arbitrary one, however, for it is based in the divergent concerns of managers at varying levels of a company. The variant educational cultures reflect enduring organizational cleavages. The diverent organizational imperatives cannot themselves be altered, but the resulting educational cultures are subject to change.

The organizational differences can be traced to the distinctive concerns faced by front-line supervisors and senior managers. Front-line supervisors are responsible for ensuring that newly hired employees make immediate contributions to the tasks at hand. In the case of the health-products company, for instance, we saw that BA-degree holders with highly specific skills are generally sought for entry-level openings. Similarly, in the high-technology company we studied, recruitment is targeted at those "who can get the job done," the primary concern of the hiring supervisor. In both firms it is recognized that "higher up in the company" they worry about whether the new employee would have the capacity to assume broader responsibilities. But on the front line, the driving concern is this year's performance, not what the new recruit may be doing in 10 years.

Senior managers, on the other hand, are responsible for an employee's current performance as well as future development. Most corporations recruit the vast majority of their middle and senior managers from the ranks, so that the development of the next generation of company leadership necessarily begins with those freshly hired from colleges and universities. Recruiters are thus caught between the immediate demand of a hiring supervisor for people who can "get the job done" and the less tangible but nonetheless important company demand for individuals who one day can also move into more general responsibilities. Without attention to the new employees' flexibility, capacity to learn, and other qualities essential for promotion, short-term-performance gains may come at the cost of future failures. "Technical experts promoted into management are bright people with a long string of successes," observes the president of a small manufacturing firm, "but they often fail because as managers they try the same methods that have worked in the past instead of learning new techniques."[6]

The survey of company managers provides systematic confirmation of the correlation between management rank and preference for liberal-arts graduates. Though the survey is limited to middle and senior managers, the differences are evident even within this restricted group. As a measure of the value the manager places on liberal learning, we focus on the manager's assessment of the importance of a liberal-arts degree of a candidate under consideration for entry-level hiring. The company managers were asked: "When you consider hiring (or recommending hiring) a college graduate for an entry-level position, which of the following . . . qualifications . . . are most important to you in evaluating the candidate?" A third of the managers (32%) placed possession of an undergraduate liberal-arts degree among the most important qualifications.[7]

For comparison, the managers are divided into two groups. The first includes officers and assistant officers, and the second consists of nonofficers with varying managerial responsibilities. Three subgroups are identified within each group, differing in their distance from front-line supervision and their responsibility for general development of the firm. The subgroups and the titles that their occupants typically carry are the following:[8]

Officers and assistant officers
    Senior officers   Chief executive, executive vice-president, senior vice-president
    Officers   Vice-president, division vice-president, regional vice-president, treasurer, comptroller, secretary

Managers
General managers	Manager of division, region, or plant
Directors	Director of sales, planning, research, manufacturing, industrial relations
Managers	Manager of accounting, engineering, auditing, field sales, administration

The study's evidence confirms that senior officers are significantly more likely than assistant officers to view a liberal-arts degree as important at the point of hiring. Of the senior officers, 43% placed such a degree at the top of the list of hiring criteria, while 28% of the assistant officers did so (Table 5.3). Similarly, 50% of the general managers looked for liberal-arts credentials, compared to only 22% of the functional managers. Moreover, the same general patterns prevail when subanalyses are performed in firms broadly divided by sector (service vs. manufacturing) and size (e.g., top third, middle third, and bottom third of the manufacturing firms). Thus the more general the responsibilities of the manager, the greater is the value placed on a liberal-arts degree for entry-level college-graduate applicants. Conversely, the more proximate is the manager to the point of hiring and supervision, the lower is the value placed on a liberal education.

Since lower-level managers are under pressure to produce immediate results, they understandably have less concern for the eventual career-development of those they hire than do upper-level managers. To the extent that their immediate needs dominate the

Table 5.3. Percentage of Company Managers Who Consider a Liberal Arts Degree Important in Hiring at the Entry Level, by Level of Manager[a]

Officers and assistant officers	Number	Percentage	Managers	Number	Percentage
Senior officers	60	43	General managers	16	50
Officers	152	34	Directors	88	32
Assistant officers	39	28	Managers	124	22

[a]The percentage differences among the officers/assistant officers are significant at less than the .05 level; the percentage differences among the managers are also significant at less than the .05 level.

hiring decisions, as they often do unless senior management intervenes, liberal-arts graduates cannot fully compete with those who have technical specializations. Yet upper-level managers can and often do intervene. When they do, they can meld short-term needs with long-term management development concerns.

We saw in the case of the consumer-products company, for instance, that the educational culture in the area of product management favored MBA holders. Yet the chairman, president, and a group vice-president were all concerned about securing the highest-quality candidates, regardless of field of training. Accordingly, they instructed the manager of college relations to search for more BA holders, including those with liberal-arts majors. Despite some resistance from the middle managers in product management for whom they would be working, the college-relations manager did hire and place additional college graduates in areas that had traditionally been the preserve of MBA holders.

Similarly, hiring supervisors in the systems-information group of the high-technology company we studied occasionally recommended hiring technically well-qualified individuals who lacked college degrees. But the division manager ordinarily refused to approve the appointments on the premise that all of those hired by the company should be expected to be promoted at least twice, and possession of a college degree was viewed as a good predictor that this would occur. Though opposed to it initially, the front-line supervisors came to accept the division's policy.

III. Conclusion

Corporate educational cultures are shaped by both individual and organizational factors. The individual factor is evident in the continuing influence of managers' educational backgrounds on the criteria they apply in making hiring and promotion decisions. If they had earned an MBA degree, they tend to prefer MBA holders; if they had graduated in the liberal arts, they are often more interested in liberal-arts graduates; if they had been trained as engineers, they tend to look for fellow engineers. Part of this intergenerational preference is related to the technology and products of the company, but it is not entirely rooted in such factors. As part of the general tendency for managers to prefer their own kind in hiring and selecting successors, they often look for those with similar educational experiences and credentials.

Individual managerial preference, however, is also shaped by organizational imperatives. Regardless of a manager's own educational background, the more senior the manager, the stronger is his or her interest in those with a liberal-arts background. Conversely, the closer the manager is to the front-line supervision of entry-level college graduates, the stronger the interest in those with technical skills. If lower-level managers are looking for people to get the job done, higher-level managers are looking for people who get the job done but *also* have high potential and might one day move up to more responsible positions. The differences in the managers' perspectives are a direct product of the contrasting organizational concerns that they carry into their decision making. The often perplexing signals that companies give on hiring—with senior managers extolling the virtues of liberal learning and college recruiters emphasizing specific skills—can be largely traced to these divergent organizational imperatives within the corporation.

While educational cultures have a powerful effect on who is hired and promoted, they are not immutable. By explicit and self-conscious intervention, cultures can be altered. Here the role of the company's chief executive is critical. If the CEO encourages the hiring of liberally educated managers, other senior officers tend to concur. When the CEO and other officers thus present a united front, company practices can and often do change. Effective communication of company policy to the managers who are making the hiring decisions is crucial. This is particularly important because organizational incentives often otherwise discourage front-line supervisors from recruiting those with liberal-arts backgrounds. With company policy clearly communicated to them, however, organizational incentives can be tipped the other way. Periodic review of subsequent recruitment achievements can also be essential if the tipping is to be consolidated.

"An effective leader knows that the ultimate task of leadership is to create human energies and human vision," writes Peter F. Drucker. Building that energy and vision requires effective recruitment at the entry level. Otherwise, the base for later recruitment of more senior managers can be too restrictive. This is one of the findings in a study of management by John Kotter. From extensive interviews industry, he finds that too often in lower and middle management there is "a certain narrowness of ability and career experience, a narrowness that undermines efforts to develop visions and strategies and to elicit cooperation and motivation."[9]

Overcoming that narrowness requires concerted company efforts on several fronts, concludes Kotter, including college recruitment. His study focused on 15 firms that are rated by other companies as having particularly strong managements and the capacity to attract, develop, and retain able people. Among their distinguishing characteristics, he reports, are two of specific interest here. One is direct involvement of line managers, often from senior levels, in the recruitment process. Observed one of those interviewed by Kotter:

> Our current senior management is in the best position to know how many and what kind of people will be needed to run the business in the future; they understand where our business strategy is taking us better than anyone. They also are better able to spot the kind of quality minds and interpersonal abilities we want in young people.

The other distinguishing characteristic is explicit attention to whether prospective recruits have the potential to move well beyond their first position and assume broader responsibility. One of the highly rated companies, for instance, asked managers who interviewed candidates to complete an evaluation form on which one of the criteria is "leadership potential." Without such explicit consideration, observed an investment banker, "we end up with a lot of smart technicians."[10]

Creating a self-conscious company focus on leadership potential, then, is the task of senior managers. Their intervention can and will make a difference in the educational cultures that prevail.

Notes

1. Collins (1971, 1979), marshals evidence pointing to the importance of educational preferences in shaping employment practices.
2. Rosenbaum (1984).
3. The managers were asked: "When you consider hiring (or recommending hiring) a college graduate for an entry level position, which of the following experiences, qualifications or achievements are most important to you in evaluating the candidate." The qualifications used here are "undergraduate-liberal arts degree," "undergraduate business degree," and "MBA degree."
4. Kanter (1977); Pfeffer 1977.
5. Pierson *et al.* (1959), pp. 98, 112; Gordon and Howell (1959), p. 117.
6. Bettman (1987).
7. The full question read: "When you consider hiring (or recommending hiring) a college graduate for an entry level position,

which of the following experiences, qualifications or achievements are most important to you in evaluating the candidate?" The referenced items were: undergraduate liberal-arts degree; undergraduate business degree; undergraduate engineering degree; strong academic record in college; involvement in student, athletic, or community activities; graduated from a high-quality college; internship or work experience in business; study-abroad experience; MBA degree; postgraduate engineering degree; and law degree.

8. The general manager, director, and manager groups included a small number of those with assistant or associate titles.
9. Drucker (1988); Kotter (1988), p. 31.
10. Kotter (1988), pp. 85–86.

6

Strategies for Educational and Corporate Change

Most company managers have hectic schedules that demand as many as 60 hours a week or more, the equivalent of five 12-hour workdays. Crisis periods can force even longer hours of work, but the typical week is already long enough. The average workweek of chief executives of large corporations, according to one national study, is over 56 hours. Each of the hours tends to be jam-packed. Studies of "what managers do," often conducted by following a manager around the office, reveal intense time pressures, recurrent interruptions, and endless rounds of meetings. Since little sustained time is ever available for reflection or contemplation on the broader context of the work, one is advised to arrive in the job with a focused understanding already well developed.[1]

A thorough, quality education should have introduced the manager to many of the readings and ideas required for an effective leadership role in the corporation. Critics of American management, however, find that many of these fundamentals have not been furnished by our educational system or, worse, have been misshapen by it. In their influential 1980 *Harvard Business Review* article on "Managing Our Way to Economic Decline," Robert H. Hayes and William J. Abernathy argue that the nation's intensifying competitive woes can be traced in part to inadequacies of the business curriculum. At the core of the managerial problem, they argued, is the overly analytic detachment of managers who have had too little "hands-on" experience and the overconcentration of managers on short-term company performance to the neglect of long-term planning. Though these shortcomings are rooted in American business practices and culture, they are also partially derived, Hayes and Abernathy suggest, from the practices and culture of American business education. In reviewing the thrust of this and other critiques of business education in the 1980's, Earl Cheit, then dean of the Business School of the University of California at Berkeley, concluded that the "new criticism is telling business schools to be technically sound, but to do more to generate those energies of mind needed to direct the skill."[2]

If business schools have been long on technical skills but short on breadth of vision, liberal-arts programs have suffered from a reverse imbalance, in the view of many business managers. Still, the call by executives for more liberal education is predicated on the belief articulated by Hayes and Abernathy and others that the next generation of corporate leadership must be educated as broadly as possible if the short-term vision so prevalent today is to be overcome, and if we are to remain creative and innovative in both product and workplace design.

Liberal-arts programs have a decisive role to play here. Roger B. Smith, chairman and chief executive of General Motors Corporation, observed that "There are many paths to educational breadth, but none, I think, better than the liberal arts. A strong grounding in these fields can greatly enhance a manager's effectiveness." His arguments are representative of those offered by many senior managers:

> The higher one rises in the managerial/executive ranks, the more far-reaching his or her decisions are likely to be, and the more critical it becomes that these decisions be colored by a strong sense of steward-ship. And this is [an] area in which liberally educated people come to us already prepared, at least conceptually. People who have studied history and philosophy find it easy to maintain a broad perspective.[3]

A foundation in the liberal arts is also useful for meeting two other goals of General Motors, suggests its CEO: product quality and the effective management of change. The "liberally educated manager understands the nature of quality in its broadest sense: the result of an attitude—a pride of workmanship—that permeates the entire organization and touches every task." Moreover, writes Smith, liberal-arts graduates "are receptive to new information, to new paths to the traditional goals, even to new goals. . . . They have learned to uncover truth in many forms. They know that although some principles endure from one time and place to another, no answer need be final."[4]

In turning to the liberal arts for assistance, business is renewing a relationship that dates to the 1920's, when attending college became a respectable means for preparing for a career in the private sector. Few business-education programs were then available, and corporations looked to liberal-arts programs in college to prepare the coming generation of business leadership. Then as now the search for a quality general education was coupled with an insistence that useful skills be provided as well, a change that liberal-arts programs were not always well prepared (then or now) to incorporate. Writes an educational historian of the 1920s: "Liberal arts colleges struggled to find a balance between the traditional classical curriculum and the new practical courses added to keep them competitive."[5]

With the great expansion of business programs during the postwar period, especially the 1970s, companies are now assured of a large and steady flow, almost wholly absent a half century earlier, of graduates well trained in the principles of management. Yet they have become less certain of whether the new generation has been adequately exposed to the lessons of a liberal education, which can be as important as the technical principles of management. The thrust of the contemporary criticism and reform proposals is thus, as we have seen in earlier chapters, to strengthen and restore a closer relationship between management and liberal education.

This chapter extends the assessment that companies and managers have offered of their experiences with liberal-arts and other college graduates in the corporate workplace. We translate the criticisms and suggestions for change into a set of guidelines for reform and renewal. The guidelines are intended to be of use in rethinking and re-shaping how education goes about its task of preparing the next generation of corporate leadership. They are also intended to focus our thinking on how companies can best undertake the subsequent task of making more effective use of the talents of the better-educated managers that our colleges and universities do produce.

Companies and managers generally view liberal learning as the objective, with liberal-arts programs seen as a major but certainly not the only avenue for achievement. Broad-based reasoning can indeed often be taught as effectively in business, engineering, or other professionally oriented curricula as liberal-arts programs. What is needed, drawing on the apt phrase of educational researcher Zelda Gamson, is a "liberating education," a pedagogical approach in which students are stimulated and challenged to think analytically and critically. Liberal arts programs possess no monopoly on the approach. "[T]he standard liberal arts are by no means necessarily nonvocational or liberating," writes David Riesman, and "[m]any vocational subjects can be taught in a liberating way." Future managers need courses in both the liberal arts and the useful arts, and both must be taught in a way that maximizes the graduates' liberal learning.[6]

I. Educational Change in Liberal-Arts Programs

The corporate managers surveyed in this study call not for more students to major in the liberal arts or in business per se, but for a more effective integration of the curricula of both fields for those intent on entering the private sector, whatever the particular discipline of study. Even those not intent on entering the business world after graduation may profit from an integrated exposure. Approximately three quarters of all college graduates, it is estimated, will find their first job in the private sector, and thus some preparation for that setting is in order for a majority of students. Among the steps that colleges and universities can take are the following:

1. *Increase opportunities for liberal-arts students to carry courses in business.* The typical liberal-arts student now completes one course in business or none at all during 4 years of undergraduate study. Nearly 9 in 10 of the surveyed companies, however, stressed the importance of a range of business-related courses for college graduates whom they expect to hire.

For liberal-arts colleges within universities that include an undergraduate business-administration college, opportunities for such enrollment are readily available. The organizational framework for cross-registration between the colleges in many cases should already be firmly established. Business students typically carry a large fraction of their coursework in the liberal-arts college (over half of their course credits on average are taken in the liberal-arts). The financial framework for accommodating large numbers of liberal-arts students in business courses, however, is far less developed. Liberal-arts colleges in universities have evolved budgetary support for the service instruction that they have long provided to students in adjoining colleges of business and engineering. Often as much as half of the credit hours taught by an arts-and-science faculty in a university go to students who are not enrolled as majors in the liberal-arts college itself. Business colleges in universities, by contrast, perform much less service teaching of this type, and the infusion of a large number of liberal-arts undergraduates into their courses could require a large infusion of instructional funds into their budget.

Liberal-arts colleges not lodged in a university with an undergraduate or graduate business school face a far more difficult task in opening opportunities for their students to take business courses. By scholarly temperament and tradition, liberal-arts faculties are typically ill-equipped to design and staff business courses within their own curriculum. Rather than attempt to develop business courses in an inhospitable environment, independent liberal-arts colleges may need to be innovative in other ways, as some already have been. For example:

• Noncredit courses in business and careers in management. Wellesley College, for instance, offers a 3-week intensive seminar in

Management Basics to "help bridge the gap from a liberal arts education to the skills and information required for entry into management careers." Held during the winter intersession period, it primarily draws advanced undergraduates from the college, but it also attracts those who have already graduated from liberal-arts programs. Topics include finance, marketing, accounting, organizational behavior, and management-information systems.

• Executives-in-residence programs that bring company managers or retired managers to campus as guest lecturers and student advisers. The State of New Jersey Business/Humanities Project, for example, promotes such visits through its New Jersey Visiting Fellows Program. Senior executives of major New Jersey corporations are invited to college campuses for a week to "help students and faculty relate a liberal education to the world of work." The managers give public lectures and classroom presentations, meet with faculty, and counsel students. The dozen participating executives in 1987–1988 included senior managers from Dow Jones & Co., Prudential Insurance, Johnson and Johnson, Merrill Lynch, and Merck, and the recently retired chairman of AT&T. Eight colleges were selected in statewide competition to host the executives, including Glassboro State College, Saint Peter's College, and William Paterson College.

• Programs to enhance faculty familiarity with regional corporate employers. Carleton College, for example, has developed a set of advisers in each of the academic departments who meet with managers and corporate leaders in the region to learn directly of career opportunities for their students.

• Cooperative arrangements for undergraduate instruction at business schools of other institutions. The University of Chicago's Graduate School of Business, for instance, operates a summer program for students enrolled in 23 liberal-arts colleges, including Bowdoin, Carleton, Haverford, Oberlin, Spelman, Swarthmore, and Wesleyan. The Chicago Business Fellows Program brings three dozen liberal-arts students between their junior and senior years to Chicago to take introductory MBA courses, and they are entitled to return to complete the MBA degree after they graduate from their liberal-arts college. Each of the cooperating liberal-arts colleges selects one or two fellows for the program, and participating students receive full-tuition fellowships from Chicago for their summer of study.[7]

2. *Establish a business minor for liberal-arts students.* The creation of a minor concentration in business administration for

arts-and-science majors, with an advisory apparatus to support it, may be one of the most efficient means of orchestrating the involvement of liberal-arts students in management courses. A minor typically identifies six or more courses that must be taken and electives that might be taken, thus ensuring that students can carry the right courses within the limited time available. A business minor is most readily created by a liberal-arts college that can draw upon the course offerings of an affiliated undergraduate business school. For independent liberal-arts colleges, however, establishing a full business minor may simply not be possible.

A business minor can also establish invaluable credentials for the liberal-arts major. Students at Pennsylvania State University, for example, may enroll in the Business/Liberal Arts Minor, requiring approximately nine courses including accounting, economics, marketing, and management. The minor is intended to provide students "with a coherent group of skills applicable to business and industry," and business and industry has come to recognize the minor's value. Studies of corporate recruiters at Pennsylvania State University and elsewhere reveal that the business minors are more likely to be selected for a campus interview than other liberal-arts majors.[8]

The existence of a business minor for liberal-arts students can also attract company employers to college placement offices that service liberal-arts students. The main placement office at one large private university, for instance, supports all undergraduate recruitment except for students in the business program, which operates its own placement service. The liberal-arts college created a business minor for its students in 1982, and the director of the main placement office found that, as a result, it became easier to attract companies to interview in the main placement office.

Still another model is a certificate program in which business courses are taken for credit, thought not for a minor. The University of Rochester, for instance, has a summer program in Management Studies for its students in liberal arts, engineering, and other fields. The six courses include accounting, statistics, economics, and computer science. The program "enables students to acquire the management and administrative skills they need for a head start in a business career, while still majoring in liberal arts." To encourage participation, undergraduates at the university can enroll in the summer program at no extra tuition cost.

3. *Increase the number of courses in the liberal-arts curriculum that draw upon business issues.* The comment of one manager that liberal-arts students have not received a liberal education in one of

America's most important institutions—business—is symptomatic of the relative underrepresentation of business issues in the liberal-arts curriculum. If it is remarkable that many of American students cannot correctly identify the location of Mexico or France, it is equally remarkable that most leave college with only the most rudimentary knowledge of how business corporations are organized. To overcome this form of cultural illiteracy, business-related courses could be readily introduced or strengthened at many points in the traditional liberal-arts curricula:

* Biotechnology (biology)
* Business and labor history (history)
* Industrial organization and labor relations (economics)
* Business ethics (philosophy)
* Business political behavior (political science)
* Industrial psychology (psychology)
* Business and society (sociology)
* Corporate culture (anthropology)
* Technology and organization (interdisciplinary)

Many colleges already offer some or all of these courses, and often little more need be done than bring their relevance to the attention of undergraduates interested in managerial careers. The customized design of a set of new courses can also be useful, however, for bringing visibility and a sense of vitality to the offerings. This has been done, for instance, by the arts-and-humanities division of the University of Maryland. The division initiated a separate honors program on Liberal Arts in Business, and students enrolled in the program must take at least seven specially designed courses, such as the law and ethics of business, while also completing a regular arts-and-humanities major.

Business-related issues can be more extensively integrated into other coursework as well. A course on the American political process could usefully discuss the impact of corporate lobbying and political-action committees; a course on law and society might cover the research literature on corporate violations of federal and state law; a course on ethics could draw upon the extensive case materials now available on ethical dilemmas in business decisions; in cultural anthropology one might study the ritual and language not only of the preliterate tribes in Borneo but of the companies on Wall Street; and a course on American history could examine the formation of the modern corporation in the early part of this century along with the more conventional topics. Whether new courses are created or old courses redesigned, a faculty committee to initiate and guide the process would be helpful.

4. *Strengthen advising on business-related studies for liberal-arts students.* An expansion of opportunities in business-related studies must be accompanied by institution-supported guidance if students are to make full use of the opportunities. We saw from the transcript study of the liberal-arts courses taken by engineering students that, whatever the formal requirements, students do not necessarily acquire breadth or depth as they cross-register in other colleges. Course catalogs are open menus with no explicit guidance on where to concentrate the limited time available. If liberal-arts students are encouraged to acquire coursework in business, they must be systematically and thoughtfully advised about the most useful courses and the best way to integrate them into the comprehensive fabric of their undergraduate experience.

The quality of course counseling and career advice for liberal-arts students interested in business careers will be a function of the faculty's and professional advisors' familiarity with the business world. Programs such as CBS Inc.'s faculty-in-residence project that bring liberal-arts faculty into direct contact with company managers are invaluable for developing that familiarity; so is the recruitment of career counselors who have worked in the private sector.

5. *Expand internship opportunities for liberal-arts students.* The surveyed corporations placed internships and work experience at the top of their list of important qualifications for the college graduates they are considering hiring. Internships and related experience are viewed as two of the very best means for testing and preparing liberal-arts students for what lies ahead. In exposing liberal-arts students to the realities of work in the private sector, they provide an early test of whether the individual may really want to embark on a corporate career. By introducing students to the language and issues of the corporate workplace, the experience also provides an invaluable firsthand education in the culture and concepts of the corporate workplace. Moreover, by bringing students into contact with one another and those already in the workplace, internships also help build enduring networks of contact and communication.

To achieve their educational purpose, internships and related forms of work experience require careful organization. Internships must be found that relate to the student's educational interests and goals. This is often a labor-intensive process requiring sustained negotiation between the student and potential placement setting. After students are placed in their work settings, the customized internship must be continually monitored and evaluated to ensure that the work assignments are educationally meaningful. Faculty contact must be maintained with the student to ensure that he or she interprets the experience in a broader learning context. Faculty contact with the company itself is important as well. One means for facilitating this is the development of private-sector internships for faculty members. St. Olaf College, for example, created a program to place faculty members in paid internships with regional companies such as Honeywell, Northwestern Bell, and General Mills. Several of the faculty participants were later able to open opportunities for their students with the same companies.[9]

Building internship programs can be costly in time and money, especially if made available to a large number of undergraduates, and colleges must take this cost into account. Still, internships may be one of the best avenues for integrating liberal learning with career preparation for the private sector. This may be particularly true at independent liberal-arts colleges that are unable to enroll their students in courses at associated business schools.

6. *Improve undergraduate awareness of the value of liberal-arts education for corporate careers.* Many institutions provide career counseling for liberal-arts students planning careers in medicine, law, or other professions, but relatively little guidance in preparing for careers in management. Improved undergraduate counseling services are needed if students are to make realistic and calculated appraisals of the course and extracurricular experiences that they will require. Counseling may be particularly important for minorities and women, groups that have traditionally found the least opportunity in company management. Minorities and women have fewer role models and informal contacts in the private sector than do white men, and campus counseling may be especially important in helping them overcome a more limited familiarity with the corporate workplace.

College counseling should also offer a nuanced view of where liberal-arts majors are likely to find private-sector employment—and where they will not. The present study would, for instance, point to the following lines of guidance:

- *Functional area.* Greatest opportunities for liberal-arts graduates are in marketing, sales, and human resources.
- *Product sector.* Financial, insurance, and other service companies hire liberal-arts graduates more often than do manufacturing firms, but there are large differences within these broadly classi-

fied groupings. Diversified financial firms are particularly strong in hiring, while savings banks are far less likely to seek liberal-arts graduates; some pharmaceutical companies hire a large number of liberal-arts graduates, while many electronics firms employ few.

- *Corporate leadership.* Regardless of product sector, some firms have a long-standing reputation for the generous hiring of liberal-arts graduates. One of the foremost defining characteristics is whether the firm's senior management believes in the value of liberal learning.

- *Company size.* Larger companies are far more likely to come to campus to recruit liberal-arts graduates. Smaller companies should not, however, be overlooked. They seek liberal-arts graduates just as often as do large firms, but are much less likely to have the resources to recruit on campus.

The present study also points to several lines of guidance that business-oriented students should consider when making their critical choices during the undergraduate years:

- *Majoring in the liberal arts.* A liberal-arts education is a suitable avenue of preparation for business management. A particularly strong combination is a liberal-arts degree, several years of work experience, and then an MBA degree. Undergraduate coursework in the liberal arts that enhances knowledge of organizations, writing and speaking abilities, and familiarity with the business world can be especially useful.

- *Business coursework.* If at all possible, one should enroll in appropriate business courses and even minor in business administration when such an option is available on campus.

- *Internships.* Internships and other opportunities that place one in a corporate work setting can be invaluable because of both the unique experience and the distinctive credential that they provide a liberal-arts student.

- *Getting started.* Compared to engineering and some business graduates, liberal-arts graduates can have a more difficult time landing the first job with a corporation. Over time, however, liberal-arts graduates on average fare at least as well as college graduates with professional undergraduate degrees. In some corporations in which engineering or MBA cultures are prevalent, their promotion prospects may be below average; in other firms, however, their communication and other distinctive abilities may lead to faster-than-average movement up the corporate ladder.

II. Educational Change in Business Programs

While a strong dose of useful education should be added to a liberal-arts education, in the corporate managers' assessment an equally strong measure of liberal-arts education should accompany business education. Engineering education should be strengthened as well, with more coursework in both liberal arts and business. There is considerable sympathy for the position offered by the president of Cornell University, Frank Rhodes, that the strongest business and undergraduate professional programs are those that embrace "liberal education, not as an 'add-on,' but as a vital component of professional study."[10] This can be achieved through several avenues.

1. *Strengthen opportunities for business students to take courses in the liberal arts.* Experienced managers in many companies urge that business students acquire a solid foundation in the liberal arts. Not all do so: senior managers of the industrial-products company that we studied expressed limited interest in seeing stronger liberal-arts records among either the engineering or the business graduates they recruit. The predominant call, however, was for more liberal-arts education, both because of the substantive content and the analytic capacities that it can impart. Liberal-arts graduates received better than above-average marks from the company managers for their communication abilities, leadership capacities, innovativeness, ethical concerns, and understanding of people. All are competencies that companies would like future business graduates to have, and exposure of business majors to liberal-arts coursework may be the vehicle for obtaining them.

2. *Increase the number of business courses that draw upon the frameworks and approaches of the arts and sciences.* Just as business issues would be fruitfully introduced into liberal-arts courses, so too should business courses borrow from the arts and sciences. This may be particularly important in independent business schools that do not have an affiliated liberal-arts college to which their students can be sent for coursework.

Many managers would concur with the thrust if not all of the specific elements of the formulation of one analyst of business programs, Raymond E. Miles. He writes in forecasting the shape of business programs in the 1990s that the

> *undergraduate business major/minor* is likely [to] provide an introduction to business and organizations built on a strong, demanding, letters and science foundation. . . . Students will learn the language of business and economics and be introduced to the major issues and approaches.

They will be essentially letters and science graduates with a firm grasp of business directions and demands. The better undergraduate business programs will bring students into contact with real organizational cases and managers and will seek to illustrate the use of broad economic and organizational theory as diagnostic and learning approaches.[11]

Yet if such initiatives are to work, a stronger tradition of research on business is required, especially in the social sciences. A distinctive contribution of social-science research to the curriculum of business courses is to offer theory-based analytic studies of corporations and their managers, investigations that go beyond case studies to identify enduring patterns of corporate organization and behavior.

3. *Strengthen advising on liberal-arts coursework for business students.* Business students already carry half or more of their coursework in the liberal arts. To ensure optimal development of the skills and capacities for which that experience is intended, student advising by both business and liberal-arts faculty can be essential. The same is true for engineering students: jointly managed guidance by the engineering, liberal-arts, and business faculties could optimize student learning experience when they seek courses in business and liberal arts.

If this advising is to be maximally effective, the faculty advisers must be trained in how it is best rendered. Moreover, a professional counseling staff can also be crucial. These advisers should be thoroughly familiar with the curriculum of both the business and the liberal-arts programs, the academic and career issues confronting students, and the outlook and concerns of private-sector employers. "Peer counseling" by students who have successfully bridged the liberal-arts and business divide can also be invaluable, as can advisory sessions with college alumni who return to campus for special counseling evenings or fairs.

4. *Stress the value of a liberal education for entry into an MBA program.* If graduate schools of business emphasize the importance of a broad undergraduate education for gaining admission to MBA programs, undergraduate students intending to seek graduate management training are more likely to pursue a diversified course of study. The message offered by the dean of the business school at Duke University, Thomas Keller, is illustrative of what more undergraduates would usefully hear:

[W]e must train managers to be less insular. Business schools should invite applicants with a broad undergraduate education. A liberal-arts background can equip students with an orientation that may be crucial for success in the global marketplace—one that instills suspicion of pat rules and formulas, an awareness of history and traditions and an understanding of the tremendous variety of the world's people.

For similar reasons, MBA coursework itself would benefit from an infusion of arts-and-sciences issues and approaches.[12]

III. Organizational Change in the Corporate Workplace

The current generation of corporate officials express widespread support for the pursuit of liberal learning by the nations's next generation of company managers. Yet this message has not yet been fully communicated either to many undergraduate students on campus or to many front-line managers in the company. If the message is to be better heard and thus heeded, companies should take several steps, and action is needed if student and parental confidence in the value of a liberal-arts education for a career in the private sector is to be restored. Effectively delivered, the message may ultimately show the 1970s to be an anomaly. The massive flow of students out of the liberal arts into business programs during the decade may prove to have been the exception in an otherwise more enduring relationship between liberal education and corporate management. Companies can take several steps to sustain the relationship.

1. *Increase emphasis on liberal learning in campus recruitment.* While top management in many companies believes in the special role of liberal learning for management development, their college-relations staff frequently does not incorporate such commitment into their recruitment policies and goals. Perhaps the most important source of resistance is the managers who will be directly supervising the newly hired college graduates. In the interest of recruiting somebody who can "get the job done," they frequently specify that the person bring relatively technical or business skills. There is no contradiction here. The immediate supervisor is indeed charged with getting the job done, not with long-term strategic management development and performance. It is senior management that is left to worry about the latter.

Our case studies illustrate, however, that concerted management can make a major difference. In the high-technology firm, for instance, supervisors in the information-systems group often wanted candidates who were technically qualified but had no college degree. The group manager resisted their appointment on the grounds that such employees were relatively unpromotable. When dossiers of candidates without a college degree were brought forward for his review, he would often refuse to approve them, and in time the message registered on both his recruiters and first-level supervisors. Similarly, in the consumer-products firm, three of the company's most-senior managers instructed the head of college recruitment to seek BA holders for the product-management ladder, a traditional stronghold of MBA hiring. Despite resistance by middle managers who typically held MBAs and who would be responsible for the work of the recruits, a new group of bachelor's degree holders—including a few with liberal-arts majors—were brought into the company.

Explicit instruction of those involved in college recruiting is thus essential. It need not focus only on the hiring of liberal-arts graduates. Equally important can be a stress on liberal-arts coursework for the business and engineering applicants who are selected for review. If college recruiters give weight to such experience in their ratings and interview questions, word will spread among students and placement counselors that their liberal-arts coursework can prove to be a major asset when they are considered for a job. Companies can send a powerful message to campuses through their recruitment actions.

Awareness of the corporate message should also be spread to high-school counselors, who increasingly play a critical role in shaping college-bound seniors' decisions about not only which college to attend, but also which course of study to pursue. Their influence may be particularly important when high-school seniors are deciding whether to enter an undergraduate liberal-arts, business, or other specialized field of study. In many cases, this decision is taken near the time of college application, long before arrival on campus.

An additional internal company step would be to create special programs for recruiting liberal-arts and other college graduates that rely on technical training after the point of hiring. These permit the recruitment of employees with strong general abilities without fear of shortcomings in their specific technical abilities. The diversified financial services company, for instance, has such a program. So does Chase Manhattan Bank, and its program is worth briefly describing, since it illustrates how effective such internal-training efforts can be.

Chase Manhattan Bank, the nation's third largest commercial bank, hires a large number of new college graduates every year (more than 340 in 1982). Both recent BA holders and MBA recipients are recruited, with the bulk of the college graduates holding a degree in a liberal-arts discipline. Two thirds enter as "relationship managers" who are responsible for overseeing the bank's contact with customers. In Chase's view, it can be difficult to teach reasoning abilities, but technical business skills can be readily taught to those who possess the first. The Chase vice-president responsible for the program observed: "Our people are able to acquire specialized characteristics for successful job performance if they have the right mental abilities and motivation for work." And Chase's own studies confirm the observation. The new BA and MBA graduates enter the same specialized training course on the development of credit and risk analysis. Seventy-nine who completed the program in the late 1970s were tracked 1 to 4 years later, and their supervisors were asked to rate their performance. The performance evaluation focused on their "application of credit skills on the job with emphasis on quantitative analytic ability," an area where MBA graduates might be expected to have an edge on BA holders. Yet Chase found that the college graduates received significantly higher rating than did the MBA holders. Of the *low* performers, 60% held MBA's, while of the *high* performers, 60% held BAs.[13]

This experience suggests that liberally educated managers without prior business training often can, if properly trained, perform as well as those with extensive formal training in business administration. Without the training opportunity, the liberal-arts graduates would have been initially disadvantaged relative to those with technical business training, but with it they were quickly placed on at least an equal footing. Later, as we have seen from evidence in preceding chapters, they bring special qualities to their management roles, qualities that the corporation would have been denied if liberal-arts graduates had been initially screened out because of their more limited technical skills.

2. *Evolve a corporate culture that values liberal learning in hiring, promotion, and management development.* Executive pacesetting is crucial. We have seen that in a company led by a chief executive who favors liberal-arts hiring, other senior managers may come to share that vision. The collectively held vision then translates into action. The greater the number of senior managers who back liberal-arts hiring, we find, the more vigorous are the company's efforts to do so. More generally, a cultural climate that emphasizes general knowledge and liberal learning will be one in which managers with such talents, whether acquired in a liberal-arts, business, or other programs, will be encouraged to express and further develop them.

Efforts to create cultural change always encounter some resistance, since culture, by definition, carries the inertial weight of tradition. One form of that resistance is the tendency for managers to pattern educational credentials similar to their own in company hiring and promotion decisions. We have seen in evidence presented here, for example, that there is a pronounced tendency for senior managers to have the same educational background as their chief executive, regardless of the type of industry, and other analysts have noted the same tendency in other settings. The educational consistency is part of a more general pattern for managers to seek people similar to themselves for positions of responsibility and trust. But whatever the origins of the practice, it can be altered by self-conscious intervention. This was evident in the consumer-products company: MBA-holding middle managers preferred to hire new managers with the same credential, but top management successfully insisted that the ranks be opened to bachelor's degree holders as well. Once recruited, several of the BA holders proved very effective (it also did not escape notice that they came at considerably lower salaries), which in turn served as a positive demonstration effect that encouraged still further BA hiring. Thus prevailing educational cultures can be altered, provided that senior management forcefully mobilizes a program to make it occur.[14]

3. *Further encourage public awareness of the importance of liberal learning for business leadership.* Student decisions on coursework, majors, and career directions are subtly but powerfully shaped by the dominant currents in American values. The private sector has achieved a special allure among American students during the 1980s. Students concentrated more on their studies for getting ahead and less on the social and political issues of the day. The focus on technical subjects and avoidance of liberal-arts subjects without direct job relevance was one way to take the career-oriented culture seriously, and it was an understandable response to the cultural cues of the moment.

A national campaign in the mid-1980s by the Association of American Colleges, backed by the National Endowment for the Humanities, to enlarge public awareness of the value of liberal learning for professional and business careers helped alter the picture. Similarly, the Council of Independent Colleges, an association representing more than 300 small liberal-arts colleges, undertook a national information campaign to improve public awareness of the value of liberal learning for management and other careers. A number of colleges and universities have initiated their own on-campus campaigns to better inform undergraduates of the importance of liberal arts for future employment. The University of Virginia, for example, assembled alumni-survey data and other persuasive and practical information in a widely circulated guide for undergraduate students on converting a liberal-arts major into a well-paying and interesting career, *Life After Liberal Arts*. Similarly, the University of Texas at Austin published a comprehensive manual to assist liberal-arts students in preparing for "successful self-placement in the job market."[15]

Supportive argument has also come from some high government officials: the chairman of the National Endowment for the Humanities, Lynne E. Cheney stated in a subtitle to a widely circulated column in 1986 that "a liberal-arts is increasingly valuable in the American corporation." Similarly, her predecessor and later U.S. Secretary of Education, William J. Bennett, had entitled a 1985 newspaper column on the subject, "Go Ahead, Major in the Liberal Arts." The founding of the Corporate Council on the Liberal Arts in 1984 added an explicit corporate voice as well.[16]

Still, it is the companies that are doing the hiring. The chief executives of AT&T, General Motors, and some other companies have already spoken out, and their commentary has been very important in restoring public perceptions of the liberal arts. What is needed now, however, is similar commentary and commitment by hundreds of other companies. It need not be more than occasional public reference to the dual importance of liberal education and business training. Yet if many company voices are expressing their concern simultaneously, the effect will be to convert a message still perceived to be tentative and arguable into one that is incontrovertible.

Notes

1. Burck (1976); Mintzberg (1975); Kotter (1982).
2. Hayes and Abernathy (1980); Cheit (1985).
3. Smith (1986), p. 30.
4. Smith (1986), p. 31.
5. Levine (1986), p. 60.
6. Gamson *et al.* (1984); Riseman (1984), pp. 218–219.
7. Mohrman and Hirsch (1986); Rice (1983); Cordisco and Walker (1983).
8. Garis *et al.* (1985).
9. Rice (1983), pp. 23–25; Haviland *et al.* (1983).
10. Rhodes (1985), p. 80.
11. Miles (1985), p. 68.
12. Keller (1987).

13. Burns (1983).
14. Powell (1969); Kanter (1977).
15. Council of Independent Colleges (1986); University of Virginia (1986); Liberal Arts Placement Office, University of Texas, (n.d.).
16. Cheney (1986); Bennett (1985).

7

Liberal Education and a New Generation of Corporate Leadership

In 10 years, most of the current top managers will have retired. Senior managers are typically in their mid-50s, and most will take retirement by their mid-60s. At the same time, a new generation of corporate managers will be coming to the fore, graduates of the late 1980s who will be reaching well into the middle-management ranks by the late 1990s. The values, perspectives, and experiences that the new generation brings to its responsibilities will be critically shaped by the actions of today's managers. What they stress in recruitment, and how this is communicated to college audiences, will have a fundamental bearing on how the new generation is educated to assume its responsibilities for guiding the nation's major institutions.

The choices are fateful for both the corporation and the individual. In the aggregate, a new generation that is long on technical skills but short on liberal learning will move companies in directions that are potentially very different from what would have been the case if the new generation had instead acquired an integrated education in the useful and the liberal arts. For the individual, the choice of a college major can be just as crucial, fundamentally shaping opportunities for employment and personal growth for the half-century of active work and adult life to come.

I. Liberal Education and Corporate Performance

Since a liberal education contributes to a manager's effectiveness, it follows that well-educated managers should make companies more effective. Evidence for this is not well developed, however, for there has been little systematic study of the impact of educational cultures on corporate performance. It is nevertheless a plausible working hypothesis, particularly when applied to corporate change and outreach.

We know, for example, that the overall educational attainment of managers can influence a company's willingness to make changes. Firms led by well-educated officers are found to be more innova-

157

tive. The type of degree has been found to make a difference as well. In one study by Rosabeth Kanter, for example, two sets of large corporations were compared: one group of 31 firms identified as "progressive" by a panel of senior human-resource executives and a second group of 19 "nonprogressive" companies selected from the same industry and size class as the first set. Progressive companies were defined as those that had adopted practices intended to (1) improve work conditions through quality-of-worklife efforts, (2) assure equal employment opportunity, and (3) address the special problems of working parents. Direct observation of the firms confirmed that the progressive companies had lived up to their reputation, for they had more often introduced such programs as quality circles, career-development training, and flexible work schedules.[1]

Among the factors that distinguished the two groups of companies was the educational background of the top managers. A lower proportion of the top managers in the progressive companies held MBA degrees than in the nonprogressive companies. Formal management training, it would appear, may direct executive attention away from the human dimension of managing the work force. That this is not necessarily a cost-effective measure is shown by the fact that the progressive companies in this study were, on average, more profitable than the otherwise similar set of nonprogressive firms.[2]

This kind if evidence does not directly confirm the importance of liberal learning, but it does reveal that the educational background of top managers can affect the company's performance. Other indirectly supportive evidence comes from studies of corporate outreach into the local community or metropolitan region. We know from the present study that liberally educated managers more often take active part in the community's social and political affairs. Other research has also shown that better educated senior managers take more active part in corporate affairs beyond the boundaries of the corporation—serving on the boards of directors of other companies or playing a leadership role in the nation's major business associations, such as the Business Roundtable. Thus firms led by liberally educated managers may acquire a better sense for the pulse of both the political and the business communities in which they operate. It is a kind of informal "environmental scan" by which the managers are continuously acquiring information about the worlds outside the company. Corporations are thus not only better informed, but, as confirmed by still other research, are perceived by the business community, government officials, and the public at large as being more responsible. A reputation for social responsibility may even be generalized into a reputation for effective management. A study of major corporations in the Minneapolis–St. Paul area shows that socially active firms are perceived as being not only more responsible corporate citizens, but also *better run* companies. The outreach efforts of externally active managers can therefore contribute to the company's reputation as a well-managed operation, a reputation that the company can often parlay into additional customers and investors.[3]

Other studies suggest that a general education may be important also for other private-sector employees. Henry M. Levin and Russell W. Rumberger, for example, examined the educational and training requirements of personnel using computers in nearly 3000 small companies in 1985. While prior specialized training in computers, quantitative skills, and related technical subjects was considered useful, the companies placed much greater stress on general educational preparation that engendered reasoning, comprehension, and communication abilities. In other research assessing the impact of technological change on future workplace demands for education and training, Levin and Rumberger also conclude that a general educational foundation may be the soundest means of preparing for future employment in a rapidly changing economy whose specific work requirements cannot be readily forecast. They conclude that the "best preparation for the future is a general rather than a specific job-focused education, one with a strong foundation in the liberal arts. Many jobs as we know them today will be different in the future. And many workers will change jobs and careers in their lives. The best preparation for a changing work-world is one that stresses flexibility and adaptability."[4]

Moreover, an investment now in the liberal education of those who will one day enter the private sector can create unanticipated new possibilities later. In their defense of the role of manufacturing in the United States, Stephen S. Cohen and John Zysman argue in *Manufacturing Matters* that "organized smarts" will have a decisive bearing on how American companies respond to world competition. "An educated, skilled labor force broadens," they suggest, "rather than forecloses choice in the competitive development and application of technologies." A well-educated work force should thus possess the requisite competence and knowledge than their companies can capitalize on presently, yet it is also a reservoir of talent that can open new directions and opportunities for corporations in the decades to come.[5]

Finally, American companies are increasingly international in scope, and managers educated in international affairs, cross-cultural communication, and foreign languages can only be an asset. The breath of involvement abroad is evident in our own survey of managers.[6] Of the 505 responding managers, only 2% worked with corporations that had no international operations. Thus not only did virtually all companies in this sample from the Fortune 1500 operate abroad, but over half—51%—of the managers in companies that are active abroad are themselves directly involved with the international operations. Moreover, the international involvement was not limited to those at a particular level in the company, in a specific function, or from a particular educational background.

The more widespread the managerial familiarity with international politics and transnational business cultures, the more effective therefore should be the company's oversight of its operations and activities outside the United States. Certainly companies involved in international operations view it this way, according to a study by Stephen J. Kobrin of 163 large industrial and banking firms with major international operations (the industrial firms, for instance, acquired at least 20% of their income from operations abroad). On the basis of interviews with senior managers of 37 of the corporations and a survey of the remainder, Kobrin concludes that most managers of multinational corporations "will have to *understand* how to operate outside of the United States; how to deal effectively, and manage, a wide variety of people. This entails being able to quickly establish ground rules and to gain an understanding of social, economic, and political conditions when necessary." As a result, "the ability to interact across borders and to manage a wide variety of people may also be necessary for effective performance within the firm." Cultivation of these abilities is laid at the doorstep of higher education:

> [I]t is critically important that students who plan managerial careers in large international firms develop at the college level the basis for acquiring international expertise. First, that means at least some language competency. Second, it means developing a systematic understanding of the differences in political and economic systems, culture, behavior, world view, and interpersonal interaction that one finds once one leaves home. That requires traditional academic courses, perhaps including comparative politics, economics, and anthropology, taught in such a way as to leave the student with a framework upon which to build further study and experience. . . . What is important is that the student develop a systematic understanding of international differences and an ability to analyze and synthesize on his or her own.[7]

Since internationalization of operations is increasingly common in major companies, a liberal education or at least exposure to many of its courses may be particularly crucial for the next generation of internationally minded corporate managers. A high degree of specialization in international affairs is not necessary, since most hiring will continue to focus on general managerial skills and abilities. Still, at least some foundation in foreign cultures, language, and related matters that are part of most liberal-arts curricula should serve well the majority of future middle and senior managers who are likely to become involved in their company's international operations.

If future research corroborates the importance of liberal education for international operations, workplace innovativeness, social responsiveness, and other areas of performance, it would confirm that an emphasis on liberal education can be important not only for individual careers but also for corporate change and social responsibility. The goal of providing the next generation of corporate leadership with as broad an education as possible may thus be as important for national competitiveness and societal goals as for the earnings and other goals of individual firms.

II. Liberal Education and the Individual Manager

For individuals intending a career in the private sector, a liberal education or strong exposure to liberal-arts courses may be important for reasons that go well beyond the issue of managerial effectiveness. A liberal education can assist managers in coping with unanticipated limitations they may face in their own career prospects. It is an era in which many companies are no longer able to assure expanding managerial opportunities, and a growing number of corporations are not able to assure continuing employment to managers who have invested their entire career in the company.

The warning signs of a generation of managers at risk are now more abundant than ever. Consider the 1987 assessment of Paul Hirsch in his guide to surviving corporate takeovers and downsizings, *Pack Your Own Parachute*, of the impact of the accelerating phenomenon of corporate restructuring:

> America's mightiest firms are firing thousands of our most talented managers. At the same time, the number of management positions at large U.S. corporations is falling. . . . [O]ther companies have been crippled, stripped down against the best judgment of their own top executives during a decade of retrenchment. Between 1980 and 1990, it is estimated that more than one million managers will have lost their jobs. With more and more companies being forced to accelerate cost

cutting and avoid taking entrepreneurial risks, the number of attractive management positions on the career ladder has nosedived.[8]

The "crash" of the stock market in the fall of 1987 further exacerbated the downsizing impetus, bringing it into the hitherto largely immune areas of investment banking and diversified financial services. Such actions, concludes Hirsch, "are destroying the lives of loyal long-term managers, the people who know a company's business best and are most committed to its continued success. The corporation's commitment to its own people has fallen at every level to the lowest point in fifty years."[9]

At the same time, employee commitment to the corporation has also sharply declined in recent years, with managers more prepared to move from company to company in search of a suitable position. If managers are thus more likely to face layoffs, periods of unemployment, and jobs with several employers during their career, flexibility and adaptability are all the more essential. So, too, are more generic skills and abilities, capacities that can be readily transferred to other work settings. One of Hirsch's central recommendations is to avoid overspecialization and build generality: "Develop and maintain transferable skills that will enhance your value to other employers as well as to your present employer." Here, again, a liberal education can be an important foundation for flexibility and generic abilities.[10]

Even without the reductions in managerial ranks of the mid-1980s, most managers are certain to reach plateau's in their careers from which further promotion is unlikely. Virtually all managerial hierarchies rapidly narrow in the middle and upper ranges. This is evident, for instance, in the distribution of managers among the seven management levels of Illinois Bell Telephone Company presented in Table 4.4. Of the more than 7000 managers with the company in 1984, fully 76% were employed on the first rung, and the second rung included another 19%. Thus the next five levels were occupied by only 5% of the managers. The width of a management level shrinks by about three quarters with each successive rise, leaving little opportunity for a majority of those in a given level to ever move to the next level. The "stayers" on each rung will of necessity far outnumber the "movers."

Detailed analysis of managers with college degrees in another large company reveals a similarly rapidly constricting corporate hierarchy. The result is a sharply declining rate of promotion for individual managers over time. Graduates of highly selective colleges who had been with the firm for 15 years were only about half as likely to be further promoted as during their first several years with the company, and the probability drops to about a third after 25 years. Promotion probabilities display similarly sharp dropoffs for college graduates of less selective institutions as well.[11]

Most company managers start relatively well and many are promoted by one or more levels, but the great majority, regardless of educational origin or other factors, experience a rapidly diminishing rate of upward mobility. A large number of managers will reach a plateau of responsibility from which they are likely to rise little further. These patterns have been intensified during the reductions in managerial ranks of the mid-1980s, but their basic structure will still prevail when expansion returns.

For even the most-career-driven student, then, it can be important to prepare for later career periods when company work may not be fully preoccupying, either because further promotions are unlikely or possibly even because there is at least momentarily no employment at all. A liberal education certainly offers no protection against such circumstances, but it can enhance making the most of them. Numerous studies confirm that a college education, and above all a liberal education, increases interest in political life, knowledge of the political process, and engagement in political activity; heightens awareness of culture and the arts and increases involvement in community and public affairs. This is evident, for instance, in the rates of participation in community and public affairs among the managers surveyed for the present study. In both the officer and nonofficer ranks, and especially in the latter, managers with a liberal-arts degree are found to be significantly more likely than those with a business degree to take active part in the local community and to serve in voluntary positions with nonprofit organizations (Table 4.14). Exposure to a liberal education can thus better prepare managers for later periods of their lives in which extracorporate involvements acquire greater significance.[12]

III. Liberally Educated Managers and the Social Fabric

The ethos of "getting ahead" and accumulating wealth acquired a special saliency in American culture during the 1980s. The values of individualism and self-interest were ascendant, while the values of collective responsibility and social involvement were in eclipse. Whatever personal benefits a linear career-mindedness might bring the individual, they come at significant costs to the broader community and even to business itself. The decline of individual attachments to voluntary organizations, community groups, and political and social causes has left many Americans without significant collective engagement and social meaning in their lives, as Robert Bellah and his colleagues have well documented in *Habits of the Heart.* With depth interviews of individuals in diverse walks of life, including several in business, their research richly confirms the loss of transcendent meaning and sense of social contribution in the lives of many.[13]

Yet both the local community and national political systems need voluntary support and participation. "Individualism," observed Alexis de Tocqueville more than a century ago in *Democracy in America,* "disposes each citizen to isolate himself from the mass of his fellows and withdraw into the circle of family and friends; with this little society formed to his taste, he gladly leaves the greater society to look after itself." The contemporary rise of individualism threatens to leave the nation's voluntary social and political affairs in an increasingly undernourished state, dependent on the energies and contributions of a dwindling minority.[14]

The context for reinvigorating American industry, too, may be undercut by the radical individualism. Robert B. Reich argues that the "atmosphere of insecurity and impermanence which characterizes all levels of American business has bred a selfish attitude among directors, managers, and employees, an egoistic mentality which is seriously undermining American enterprise." The undermining ranges from the sacrifice of long-term corporate planning to weakened management teamwork and an environment more hostile to cooperative endeavors between business and government to improve the nation's competitive advantage. Similarly, drawing on the results of a comparative study of industry and government in nine countries including the United States and Japan, Ezra Vogel concludes that corporations in societies such as the United States that "are dominated by individualism confront special problems of governability. Private enterprises in a free-wheeling environment devote much of their time and energy to promoting or preventing mergers and takeovers, thereby slighting issues that are fundamental to the long-term health of corporations." In his comparative studies of industry and politics in the United States and Japan, William Ouchi reaches much the same assessment, observing that an integrated social fabric is integral to the success of Japanese corporations and the nation's industrial growth and that new forms of social integration will be essential in the United States if it is to successfully compete.[15]

Education can play a critical role in rebuilding that social fabric. Studies of the voluntary activities and charitable contributions of individuals generally indicate that education is one of the best predictors of the amount of time and the proportion of personal income contributed to nonprofit causes, a far better predictor than an individual's occupation or income. Those with a college education, according to a national survey of a representative sample of more than 1100 adults in 1985, give at a nearly 50% higher rate than do those with a high-school education. While people at all educational levels give to religious organizations at about the same rate, the college educated give two to three times more than do others to nonreligious organizations ranging from human services to art. Education has a similar impact, according to other studies, on the voluntary giving of *time* to nonreligious charitable organizations. A nationwide study of more than 800 middle-level plant and production managers in 1981, for example, reveals that their educational background is among the best predictors of whether they participated actively in area civic, cultural, professional, and other voluntary organizations.[16]

The value of a liberal education in generating greater civic-mindedness is arguably unique, though there is little direct evidence to bolster the point at present. This study's finding that liberally educated managers are more active in the community than those with business degrees is certainly suggestive of the confirming evidence that could be expected from more comprehensive studies of the linkage between liberal education and social engagement.

If the linkage is more extensively confirmed, as should be expected, it would indicate that liberally-educated managers constitute a more active and responsible citizenry. It would also confirm John Gardner's more general point that liberal education can be a critical foundation of national leadership, whether in public or private life. "Today's leaders must have a grasp of economic realities and some comprehension of the basic framework within which scientific and technological change takes place," writes the former Cabinet Secretary and founder of Common Cause. He goes on to say that

> whether they are mayors, corporate leaders, or heads of state, they cannot limit their view to the system over which they preside. Mayors must understand the levels of government above them and the other governments in the metropolitan area. Corporate executives must understand the relationship between government and the private sector, and must comprehend the national and world economy.

The best avenue of preparation for young leaders who will be moving into both the public and private sectors, Gardner concludes, is a liberal education.[17]

IV. College Education and Corporate Employment

The evidence presented here confirms an originating hypothesis that the degree area of a college education can have lasting effects on white-collar company careers. In thinking about and analyzing the impact of higher education on managerial careers, it is no longer sufficient to know that an individual has completed a college education. The quality and reputation of the institution must be taken into account, as should the academic performance of the student. And so too should the field of study.

The importance of earning a college degree for entry into business is reconfirmed by the educational profile of the 505 surveyed managers. Nearly 9 out of 10 had graduated from college, signifying again that without a college credential one's prospects for advancement in the corporate hierarchy are very limited.

The quality of the college is also important, according to indirect evidence produced in the present study. When the 535 surveyed companies were asked to evaluate the importance of a number of factors in a college graduate's record, the quality of the undergraduate institution was viewed as an important hiring criterion by four out of five corporations. As a result, companies tend to concentrate their recruitment efforts at a limited number of relatively high-quality institutions, a common practice at the major companies studied in more detail here. The high-technology company, for instance, conducted campus recruiting visits at only 34 colleges and universities during the spring of 1988, and all were well-known, selective institutions. Similarly, college recruitment by the health-products corporation was concentrated at 33 institutions during the 1986–1987 recruitment cycle, and these too were well-established institutions. The health-products company hired 203 new college graduates from 104 colleges and universities, but half of the new employees came from the 33 most select institutions. Put differently, for college students interested in working for either the high-technology or health-products company, enrollment at one of a handful of select institution provided a pronounced advantage at the time of recruitment.

The graduate's academic record has also been found to make a difference, corroborating other research finding summarized earlier. Virtually all—96%—of the surveyed corporations stressed a "strong academic record on campus" in the hiring of a new graduate. This factor was viewed as important by more companies than any of the other nine factors considered. The recruitment practices of the companies examined in more detail confirm the importance of academic performance. In recruiting liberal-arts graduates, the consumer-products company required an undergraduate grade-point average of at least 3.0 and preferably 3.5. The high-technology company and the industrial-products corporation considered a grade-point average of at least 3.0 in the core field of study to be essential. Similarly, the diversified financial company stressed a grade-point average of at least 3.5 in the candidates it sought.

A college education, the reputation of the graduating institution, and the graduate's academic record are thus all found to make a significant difference, and it was hypothesized that the field of the college degree should also make a difference for those who enter the private sector. This expectation has been repeatedly confirmed in the present study, though not always in expected ways.

We have found little difference in the vertical distribution of managers as a function of their general field of college study. Liberal-arts, business, and engineering graduates fare about equally well. The aggregate pattern, however, masks significant variation from company to company. In some companies, such as AT&T, liberal-arts graduates are found to have accelerating prospects for further advancement as their career develops. In others, such as the industrial-products company, few liberal-arts graduates are hired, and a dominant engineering culture impedes the advancement of those who are employed. In still other companies, such as the consumer-products corporation, MBA graduates with liberal-arts undergraduate degrees displayed particularly strong staying power: all of the product managers who had been hired by the company 5 or 10 years earlier and were still with the company in 1987 held both an MBA degree and a liberal-arts degree.

Yet overall vertical differentiation among college-degree holders is not prevalent. Liberal-arts, business, and engineering graduates are about equally likely to "get ahead" in business at large. Horizontal differentiation, however, is considerable. The field of undergraduate study has a major bearing on the kind of company a graduate is likely to enter and the kind of work performed in the company. Liberal-arts graduates are found to be more prone than other graduates to work for service companies, to acquire responsibilities for consumer rather than industrial goods and services, and to become involved in marketing and sales. Engineering graduates, by contrast, tend to acquire managerial responsibilities for industrial rather than consumer goods and services, and business graduates are far more likely to work on the financial and accounting side of a company.

The field of undergraduate study has also been found to affect the likelihood of a manager's involvement in external affairs. Compared to business graduates, liberal-arts graduates are serving significantly more often as company representatives to the local community and more often as volunteers in nonprofit organizations or advisers to government. The field of the college degree thus also makes a difference in the experiences of managers in representing a company to its external world.

The understanding of white-collar-career paths, then, requires information about more than the level of college completed. To forecast and analyze such paths more fully, it is essential to know the individual's academic performance in college, the selectivity and reputation of the college, and the general field of undergraduate study. While this has been demonstrated here for careers in business management, the proposition probably stands as well for other professional careers, including those in law, health, architecture, and teaching.[18]

It should be noted, however, that majoring in the liberal arts is not necessarily a superior way to acquire a liberal education or to prepare for a career in corporate management. The most generic elements of a liberal-arts program, such as learning how to learn and to lead, are often incorporated into undergraduate business and engineering programs. Many of these programs stress liberal learning as a central part of their curricula. Moreover, some liberal-arts courses are so narrowly conceived that they qualify as part of a liberal-arts curriculum in name only. If we turn to an outcome measure, such as ascent to the higher levels of corporate management, we have also found that liberal-arts graduates on average fare no better than do business and engineering graduates. Liberal-arts graduates gravitate toward companies and functional areas within companies that are somewhat different from those of business and engineering graduates. Yet overall it cannot be said that a liberal-arts degree is necessarily a preferred way to prepare for a career in company management.

V. The Dynamics of Corporate Change

A stress on one undergraduate field or another within a company, we have found, is often the product of prevailing educational cultures. The fostering and perpetuation of these cultures can be traced in part to the outlook of the company's top management. In the high-technology company we studied, for example, most college recruitment occurred in the science and engineering fields. Yet some exposure to the humanities was valued in the college graduates recruited by the company, and this emphasis could be traced back to the company's founder. The founder had expected his managers to be effective communicators and innovators, and he believed that humanistic studies were important for both. When the founder retired after many years as chief executive, he was succeeded by managers who shared a similar vision, institutionalizing a culture that had been individually created.

More generally, this study reveals that one of the best predictors of a company's record in hiring liberal-arts graduates is the stance of the chief executive. Firms headed by CEOs encouraging recruitment of liberal-arts graduates are twice as likely to actively recruit them, half again more likely to have recruited an above-average number of liberal-arts graduates in the immediate past, and twice as prone to forecast an increase in their hiring in the future. The attitude of the chief executive also has a critical bearing on how other senior managers look at the issue. If a CEO has been advocating the hiring of liberal-arts graduates, the likelihood that his or her senior managers have been doing the same is increased by a factor of 3 to 10. The more extensive the top management's commitment to recruiting liberal-arts graduates, the more aggressive is the company in actually doing so.

These findings are consonant with a growing research literature demonstrating that top-executive actions often make a crucial difference in the policies of large companies, whether employment, social outreach, or even financial performance. This research literature runs counter to some traditional conceptions of the large corporation, which stress the overwhelming importance of market and organizational structures in determining company policies. In the context of market constraints and bureaucratic limitations, it is sometimes suggested, limited opportunities remain for the exercise of individual preference. It matters little who the top incumbents are, since their decisions will be largely shaped by the economic context and organizational structure of the company.

Studies of corporate financial performance, however, indicate that the identity of the incumbent CEO can often make a major difference in financial affairs. One analysis of turnover in the top management of 167 major corporations during a 20-year period found that a company's profitability could at least in small part be attributed to turnover in the chief-executive suite. A subsequent analysis of 193 companies over a similar period found that executive succession explained a substantially larger portion of the variation in financial performance, ranking ahead of many market and organizational factors. Still another indirect confirmation of the importance of executive identity comes form a study of stock prices of companies following the sudden death of a chief executive: the market generally reacts negatively to a CEO's death announcement, with stock prices sharply declining, implying that investors fear a period of lessened financial returns.[19]

Corporate leadership has also been found to have a major bearing on such organizational questions as whether a company adopts a multidivisional form or disperses its operations geographically. A study of 147 large manufacturing firms, for instance, reveals that owner-dominated companies are, in comparison with management-controlled corporations, less likely either to utilize a multidivisional structure or to locate its plants and offices widely. Explanation for the difference probably lies in the preference of owning families to maintain tight control over their operations. Whatever the interpretation, the fact remains that the identity of top management makes a significant difference in these areas of corporate decision making.[20]

Similarly, top executives are known to have a distinctive major impact on corporate outreach to the social and political environments. Thus many corporate political-action committees (PACs) concentrate their resources on congressional incumbents, but some give virtually all of their money to conservative challengers. An explanation for the latter can often be traced back to the vigorous political preferences of the company's top executive, regardless of the corporation's organization or market interests. Similarly, studies of corporate giving reveal that the chief executive's personal interest has a major bearing on whether a company gives generously or miserly, and it even affects the specific targets of company giving. Corporations whose chief executive had a special concern for culture and the arts were, according to one study, more than twice as likely to increase their gift budget for this area during one 2-year period.[21]

Concerted action by the chief executive and other senior managers, then, can be decisive in many areas of company activity. Once committed to a course of action, they possess the resources for overcoming organizational inertia. This has been seen in the case of the consumer-products company studied here: forceful instructions by top management to the company's recruiting staff led to an altering of the firm's hiring practices despite the opposition of many front-line supervisors. Individual change in corporate practices in the hiring and promotion of college graduates, then, can be initiated by senior managers. Indeed, the lower-level resistance to the hiring of broadly educated college graduates can often be overcome only by the direct intervention of senior managers. The willingness of top executives to take the initiative, however, depends in part on the existence of a national movement and agenda to do so.

VI. The Dynamics of National Change

The call for an integration and more effective use of liberal-arts and business subjects has been on the corporate agenda for educational change for several decades. The 1959 study of business education sponsored by the Ford Foundation had urged such a joining: "The issue, as we see it, is not simply a choice between liberal education and business education. The issue is to combine both." The same recommendation was made in the companion 1959 assessment of business education sponsored by the Carnegie Corporation: "Undergraduate preparation for business necessarily rests on a number of subjects in the liberal arts area. The work in these subjects should be pursued beyond the first-year introductory level. The student should be given every opportunity to transfer general knowledge to applications in the business area."

A follow-up study in 1964 by the Committee for Economic Development, an organization of top business leaders and educators, again confirmed the need for both emphases. One "cannot be considered a liberally educated person in our society without a knowledge of the nature and role of business institutions. Nor is there any necessary conflict between a liberal and a professional education; on the contrary, each should be shaped to enrich and strengthen the other."[22]

Major changes have been achieved since these reports were issued, as the 1988 report by the American Assembly of Collegiate Schools of Business makes clear in its assessment of the state of business education. Undergraduate business students, as we have seen, now carry a majority of their course credits in the arts and sciences. Many companies would urge still further strengthening of the exposure of business and engineering students to the liberal arts, but above all they stress the need for liberal-arts students to acquire exposure to a business curriculum and business experience. Presently, for most liberal-arts graduates, the undergraduate exposure is practically nonexistent: only 1% of their course credits, on average, are in business subjects, and few participate in business internships or other opportunities for practical experience in business.[23]

If there is a singular message for prospective and current college students and their parents, it is to seek a suitable combination of the liberal arts and the useful arts when anticipating a career in the private sector. Majoring in the liberal arts can be an entirely acceptable way, though certainly not the only preferable way, to obtain an appropriate grounding. Yet the trends in college enrollments in the late 1970s and early 1980s suggest that the latter point had been largely lost on a generation of students and parents anxious about the future. That a liberal arts degree can be a suitable path to a managerial career was a message that corporate employers had not effectively communicated to the campus. Questions raised by the Carnegie Corporation report in 1959 remain salient today:

> Will the demand from business firms for liberal arts graduates be strong enough to induce relatively more students interested in business careers to study liberal arts rather than business administration in colleges? In other words, are increasing numbers of students, parents, and employers convinced that liberal arts education is of practical value in opening up jobs leading toward management opportunities?[24]

Articulation of that demand can only come from the private sector. While individual corporations and their managers have expressed such preferences from time to time, effective communication to the more than 10 million students presently enrolled in college and their parents will depend on collective endeavor. If the demand is to be heard, companies and general business associations must repeatedly express it in both statements of hiring philosophy and direct action in recruitment.

American business has no single, formal voice with which to represent and express such concerns. In contrast to Japan and other industrialized nations, no organization can purport to speak for business. Yet there is a select informal network of senior managers from large corporations who can and often do play a critical role in engineering corporate change in matters of general business interest, including educational policy. These managers, whom I have elsewhere termed a corporate "inner circle," hold the top positions of the nation's several thousand largest corporations; they serve on the board of directors of several companies in addition to their own; they play leading roles in the nation's major business associations, such as the Business Roundtable; and they typically serve on the governing boards of several nonprofit organizations, frequently including a college or university. By virtue of their active involvement in the affairs of other corporations and institutions in addition to their own company, these senior managers acquire a more general appreciation for the issues of general concern to business. Among those issues are the quality and preparation of college graduates entering the corporate sector and the internal development of future leadership within the company.[25]

Not only is this inner circle of senior managers more aware of the shared concerns of the nation's major private employers, but it can also be instrumental in bringing those issues to broader attention. Actions may be taken both within and outside the business community. Within the business community, these senior managers can approach their counterparts in other firms to encourage an active expression of support for liberal education. CEO-to-CEO persuasion is as strong a lever for corporate change as any, and there is evidence from several areas of corporate outreach that it works.[26]

Outside the business community, these senior managers can also be particularly effective proponents of change. Because they are known to be broadly informed about corporate affairs, they are more often sought out by journalists, giving them more of a media forum than is available to most company executives. For similar reasons, they are also more often recruited to serve in policy associations concerned with education, such as the Committee for Economic Development, and on the board of trustees of colleges and universities. They are thus well positioned not only to influence other business executives on questions of educational policy, but also to directly shape the policies of colleges and universities. Available evidence suggests that they are particularly effective compared to other business managers in such settings.[27]

These well-positioned and highly informed senior managers can thus serve as a driving force in reconstituting both corporate and campus cultures vis-à-vis the importance of liberal learning for company management. Also critically important are individuals within the firm or college who are prepared to initiate that change as well. When supported by top management, these change-oriented individuals can undertake and guide the detailed planning and follow-up steps that are essential if confidence in the broader mission of liberal education is to be restored.[28]

While the change will be largely driven by those in higher education and the private sector, public agencies can play a critical catalytic role. A call to such action came from the Commission of

National Challenges in Higher Education, a panel of 33 college and university presidents and other leaders in higher education convened by the American Council on Education. In its 1988 *Memorandum to the 41st President of the United States,* the commission urged that higher education help meet the national challenges of revitalizing the economy and improving the quality of life, and to that end a renewed partnership with the federal government would be essential. Among the partnership's critical ingredients, urged the commission, would be action by the new national administration to strengthen international studies, improve foreign-language instruction, and, more generally, "reaffirm the importance of the liberal arts tradition in our society."[29] If those in business, education, and government take joint action to reaffirm the importance of the nation's liberal-arts tradition, students, educators, and corporate recruiters should hear the message.

Notes

1. Hambrick and Mason (1984); Kanter (1984).
2. Kanter (1984).
3. Useem (1982, 1984, 1987); Useem and Karabel (1986); Galaskiewicz (1985); Wokutch and Spencer (1987).
4. Levin and Rumberger (1986); Levin and Rumberger (1987), p. 350.
5. Cohen and Zysman (1987), p. 228.
6. The managers were asked: "Are you involved in any way with international operations or activities your company may have?"
7. Kobrin (1984), pp. 50, 55.
8. Hirsch (1987), p. 17
9. Hirsch (1987), pp. 17–18.
10. Hirsch (1987), p. 128.
11. Rosenbaum (1984), p. 172.
12. Feldman and Newcomb (1969); Bowen (1977); DiMaggio and Useem (1978).
13. Bellah *et al.* (1985).
14. de Tocqueville (1969), p. 506 (originally published in 1835).
15. Reich (1983), p. 166; Vogel (1987), pp. 306–308; Ouchi (1981, 1984).
16. Independent Sector (1986), p. 5; Shepard and Hougland (1984); Hougland and Shepard (1985).
17. Gardner (1987), p. 12.

18. Evidence of the impact of collegiate academic performance and the quality of the college attended on later career achievements for a variety of professions is summarized in Klitgaard (1985).
19. Leiberson and O'Connor (1972); Weiner and Mahoney (1981); Worrell *et al.* (1986).
20. Palmer *et al.* (1987).
21. Useem and Kutner (1986).
22. Gordon and Howell (1959), p. 126; Pierson *et al.* (1959), p. 163; Committee for Economic Development (1964), p. 26.
23. Porter and McKibbin (1988).
24. Pierson *et al.* (1959), p. 663.
25. Useem (1984).
26. Useem and Kutner (1986); Useem (1988).
27. Useem (1981).
28. Kanter (1983).
29. Commission on National Challenges in Higher Education (1988), pp. 6, 9.

Bibliography

American Association of Colleges of Nursing (1986). *Essentials of Colleges and University Education for Professional Nursing.* Washington, D.C.: American Association of Colleges of Nursing.

American Association of Community and Junior Colleges (1988). *Building Communities: A Vision for a New Century.* Alexandria, Va.: American Association of Community and Junior Colleges.

Association of American Colleges (1985). *Integrity in the Curriculum: A Report to the Academic Community.* Washington, D.C.: Association of American Colleges.

Astin, Alexander W., Green, Kenneth C., and Korn, William S. (1987). *The American Freshman: Twenty Year Trends.* Los Angeles: Higher Education Research Institute, University of California, Los Angeles.

Astin, Alexander W., Green, Kenneth C., Korn, William S., and Schalit, Marilynn (1987). *The American Freshman: National Norms for Fall 1986.* Los Angeles: Higher Education Research Institute, University of California, Los Angeles. (a)

Astin, Alexander W., Green, Kenneth C., Korn, William S., and Schalit, Marilynn (1987). *The American Freshman: National Norms for Fall 1987.* Los Angeles: Higher Education Research Institute, University of California, Los Angeles. (b)

Austin, Gilbert R., and Garber, Herbert (eds.) (1982). *The Rise and Fall of National Test Scores.* New York: Academic Press.

Bellah, Robert N., Madsen, Richard, Sullivan, William M., Swidler, Ann, and Tipton, Steven M. (1985). *Habits of the Heart: Individualism and Commitment in American Life.* Berkeley, Ca.: University of California Press.

Bennett, William J. (1984). *To Reclaim a Legacy: A Report on the Humanities in Higher Education.* Washington, D.C.: National Endowment for the Humanities.

Bennett, William J. (1985). "Go ahead, major in the liberal arts." *Washington Post,* January 13:B7.

Berle, Adolf, Jr., and Means, Gardiner C. (1967). *The Modern Corporation and Private Property.* (Reprint ed.). New York: Harcourt, Brace and World.

177

Bettman, Ralph B. (1987). "Technical managers mismanaged: Turnover or turnaround?" *Personnel Journal* 66 (April):65–70.

Bisconti, Ann S. (1978). *Who Will Succeed? College Graduates as Business Executives.* Bethlehem, Pa.: College Placement Council Foundation.

Bisconti, Ann S., and Kessler, J. G. (1980). *College and Other Stepping Stones: A Study of the Learning Experiences That Contribute to Effective Performance in Early and Long-Run Jobs.* Bethlehem, Pa.: College Placement Council Foundation.

Bloom, Allan (1987). *The Closing of the American Mind.* New York: Simon and Schuster.

Bonfield, Patricia (1980). *U.S. Business Leaders: A Study of Opinions and Characteristics.* New York: Conference Board.

Bowen, Howard R. (1977). *Investment in Learning: The Individual and Social Value of American Higher Education.* San Francisco: Jossey-Bass.

Bowles, Sandy Quadros (1987). "Liberal arts grads find few jobs in high tech firms." Special Newspaper Supplement from Beacon Communications Corporation, August 27.

Boyer, Ernest L. (1987). *College: The Undergraduate Experience in America.* New York: Harper and Row.

Burck, Charles G. (1976). "A group profile of the Fortune 500 executive." *Fortune,* May:173ff.

Burns, Stanley T. (1983). *From Student to Banker: Observations from the Chase Bank.* Washington, D.C.: Assoc. of American Colleges.

Business–Higher Education Forum (1985). *America's Business Schools: Priorities for Change.* Washington, D.C.: ACE.

Calvert, Robert, Jr. (1969). *Career Patterns of Liberal Arts Graduates.* Cranston, R.I.: Carroll Press Publishers.

Carnegie Foundation for the Advancement of Teaching (1987). "Academe and the boom in business studies." *Change* 19 (September/October):37–42.

Carnegie Task Force on Teaching as a Profession (1986). *A Nation Prepared: Teachers for the 21st century.* New York: Carnegie Forum on Education and the Economy.

Center for Educational Statistics (1986). "Curricular Content of Bachelor's Degrees." Washington, D.C.: Center for Educational Statistics, U.S. Department of Education.

Chandler, Alfred D. (1977). *The Visible Hand: The Managerial Revolution in America.* Cambridge, Mass.: Harvard University Press.

Cheit, Earl F. (1975). *The Useful Arts and the Liberal Tradition.* New York: McGraw-Hill.

Cheit, Earl F. (1985). "Business schools and their critics." *California Management Review* 27 (Spring):43–62.

Cheney, Lynne E. (1986). "Students of success: A liberal-arts training is increasingly valuable in the American corporation." *Newsweek,* September 1:7.

Cheney, Lynne E. (1987). *American Memory: A Report on the Humanities in the Nation's Public Schools.* Washington, D.C.: National Endowment for the Humanities.

Cohen, Stephen S., and Zysman, John (1987). *Manufacturing Matters: The Myth of the Post-Industrial Economy.* New York: Basic Books, Inc.

Collins, Randall (1971). "Functional and conflict theories of educational stratification." *American Sociological Review* 36:1002–1019.

Collins, Randall (1979). *The Credential Society: An Historical Sociology of Education and Stratification.* New York: Academic Press.

Commission on National Challenges in Higher Education (1988). *Memorandum to the 41st President of the United States.* Washington, D.C.: American Council on Education.

Committee for Economic Development (1964). *Educating Tomorrow's Managers: The Business Schools and the Business Community.* New York: Committee for Economic Development.

Cordisco, Jane H., and Walker, Janet L. (1983). "Business basics for liberal arts graduates." *Journal of Career Planning and Employment,* Spring:18–19.

Council of Independent Colleges (1986). *American Business Corporations and Liberal Arts Colleges.* Washington, D.C.: Council of Independent Colleges.

De Pasquale, John A., and Lange, Richard A. (1971). "Job-hopping and the MBA." *Harvard Business Review* 49 (November-December):4–11, 151–154.

de Tocqueville, Alexis (1969). *Democracy in America.* Garden City, N.Y.: Anchor Books.

DiMaggio, Paul, and Useem, Michael (1978). "Cultural democracy in a period of cultural expansion: The social composition of arts audiences in the United States." *Social Problems* 26 (December):179–197.

Directors and Boards (1987). "The making of a global manager." *Directors and Boards* 11 (Winter):6ff.

Donaldson, Gordon, and Lorsch, Jay W. (1983). *Decision Making at the Top: The Shaping of Strategic Direction.* New York: Basic Books.

Drucker, Peter F. (1988). "Leadership: More doing than dash." *Wall Street Journal*, January 5.

Educational Leadership Project (1988). *Liberal Education: A Concept for American High Schools*. New York: Educational Leadership Project.

Feldman, K. A., and Newcomb, T. M. (1969). *The Impact of College on Students*. San Francisco: Jossey-Bass.

Finn, Chester E., Jr., and Ravitch, Diane (1987). *What Do Our 17-Year Olds Know?* New York: Harper & Row.

Fiske, Edward B. (1986). "Liberal arts, long in decline, are reviving around nation." *New York Times*, November 9:1ff.

Fiske, Edward B. (1987). "M.I.T. widens engineering training." *New York Times*, June 1:1, 14. (a)

Fiske, Edward B. (1987). "Schools Criticized on the Humanities." *New York Times*, September 8:1, 8. (b)

Freeman, Richard B. (1971). *The Market for College-Trained Manpower: A Study in the Economics of Career Choice*. Cambridge, Mass.: Harvard University Press.

Galaskiewicz, Joseph (1985). *Social Organization of an Urban Grants Economy: A Study of Business Philanthropy and Nonprofit Organizations*. New York: Academic Press.

Gamson, Zelda, Black, Nancy B., Catlin, Jamie Beth, Hill, Patrick J., Mills, Michael R., Nichols, John, and Rogers, Terry Heitz (1984). *Liberating Education*. San Francisco: Jossey-Bass.

Gardner, John W. (1987). *Leadership Development*. Washington, D.C.: Independent Sector.

Garis, Jeff W., Hess, Richard H., and Marron, Deborah J. (1985). "Curriculum counts—for liberal arts students seeking business careers." *Journal of Career Planning and Employment* 45 (Winter):32–37.

Gordon, Robert Aaron, and Howell, James Edwin (1959). *Higher Education for Business*. New York: Columbia University Press.

Hambrick, D. C., and Mason, P. A. (1984). "Upper echelons: The organization as a reflection of its top managers." *Academy of Management Review* 9:193–206.

Haviland, Mark G., Weaver, Kenneth L., and Taylor, Shannon V. (1983). "Good grades for liberal arts internships." *Journal of Career Planning and Employment*, Winter:57–60.

Hayes, Robert H., and Abernathy, William J. (1980). "Managing our way to economic decline." *Harvard Business Review*, July-August:66–77.

Herman, Edward S. (1981). *Corporate Control, Corporate Power.* New York: Cambridge University Press.

Hildebrandt, H. H. (1985). *Learning From Top Women Executives— Their Perceptions on Business Communication, Careers, and Education.* Ann Arbor, Mich.: Graduate School of Business, University of Michigan.

Hirsch, Paul (1987). *Pack Your Own Parachute: How to Survive Mergers, Takeovers, and Other Corporate Disasters.* Reading, Mass.: Addison-Wesley.

Holmes Group (1986). *Tomorrow's Teachers: A Report of the Holmes Group.* East Lansing, Mich.: The Holmes Group.

Hougland, James G., Jr., and Shepard, Jon M. (1985). "Voluntarism and the manager: The impacts of structural pressure and personal interest on community participation." *Journal of Voluntary Action Research* 14:65–78.

Howard, Ann (1984). *College Experience and Managerial Performance: Report to Management.* New York: American Telephone and Telegraph.

Howard, Ann (1986). "College experience and managerial performance." *Journal of Applied Psychology* 71:530–552.

Howard, Ann, and Bray, Douglas W. (1988). *Managerial Careers in Transition: Advancing Age and Changing Times.* New York: Guilford Publications.

Independent Sector (1986). *The Charitable Behavior of Americans: A National Survey.* Washington, D.C.: The Independent Sector.

Johnston, Joseph S., Jr. (1986). "Educating managers for change." In *Educating Managers: Executive Effectiveness Through Liberal Learning.* Joseph S. Johnston, Jr., *et al.* (eds.). San Francisco: Jossey-Bass.

Johnston, Joseph S., Jr., Burns, Stanley T., Butler, David W., Hirsch, Marcie Schorr, Jones, Thomas B., Kantrow, Alan M., Mohrman, Kathryn, Smith, Roger B., and Useem, Michael (1986). *Educating Managers: Executive Effectiveness Through Liberal Learning.* San Francisco, Jossey-Bass.

Johnston, Joseph S., Jr., Shaman, Susan, and Zemsky, Robert (1988). *The Unfinished Design: The Humanities and Social Sciences in Undergraduate Engineering Education.* Washington, D.C.: Association of American Colleges.

Kanter, Rosabeth Moss (1977). *Men and Women of the Corporation.* New York: Basic Books.

Kanter, Rosabeth Moss (1983). *The Change Masters: Innovation for*

Productivity in the American Corporation. New York: Simon and Schuster.

Kanter, Rosabeth Moss (1984). *The Roots of Corporate Progressivism: How and Why Corporations Respond to Changing Societal Needs and Expectations.* New York: Russell Sage Foundation.

Katchadourian, Herant A., and Boli, John (1985). *Careerism and Intellectualism Among College Students: Patterns of Academic and Career Choice in the Undergraduate Years.* San Francisco: Jossey-Bass.

Keim, Gerry (1985). "Corporate grassroots programs in the 1980s." *California Management Review* 28 (Fall):110–123.

Keller, Thomas (1987). "The trade crisis begins at home." *U.S. News and World Report,* August 31.

Kephart, William, *et al.* (1963). *Liberal Education and Business.* New York: Columbia University Press.

Klitgaard, Robert (1985). *Choosing Elites.* New York: Basic Books.

Kobrin, Stephen J. (1984). *International Expertise in American Business.* New York: Institute of International Education.

Koppett, Leonard (1987). "At Princeton, they call it an education." *New York Times,* August 15:27.

Kotter, John P. (1982). *The General Managers.* New York: Free Press.

Kotter, John P. (1988). *The Leadership Factor.* New York: Free Press.

Krukowski, Jan (1985). "What do students want? Status." *Change,* May/June:21–28.

Kutshcher, Ronald E. (1988). "Overview and implications of the projections to 2000." In *Projections 2000.* Washington, D.C.: U.S. Bureau of Labor Statistics.

Levin, Henry M., and Rumberger, Russell W. (1986). "Education and training needs for using computers in small businesses." *Educational Evaluation and Policy Analysis* 8 (Winter):423–434.

Levin, Henry M., and Rumberger, Russell W. (1987). "Educational requirements for new technologies: Visions, possibilities, and current realities." *Educational Policy* 1:333–354.

Levine, David O. (1986). *The American College and the Culture of Aspiration, 1915–1940.* Ithaca: Cornell University Press.

Liberal Arts Placement Office, University of Texas (n.d.). *Liberal Arts Job Search: A Guide for Successful Self-Placement in the Job Market.* Austin, Texas: University of Texas.

Lieberson, Stanley, and O'Connor, James F. (1972). "Leadership and organizational performance: A study of large corporations." *American Sociological Review* 37:117–130.

Lindquist, Victor R. (1983). "The Northwestern Endicott Report: Trends in the Employment of College and University Graduates in Business and Industry, 38th Annual Report." Evanston, Ill.: Placement Center, Northwestern University.

Louis, Meryl (1985). "The First Years Out Study: A Report Card on MBA Programs." Boston: Boston University, Center for Applied Social Science, unpublished manuscript.

Lusterman, Seymour (1981). *Managerial Competence: The Public Affairs Aspect.* New York: Conference Board.

McComas, Maggie (1986). "Atop the Fortune 500: A survey of the C.E.O.'s." *Fortune,* April 28:26–31.

McGrath, Phyllis S. (1980). *Developing Employee Political Awareness.* New York: Conference Board.

Massachusetts Institute of Technology School of Engineering (1986). "Progress Report of the Commission on Engineering Undergraduate Education." Cambridge, Mass.: M.I.T. School of Engineering.

Medoff, James L., and Abraham, Katharine G. (1981). "Are those paid more really more productive? The case of experience." *Journal of Human Resources* 26 (Spring):187–216.

Merenda, Michael J. (1981). "The process of corporate social involvement: Five case studies." In *Research in Corporate Social Performance and Policy,* Lee E. Preston (ed.). Greenwich, Conn.: JAI Press.

Miles, Raymond E. (1985). "The future of business education." *California Management Review,* Spring:63–73.

Mills, Robert H. (1987). *Managing the Corporate and Social Environment: A Grounded Theory.* Englewood Cliffs, N.J.: Prentice-Hall.

Mintzberg, Henry (1975). "The manager's job: Folklore and fact." *Harvard Business Review,* July-August:49–61.

Mohrman, Kathryn, and Hirsch, Marcie Schorr (1986). "Preparing liberal arts students for business." In *Educating Managers: Executive Effectiveness Through Liberal Learning,* Joseph S. Johnston, Jr., *et al.* (eds.). San Francisco: Jossey-Bass.

National Assessment of Educational Progress (1978). *Three National Assessments of Science: Changes in Achievement, 1969–77.* Washington, D.C.: National Center for Educational Statistics.

National Assessment of Educational Progress (1983). *The Third National Mathematics Assessment: Results, Trends and Issues.* Denver: National Assessment of Educational Progress.

National Governors' Association (1987). *Educating Americans for Tomorrow's World: State Initiatives in International Education.* Washington, D.C.: National Governors' Association.

National Institute of Education, Study Group on the Conditions of Excellence in American Higher Education (1984). *Involvement in*

Learning: Realizing the Potential of American Higher Education.
Washington, D.C.: National Institute of Education.

Newcomer, Mabel (1955). *The Big Business Executive: The Factors That Made Him, 1900–1950*. New York: Columbia University Press.

O'Neill, Dave M., and Sepielli, Peter (1985). *Education in the United States: 1940–1983*. Washington, D.C.: U.S. Bureau of the Census.

Ouchi, William (1981). *Theory Z*. Reading, Mass.: Addison-Wesley.

Ouchi, William (1984). *The M-Form Society: How American Teamwork Can Recapture the Competitive Edge*. Reading, Mass.: Addison-Wesley.

Palmer, Donald, Friedland, Roger, Jennings, P. Devereaux, and Powers, Melanie E. (1987). "The economics and politics of structure: The multidivisional form and the large corporation." *Administrative Science Quarterly* 32:25–48.

Pfeffer, Jeffrey (1977). "Toward an examination of stratification in organizations." *Administrative Science Quarterly* 22:553–567.

Pierson, Frank C., *et al.* (1959). *The Education of American Businessmen: A Study of University-College Programs in Business Administration*. New York: McGraw-Hill.

Porter, Lyman W., and McKibbin, Lawrence E. (1988). *Management Education and Development: Drift or Thrust into the 21st Century*. New York: McGraw-Hill.

Powell, Reed M. (1969). *Race, Religion, and the Promotion of the American Executive*. Columbus, Ohio: Ohio State University Press.

Professional Preparation Network (1988). *Strengthening the Ties That Bind: Integrating Undergraduate Liberal and Professional Study*. Ann Arbor, Mich.: School of Education, University of Michigan.

Queens College (1987). "The Preferred College Graduate as Seen by the New York Business Community." New York: Queens College, Office of the President.

Raisen, Senta A., and Jones, Lyle V. (eds.) (1985). *Indicators of Precollege Education in Science and Mathematics*. Washington, D.C.: National Academy Press.

Reich, Robert B. (1983). *The Next American Frontier*. New York: Penguin Books.

Rhodes, Frank H. T. (1985). "Reforming higher education will take more than just tinkering with curricula." *Chronicle of Higher Education* 30, No. 12:80.

Rice, R. Eugene (1983). *Strategies for Relating Career Preparation and Liberal Learning*. Saint Paul, Minn.: Northwest Area Foundation.

Riesman, David (1950). *The Lonely Crowd: A Study of the Changing American Character.* New Haven, Conn.: Yale University Press.

Riesman, David (1984). "Afterword." In *Liberating Education,* Zelda Gamson *et al.* San Francisco: Jossey-Bass.

Rosenbaum, James E. (1984). *Career Mobility in a Corporate Hierarchy.* New York: Academic Press.

Rumberger, Russell W. (1981). *Overeducation in the U.S. Labor Market.* New York: Praeger Publishers.

Rumberger, Russell W. (1984). "The job market for college graduates, 1960–90." *Journal of Higher Education* 55 (July/August):433–454.

Rush, James C., and Evers, Frederick T. (1986). *Making the Match: Canada's University Graduates and Corporate Employers.* Montreal: Corporate-Higher Education Forum.

Ryan, Mike H., Swanson, Carl L., and Buchholz, Rogene A. (1987). *Corprate Strategy, Public Policy & The Fortune 500: How America's Major Corporations Influence Government.* New York: Basil Blackwell.

Schaeffer, Ruth G. (1982). *Top Management Staffing Challenges: CEOs Describe Their Needs.* New York: Conference Board.

Sharp, Laure M. (1970). *Education and Employment: The Early Careers of College Graduates.* Baltimore: The Johns Hopkins Press.

Sharp, Laure M., and Weidman, John C. (1986). *Early Career Patterns of Undergraduate Majors in the Humanities.* Pittsburgh: Department of Administrative and Policy Studies, University of Pittsburgh.

Shepard, Jon M., and Hougland, James G., Jr. (1984). "Organization size, managerial mobility, and corporate policy: A study of community participation of managers." In *The Impact of the Modern Corporation,* B. Beck, H. Goldschmid, I. Millstein, and F. Scherer (eds.). New York: Columbia University Press.

Shingleton, J. D., and Scheetz, L. P. (1984). *Recruiting Trends 1984–85.* East Lansing: Placement Services, Michigan State University.

Silk, Leonard, and Vogel, David (1976). *Ethics and Profits: The Crisis of Confidence in American Business.* New York: Simon and Schuster.

Smith, Roger B. (1986). "The liberal arts and the arts of management." In *Educating Managers: Executive Effectiveness Through Liberal Learning,* Joseph S. Johnston, Jr., *et al.* (eds.). San Francisco: Jossey-Bass.

Solmon, L. C. (1981). "New findings on the links between college education and work." *Higher Education* 10: 615–648.

Taussig, F. W., and Joslyn, C. S. (1932). *American Business Leaders.* New York: Macmillan.

Unger, D. (1985). "Educating tomorrow's managers: Liberal arts or business school?" *Professional Training,* Winter:1, 12.

U.S. Bureau of the Census (1987). *Money Income of Households, Families, and Persons in the United States: 1985,* Current Population Reports, Series P-60, n. 156. Washington, D.C.: U.S. Government Printing Office.

U.S. Department of Education (1986). "Curricular Content of Bachelor's Degrees." Washington, D.C.: Office of Educational Research and Improvement, U.S. Department of Education.

U.S. Department of Education (1987). *Digest of Educational Statistics, 1987.* Washington, D.C.: Center for Educational Statistics, U.S. Department of Education. (a)

U.S. Department of Education (1987). Tables on bachelor's degrees conferred in higher education, 1985–86. Washington, D.C.: Center for Educational Statistics, U.S. Department of Education. (b)

University of Virginia (1986). *Life After Liberal Arts.* Charlottesville, Va.: University of Virginia.

Useem, Elizabeth L. (1986), *Low Tech Education in a High Tech World: Corporations and Classrooms in the New Information Society.* New York: Free Press and American Association for the Advancement of Science.

Useem, Michael (1981). "Business segments and corporate relations with American universities." *Social Problems* 29 (December): 129–141.

Useem, Michael (1982). "Classwide rationality in the politics of managers and directors of large corporations in the United States and Great Britain." *Administrative Science Quarterly* 27:199–226.

Useem, Michael (1984). *The Inner Circle: Large Corporations and the Rise of Business Political Activity in the U.S. and U.K.* New York: Oxford University Press.

Useem, Michael (1985). "The rise of the political manager." *Sloan Management Review.* 27 (Fall):15–26.

Useem, Michael (1986). "What the research shows." In *Educating Managers: Executive Effectiveness Through Liberal Learning,* Joseph S. Johnston, Jr., *et al.* (eds.). San Francisco: Jossey-Bass.

Useem, Michael (1987). "Managerial Education and the Public Role of the Corporation." New York: Corporate Council on the Liberal Arts.

Useem, Michael (1988). "Market and institutional factors in corporate contributions." *California Management Review* 30 (Winter): 77–88.

Useem, Michael, and Karabel, Jerome (1986). "Pathways to top corporate management." *American Sociological Review* 51 (April): 184–200.

Useem, Michael, and Kutner, Stephen I. (1986). "Corporate contributions to culture and the arts: The organization of giving, and the influence of the chief executive officer and other firms on company contributions in Massachusetts." In *Nonprofit Organizations in the Production and Distribution of Culture*, Paul DiMaggio (ed.). New York: Oxford University Press.

Vogel, Ezra (1987). "Conclusion." In *Ideology and National Competitiveness: An Analysis of Nine Countries*, George C. Lodge and Ezra F. Vogel (eds.). Boston: Harvard Business School Press.

Wade, Ormand J. (1984). "Remarks," Conference on the Humanities and Careers in Business. Evanston, Ill.: Northwestern University.

Wall Street Journal (1987). "Life among the business elite." March 20.

Warren, R. G. (1983). *New Links Between General Education and Business Careers*. Washington, D.C.: Association of American Colleges.

Weiner, N., and Mahoney, T. A. (1981). "A model of corporate performance as a function of environmental, organizational, and leadership influences." *Academy of Management Journal* 24:453–470.

Whyte, William H. (1956). *The Organization Man*. New York: Simon and Schuster.

Willis, Rod (1987). "What's happening to America's middle managers?" *Management Review* 76 (January):24–33.

Winter, David G., McClelland, David C., and Stewart, Abigail J. (1981). *A New Case for the Liberal Arts: Assessing Institutional Goals and Student Development*. San Francisco: Jossey-Bass.

Wise, David A. (1975). "Academic achievement and job performance." *American Economic Review* 65, No. 3:350–366. (a)

Wise, David A. (1975). "Personal attributes, job performance and probability of promotion." *Econometrica* 43:913–931. (b)

Wokutch, Richard F., and Spencer, Barbara A. (1987). "Corporate saints and sinners: Philanthropy, crime, and organizational performance." *California Management Review* 29:62–77.

Worrel, Dan L., Davidson III, Wallace N., Chandy, P. R., and Garrison, Sharon L. (1986). "Management turnover through deaths of key executives: Effects on investor wealth." *Academy of Management Journal* 29:674–694.

Zeithaml, Carl P., Keim, Gerald D., and Baysinger, Barry D. (1988).
    "Toward an integrated strategic management process: An empir-
    ical review of corporate political strategy." In *Research in Corpo-
    rate Social Performance and Policy*, Lee E. Preston (ed.). Green-
    wich, Conn.: JAI Press.

Appendix I. Company Survey Form

LIBERAL ARTS AND
THE CORPORATE WORKPLACE

SPONSORED BY THE CORPORATE COUNCIL ON THE LIBERAL ARTS
IN COLLABORATION WITH THE PRESIDENT'S COMMITTEE ON THE ARTS AND THE HUMANITIES

Conducted by

Opinion Research Corporation

DESCRIPTION OF THE QUESTIONNAIRE. The questionnaire seeks general information about your company and your own assessments of the experience of liberal arts graduates within your company. When specific information is unavailable, please provide your best estimate. If you are unable to answer a particular question, leave it blank.

COMPANY DIVISIONS. If your company maintains separate personnel records and procedures for its major divisions and subsidiaries, and you are unable to provide overall data, please provide information on the largest division or subsidiary for which it is available.

DEFINITION OF LIBERAL ARTS GRADUATE. For purposes of this study, a liberal arts graduate is defined as an individual whose highest degree is a four-year undergraduate degree in the humanities, social sciences, or natural sciences (but not in business or engineering). A liberal arts education and liberal arts background are defined in the same way.

CONFIDENTIALITY. The information you provide will be treated as confidential. No names of responding firms or individuals will be revealed. Questionnaires and return postcards are numbered to assist Opinion Research Corporation in follow up with non-participants and to enable ORC to send a summary of the research findings to participants and their Chief Executive Officers.

RETURNING COMPLETED QUESTIONNAIRE. Please return your completed questionnaire directly to Opinion Research Corporation by June 19th in the pre-paid return envelope provided. If you have questions regarding the survey, either before or after your participation, please feel free to call Mr. Kenneth Patrick, Jr., ORC Survey Manager, at (609) 924-5900.

189

Part I. GENERAL INFORMATION

1. How many years have you been with the company? (*Circle **one** number.*)

    1   Less than two years

    2   Between two and five years

    3   More than five years

2. How many years have you worked in your present position? (*Circle **one** number.*)

    1   Less than two years

    2   Between two and five years

    3   More than five years

3. Does your company have any of the following programs or policies? (*Circle **one** number at right for each statement, a-j.*)

		YES	NO
a.	On-campus recruitment of liberal arts graduates.	1	2
b.	Other active efforts to recruit liberal arts graduates.	1	2
c.	Training programs open to new employees with liberal arts degrees.	1	2
d.	Internship or cooperative education programs open to liberal arts students.	1	2
e.	Employee tuition and fees program that permits study in the liberal arts.	1	2
f.	Arrangement with a college or university to offer liberal arts courses or degrees to employees.	1	2
g.	Matching-gift program for employee contributions to education.	1	2
h.	Company contributions of money or equipment to higher education.	1	2
i.	Use of executive program in the liberal arts (e.g., Aspen Institute).	1	2
j.	Company-operated seminars and programs in the liberal arts.	1	2

4. During the past five years (that is, since 1981), which of the following individuals or groups in your company have formally or informally encouraged or discouraged the hiring of liberal arts graduates for entry-level positions? (*Circle **one** number for each row, a-h.*)

	ENCOURAGED THE HIRING	NEITHER ENCOURAGED NOR DISCOURAGED	DISCOURAGED THE HIRING	DON'T KNOW
a. Chief executive officer	1	2	3	4
b. Chief financial officer	1	2	3	4
c. Marketing executives	1	2	3	4
d. Sales executives	1	2	3	4
e. Manufacturing executives	1	2	3	4
f. Yourself	1	2	3	4
g. Other human resources executives	1	2	3	4
h. Other (Specify): _____	1	2	3	4

5. What is the educational background of each of the following executives in your company? (*Circle **as many** as apply for each person.*)

a. Undergraduate College Education

Chief executive officer
   Chief operating officer (or equivalent)
      Yourself

1	1	1	Did not attend college
2	2	2	Attended, no degree received
3	3	3	Liberal arts degree
4	4	4	Business degree
5	5	5	Engineering degree
6	6	6	Degree in another field

b. Graduate or Professional Education

Chief executive officer
   Chief operating officer (or equivalent)
      Yourself

1	1	1	Did not attend graduate or professional school
2	2	2	Attended, no degree received
3	3	3	M.B.A.
4	4	4	Masters in engineering
5	5	5	Masters in liberal arts field
6	6	6	Law degree
7	7	7	Ph.D.
8	8	8	Other

Part II. YOUR ASSESSMENTS

6. When you consider hiring (or recommending hiring) a college graduate for an entry-level position, how important is it that the person had or did any of the following? (*Circle **one** number for each row, a-j.*)

	VERY IMPORTANT	SOMEWHAT IMPORTANT	NOT TOO IMPORTANT	NOT AT ALL IMPORTANT	DON'T KNOW
Undergraduate coursework					
a. Business, finance, accounting	1	2	3	4	5
b. Humanities (e.g., literature, philosophy, language)	1	2	3	4	5
c. Computer science, mathematics	1	2	3	4	5
d. History, political science	1	2	3	4	5
e. Psychology, industrial relations	1	2	3	4	5
Undergraduate performance					
f. Strong academic record on campus	1	2	3	4	5
g. Involvement in student, athletic, or community activities	1	2	3	4	5
Undergraduate institution					
h. Graduated from a high quality college	1	2	3	4	5
Experience					
i. Internship or work experience in business	1	2	3	4	5
j. Study abroad experience	1	2	3	4	5

7. When you consider hiring (or recommending hiring) a college graduate for an entry-level position, how important is it that the person have any of the following? (*Circle **one** number for each row, a-f.*)

	VERY IMPORTANT	SOMEWHAT IMPORTANT	NOT TOO IMPORTANT	NOT AT ALL IMPORTANT	DON'T KNOW	Q.8
Undergraduate degree area						
a. Liberal arts degree	1	2	3	4	5	1
b. Business degree	1	2	3	4	5	2
c. Engineering degree	1	2	3	4	5	3
Postgraduate degree area						
d. M.B.A. degree	1	2	3	4	5	1
e. Postgraduate engineering degree	1	2	3	4	5	2
f. Law degree	1	2	3	4	5	3

8. From the list above in Question 7, assuming that other factors are equal, which **one undergraduate degree area** and which **one postgraduate degree area** are most important to you when you consider hiring (or recommending hiring) a college graduate for an entry-level position? (*Circle **only two** numbers: **one** undergraduate degree area, **one** postgraduate degree area.*)

9. How would you assess the rates of advancement for the following groups during their first ten years with your company? (*Circle **one** number for each row, a-e.*)

		SIGNIFICANTLY ABOVE AVERAGE OF ALL HIRES	ABOVE AVERAGE OF ALL HIRES	AVERAGE OF ALL HIRES	BELOW AVERAGE OF ALL HIRES	SIGNIFICANTLY BELOW AVERAGE OF ALL HIRES
a.	Liberal arts graduates	1	2	3	4	5
b.	Business graduates	1	2	3	4	5
c.	Engineering graduates	1	2	3	4	5
d.	M.B.A.s with liberal arts degrees	1	2	3	4	5
e.	M.B.A.s with other undergraduate degrees	1	2	3	4	5

10. In your judgment, how useful is a liberal arts background to be a successful manager in the following levels and areas of the company? (*Circle **one** number for each row, a-k.*)

		HIGHLY USEFUL	SOMEWHAT USEFUL	NOT TOO USEFUL	NOT AT ALL USEFUL	DON'T KNOW
	Level					
a.	Top corporate management	1	2	3	4	5
b.	Middle management	1	2	3	4	5
c.	Entry-level management	1	2	3	4	5
	Area					
d.	Finance	1	2	3	4	5
e.	Marketing, sales	1	2	3	4	5
f.	Manufacturing	1	2	3	4	5
g.	Plant or facilities management	1	2	3	4	5
h.	Research and development	1	2	3	4	5
i.	Planning	1	2	3	4	5
j.	Human resources or personnel	1	2	3	4	5
k.	Public affairs or government relations	1	2	3	4	5

11. On average, how would you assess liberal arts graduates on the following characteristics and skills? (*Circle one number for each row, a-m.*)

		SIGNIFICANTLY ABOVE AVERAGE	ABOVE AVERAGE	AVERAGE	BELOW AVERAGE	SIGNIFICANTLY BELOW AVERAGE
a.	General business knowledge and skills	1	2	3	4	5
b.	Technical knowledge and skills	1	2	3	4	5
c.	Analytic skills	1	2	3	4	5
d.	Quantitative skills	1	2	3	4	5
e.	Communication (oral and written) skills	1	2	3	4	5
f.	Leadership skills	1	2	3	4	5
g.	Ability to organize and prioritize	1	2	3	4	5
h.	Understanding the company's environment	1	2	3	4	5
i.	Understanding the company's internal world	1	2	3	4	5
j.	Understanding people	1	2	3	4	5
k.	Innovativeness	1	2	3	4	5
l.	Appreciating ethical concerns	1	2	3	4	5
m.	Disposition toward business	1	2	3	4	5

12. What forecast do you make regarding entry-level hiring in 1987 and 1988 compared to 1986? (*Circle **one** number for each row, a-b, and enter percent increase or decrease as appropriate. REMEMBER: If you are unable to provide overall data, please provide information based on the largest division or subsidiary for which it is available. If specific information is not available, please provide your best estimate.*)

a. All entry-level hires

1 _____ % increase   2 _____ % decrease   3 no change

b. Liberal arts graduates only (entry-level)

1 _____ % increase   2 _____ % decrease   3 no change

Part III. HIRING AND RETENTION

13. Please indicate the numbers of individuals hired for entry-level positions in 1986. (*If you are unable to provide overall data, please provide information based on the largest division or subsidiary for which it is available. If specific information is not available, please provide your best estimate.*)

_____ Total entry-level hires

_____ Liberal arts graduates

_____ Business graduates

_____ Engineering graduates

_____ M.B.A.s with liberal arts degrees

_____ M.B.A.s with other undergraduate degrees

14. Compared to 1983, would you estimate that the number of each type of graduate listed below hired for entry-level positions in 1986 increased, decreased, or stayed about the same? (*Circle **one** number for each row, a-f.*)

		INCREASED	STAYED ABOUT THE SAME	DECREASED
a.	All entry-level hires	1	2	3
b.	Liberal arts graduates	1	2	3
c.	Business graduates	1	2	3
d.	Engineering graduates	1	2	3
e.	M.B.A.s with liberal arts degrees	1	2	3
f.	M.B.A.s with other undergraduate degrees	1	2	3

15. Of those liberal arts graduates hired at the entry-level within the past three years (that is, since 1983), identify the two or three areas where the largest numbers have been placed. (*Circle **two or three** areas.*)

1 Sales and marketing

2 Entry-level management

3 Clerical/support staff

4 Manufacturing

5 Planning

6 Research and development

7 Human resources or personnel

8 Public affairs or government relations

16. What is the total number of U.S.-based employees your company had at the end of 1986 and 1983? (*If you are unable to provide overall data, please provide information based on the largest division or subsidiary for which it is available. If specific information is not available, please provide your best estimate.*)

a. _____ end of 1986   b. _____ end of 1983

17. Does your company have an international division or operation? (*Circle **one** number.*)

1 Yes   2 No

18. If you were to address a college audience, what course of study and set of educational experiences would you recommend to today's students who wish to enter the business world?

_____

_____

_____

_____

_____

19. What could colleges do to better prepare liberal arts graduates for careers in your company and the business world?

_____

_____

_____

_____

_____

Thank you for your assistance. Please return your completed questionnaire directly to ORC by June 19th in the postage paid envelope provided. Upon completion of this study, we will send you and your Chief Executive Officer a report on the results of this survey.

Appendix II. Manager Survey:
Interview Schedule

Manager Survey

1. Please look over this list, and read me the number or numbers of all the categories that describe your educational background.
   1. Never attended college
   2. Attended college, did not graduate
   3. Received an undergraduate degree in business
   4. Received an undergraduate degree in engineering
   5. Received an undergraduate degree in liberal arts (including mathematics and the natural sciences)
   6. Attended a postgraduate program, did not graduate
   7. Received a postgraduate degree in business (M.B.A.)
   8. Received a postgraduate degree in engineering
   9. Received a postgraduate degree in law
   10. Received a postgraduate degree in a liberal arts field (M.A., M.S., Ph.D.)
   11. Received a postgraduate degree in other areas

2. In which areas of your work do you find that your undergraduate college education is particularly useful?
   1. General knowledge and information
   2. Technical knowledge and procedures
   3. Analytic skills
   4. Quantitative skills
   5. Communication (written and oral) skills
   6. Leadership skills
   7. Ability to organize and prioritize
   8. Understanding the company's environment
   9. Understanding the company's internal world
   10. Understanding people
   11. Innovativeness
   12. Appreciating ethical concerns
   13. None of these

3. In your judgment, in which of the following levels and areas of your company would an undergraduate liberal arts degree provide a useful educational background?
   1. Top corporate management
   2. Middle management
   3. Entry-level management
   4. Finance
   5. Marketing, sales
   6. Manufacturing
   7. Plant or facilities management
   8. Research and development
   9. Corporate planning
   10. Human resources or personnel
   11. Public affairs or government relations
   12. International assignments
   13. None

4. When you consider hiring (or recommending hiring) a college graduate for an entry-level position, which of the following experiences, qualifications or achievements are most important to you in evaluating the candidate?
   1. Undergraduate liberal arts degree
   2. Undergraduate business degree
   3. Undergraduate engineering degree
   4. Strong academic record in college
   5. Involvement in student, athletic, or community activities
   6. Graduated from a high quality college
   7. Internship or work experience in business
   8. Study abroad experience
   9. M.B.A. degree
   10. Postgraduate engineering degree
   11. Law degree
   12. None

5. Please look over this list of statements concerning college education, and read me the numbers of those with which you agree.
   1. Liberal arts education should include more business and technical courses.
   2. Business and engineering education should include more liberal arts courses.
   3. During a period of work-force reduction, the hiring of liberal arts graduates is more adversely affected than other graduates.

4. During a period of work-force expansion, the hiring of liberal arts graduates is more positively affected than other graduates.
5. The personnel office is less likely than top management to want to hire liberal arts graduates.
6. Liberal arts graduates are, on average, more anti-business than other college graduates.
7. Liberal arts graduates are, on average, more adept at working with other people and teams of people.
8. Liberal arts graduates are more likely to become obsolete in an increasingly technological society.
9. Future political leaders in America should have at least some liberal arts education.
10. Future business leaders in America should have at least some liberal arts education.
11. Liberal arts graduates seem to be more loyal and responsive than are M.B.A. graduates.
12. M.B.A. graduates require a higher starting salary than liberal arts graduates, but they are worth it.

6. I am going to read a list of activities and company policies. As I read each one, please tell me which you have done in the past 2 or 3 years. Just answer yes or no.
   1. Represented your company to a community organization or in a community setting.
   2. Represented your company to a government agency or unit.
   3. Represented your company to a trade or industry association.
   4. Served as a trustee or advisor to a nonprofit organization.
   5. Served as a volunteer or fundraiser for a nonprofit organization.
   6. Served as an advisor or consultant to a government agency.
   7. Been expected by your company to participate in community or public affairs.
   8. Had your community or public affairs participation reviewed by your company as part of an annual performance appraisal.
   9. None of these.

7. Which one of the items listed on this card best describes your main area of responsibility? For example, are you primarily concerned with marketing, accounting, manufacturing, or what? Just read me the number of your *one main* area of responsibility.
   1. Distribution Management: export management, traffic, warehousing

2. Marketing Planning: market analysis, market development, market planning, market research, product development
3. Sales Support: art direction, merchandising, packaging, promotions, advertising
4. Sales: customer relations, customer services, field sales
5. Personnel: pension administration, industrial relations, recruiting
6. Data Processing
7. Finance, Accounting, Cost Control
8. Purchasing
9. Production Management: maintenance, manufacturing, operations, quality control, material control, inspection
10. Plant Management: manager, director, superintendent of plant, mill, refinery, works
11. Corporate and Subsidiary General Management and Administration
12. Other Engineering or Technical
13. Research & Development
14. Corporate Planning
15. Other function (Please specify)

8. Are the company activities that you are concerned with mainly related to *consumer* goods or services or *industrial* goods or services?
   1. Consumer goods or services
   2. Industrial goods or services
   3. Both about equally
   4. Neither of these
   5. No opinion

9. Do you ever get involved in any way at all in company decisions regrading the location of plant or business facilities?
   1. Advisory
   2. Final decision
   3. Both advisory and final decisions
   4. Other (specify): _____
   5. No response

10. Are you involved in any way with international operations or activities your company may have?
    1. Yes
    2. No
    3. Company has no international operations
    4. No response

If *yes* on question 10, which one of these best describes how you are involved?
1. Suggest, recommend
2. Evaluate, select
3. Approve, authorize
4. No response

11. Would you pick the category on this card that approximates the present value of your personal stockholdings as of now? This includes common, preferred, over-the-counter stocks and stock mutual funds you now own or have a beneficial interest in, but excludes stock options.
    1. None
    2. Less than $5,000
    3. $5,000 - $9,999
    4. $10,000 - $24,999
    5. $25,000 - $49,999
    6. $50,000 - $99,999
    7. $100,000 - $249,999
    8. $250,000 - $499,999
    9. $500,000 or more

12. Using this card, please select the letter corresponding to the income from your *job*, before taxes. Include salary and bonus payments, but *not* stock options.
    1. Less than $25,000 a year
    2. $25,000 to $29,999
    3. $30,000 to $39,999
    4. $40,000 to $49,999
    5. $50,000 to $74,999
    6. $75,000 to $99,999
    7. $100,000 or over
    8. Refused

13. Which category in this exhibit indicates the amount of formal education you have received? Just read me the number.
    1. Less than 8th grade
    2. 8th grade
    3. High school incomplete (9th-11th grade)
    4. High school completed (12th grade)
    5. College incomplete
    6. College completed
    7. Graduate work
    8. Graduate degree

14. What is your age?
    1. Less than 30 years
    2. 30 to 39 years
    3. 40 to 49 years
    4. 50 to 59 years
    5. 60 to 65 years
    6. Over 65 years
    7. Refused

15. How long have you worked for this company?
    1. Less than 5 years
    2. 5 to 9 years
    3. 10 to 19 years
    4. 20 to 29 years
    5. 30 years and over
    6. Don't know/refused

16. Which category on this exhibit best describes your title? If you have more than one title, please choose the highest level.

    Top Management Officers
    1. Chairman of the Board, Vice Chairman, President, Chief Executive Officer
    2. Executive Vice President, Senior Vice President
    3. Vice President, Regional Vice President, Divisional Vice President
    4. Other Senior Officer: Treasurer, Controller, Secretary

    Other Executive/Managerial Jobs
    5. Assistant Vice President, Second Vice President
    6. Other Assistant Officer: Treasurer, Controller, Secretary, etc.
    7. General or Plant Manager: Corporate Division, Regional, Plant, etc.
    8. Associate or Assistant General Manager
    9. Manager: Accounting, Engineering, Auditing, Field Sales Administration, etc.
    10. Associate or Assistant Manager
    11. Director: Sales, Planning, Research, Manufacturing, Industrial Relations, etc.
    12. Associate or Assistant Director
    13. Professional: Attorney, Physician, Chemist, Engineer, Counsel, Editor, etc.
    14. Superintendent: General, Plan, Division, etc.
    15. Assistant Superintendent

16. Administrator
17. Executive Assistant: Assistant to the President, Vice President, Secretary, etc.
18. Purchasing Agent, Buyer

17. From what you know of politics and political parties, which of these best describes what you now consider your own political position?
    1. Conservative Republican
    2. Liberal Republican
    3. Independent leaning toward Republican
    4. Independent
    5. Independent leaning toward Democrat
    6. Conservative Democrat
    7. Liberal Democrat
    8. Other (Specify): _____
    9. Don't know

18. Sex:
    1. Man
    2. Woman

Author Index*

Abernathy, William J., 139, 140, 155, *180*

Abraham, Katharine G., 18 fn, 24, *183*

Astin, Alexander W., 4, 9, 10, 11 fn, 19 fn, 23, 24, 103, *177*

Austin, Gilbert R., 11 fn, 23, *177*

Baysinger, Barry D., 111 fn, 118, *188*

Bellah, Robert N., 164, 174, *177*

Bennett, William J., 12 fn, 13, 23, 155, 156, *177*

Berle, Adolf, Jr., 25, 26 fn, 49, *177*

Bettman, Ralph B., 132 fn, 136, *178*

Bisconti, Ann A., 21 fn, 24, 93 fn, 94, 117, *178*

Black, Nancy B., 141 fn, 155, *180*

Bloom, Allan, 11, *178*

Boli, John, 9 fn, 23, *182*

Bonfield, Patricia, 25 fn, 49, *178*

Bowen, Howard R., 163 fn, 174, *178*

Bowles, Sandy Quadros, 28 fn, 49, *178*

Boyer, Ernest L., 14, 16, 23, 63, 82, *178*

Bray, Douglas W., 95 fn, 117, *181*

Buchholz, Rogene A., 111 fn, 118, *185*

Burck, Charles G., 139 fn, 155, *178*

Burns, Stanley T., 153 fn, 156, *178*, *181*

Butler, David W., *181*

Calvert, Robert Jr., 21 fn, 24, *178*

Catlin, Jamie Beth, 141 fn, 155, *180*

Chandler, Alfred D., 1, 23, *178*

Chandy, P.R., 170 fn, 175, *188*

Cheit, Earl F., 64, 139, *178*, *179*

Cheney, Lynne E., 11 fn, 12, 23, 155, 156, *179*

Cohen, Stephen S., 159, 174, *179*

Collins, Randall, 17 fn, 66 fn, 82, 123 fn, 136, *179*

Cordisco, Jane H., 141 fn, 155, *179*

Davidson, Wallace N., III, 170 fn, 175, *188*

De Pasquale, John A., 95 fn, 117, *179*

de Tocqueville, Alexis, 164, 174, *179*

Di Maggio, Paul, 163 fn, 174, *179*

Donaldson, Gordon, 116 fn, 119, *179*

Drucker, Peter F., 135 fn, 136, *180*

Evers, Frederick T., *185*

Feldman, K.A., 163 fn, 174, *180*

Finn, Chester E., Jr., 11 fn, 23, *180*

Fiske, Edward B., 3 fn, 11 fn, 15, 23, *180*

Freeman, Richard B., 21 fn, 24, *180*

Friedland, Roger, 170, 175, *184*

Galaskiewicz, Joseph, 116 fn, 119, 159 fn, 174, *180*

*Numbers in italics indicate the page where the complete reference is given.

Swarthmore College, business
    program in, 143

Teachers, 7
Technical training, for careers, 26,
    93
Training programs of corporations,
    29–30, 121, 152–153
Transamerica, 36
Travelers Corp., 36

Undergraduate studies
    areas of, 3–8, 104–105
    and career path, 21–23, 109
    and corporation type, 109–110
    and employment, areas of, 104
    manager area of, 105–108
    and responsibility, area of, 110
University of California, Berkeley,
    93
University of California, Los
    Angeles, 93
University of Chicago Graduate
    School of Business, 143
University of Maryland, 81, 145
University of Michigan, 15, 21

University of Rochester,
    Management studies, 144
University of Southern California,
    93
University of Texas at Austin,
    manual, 155
University of Virginia, career guide,
    154, 155, 156, 186
U.S. Bureau of the Census, 8, 186
U.S. Bureau of Labor Statistics, 40
U.S. Department of Education, 5,
    17, 23, 70, 103, 117, 186
Useful arts and liberal arts, 13–14,
    16, 63–66, 80–82
*Useful Arts and the Liberal
    Tradition, The* (Cheit), 64

"Visible hand," 1

Wall Street Journal, 25, 49, 187
Wellesley College, business program
    in, 142–143
Wesleyan University, business
    program in, 143
William Paterson College, business
    program in, 143
Williams College, 27
Work force growth, 38–41